DISCOVERY

Interviewing and Investigation

By Michael A. Pener

Third edition

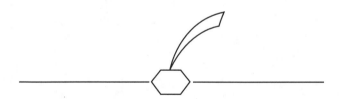

Pearson Publications Company
Dallas, Texas

ISBN: 0-929563-43-3

Factual research is important to all legal assistants and paralegals because it goes to the heart of what they do. This book is one of the most thorough and comprehensive treatments of this subject.

Legal assistants and paralegals are information gatherers and processors. *Discovery: Interviewing and Investigation* definitively examines and presents clearly everything this statement implies. It focuses on what paralegals and lawyers do most of the time – pull information together and do something with it.

Michael Pener's focus on the gathering and preliminary processing of information is impressive. He provides a thorough treatment of all considerations related to the discovery process. His book does not just start and end with the techniques of interviewing and investigation. He covers many essential areas we must know before beginning factual research. Pener defines the legal environment in which interviewing takes place and guides us through the legal process. He identifies the sources of information sought in factual research and he describes the ethical concerns involved. By the time he discusses specific interviewing and investigation techniques, Pener has given us a clear basis for understanding them.

As an attorney and educator, Mike Pener is notably experienced in factual research. He has recognized the pivotal role of this subject in the practice of law. In the 14 years I have known him, he has often discussed the interviewing and investigation course he teaches at Johnson County Community College. He has explored the intricacies of interviewing and investigation, and he has gained tremendous insight in the teaching of these subjects. *Discovery: Interviewing and Investigation* gives teachers, students, and practicing paralegals and lawyers a valuable text and resource to this essential area of law practice.

David A. Dye
Director of Education
Consortium for Advanced Legal Education

Dedication

This book is dedicated to my wife, Marlene, and my children, who survived its writing; to my father, Ben E. Pener, who in the early years of his law practice took me along when he filed pleadings with the clerk of the court or looked at ownership records and then showed me how to do it; and to all the legal assistants and paralegals everywhere in recognition of their uncommon professionalism.

Acknowledgments

I want to acknowledge the time and effort put into this book by Linda Furlet, a paralegal with extensive litigation experience, and George Schrader, a long-time paralegal educator at Auburn University. A Certified Legal Assistant Specialist in civil litigation, Linda made a wonderful transformation, especially of the beginning chapters. George expertly applied the thoroughness for which he is known through his many publications. I am also expressing special thanks to my publisher, Enika Pearson Schulze, who patiently waited for the completion of this book.

Michael A. Pener

TABLE OF CONTENTS

Introduction to the Third Edition

In 1976, when I developed the paralegal program at Johnson County Community College, the electric typewriter was considered "state-of-the-art" technology in most law offices. Now, I have students who have never used a typewriter, but by necessity have "keyboarding" skills because entry-level legal assistant positions require basic computer skills in word processing, spreadsheet development, and database development and accessing.

Presently, we have crossed over the threshold of the electronic age and are using computer technologies that were considered science fiction a mere twenty years ago. It is interesting to note that at this time we're still typing, or keyboarding if you prefer. Yet we now have software available for computerized voice-recognition transcription and electronic activities that, when perfected, will render keyboarding skills obsolete.

Soon, textbooks such as this will become electronic devices educationally personalized for optimum learning with multimedia, data links, and virtual reality components. Until then, this edition has been substantially revised to reflect the impact of the Internet and other aspects of the electronic age upon the fundamental functions of the legal assistant in the discovery process.

Anticipating the future, I would appreciate your suggestions and ideas for improving the content of this book. Send your e-mail to the following address. Thank you for your help.

Mike Pener
June, 1997

mpener@johnco.cc.ks.us

Chapter One

DISCOVERY IN TODAY'S LAW PRACTICE

THE PURPOSE OF DISCOVERY

Discovery is just what its name implies: determining the facts of a situation through the gathering of information. Discovery commences with the formation of the lawyer-client relationship on a specific matter and ends with resolution of that matter. During discovery, the lawyer:

- ascertains the facts necessary to determine the merit of the client's claim or position;

- evaluates the matter for settlement or satisfactory disposition before trial or formal adjudication; and

- preserves testimony and physical evidence to be used at trial or formal adjudication.[1]

THE NEED FOR DISCOVERY

The field of litigation has changed dramatically within the last thirty years. Lawyers who once conducted a lawsuit as if the client's pockets were bottomless and the court's time limitless have awakened to a new world — clients now keep a sharp eye on the cost and demand a full accounting, and the courts have imposed sharp limitations on the conduct of a lawsuit.

Other changes have occurred. Today, the full-scale litigation approach to dealing with the client's problem is losing its dominance as the ultimate form of dispute resolution. Clients want disputes settled quickly and economically, using techniques such as arbitration, mediation, and negotiated settlements as alternatives to the expense of trial. Through rules and statutes, the courts and legislatures have set litigation timetables, and sanctions for delays and meritless claims and defenses have become more commonplace.

The discovery process has become vitally important to successful litigation and case management. Lawyers, learning through experience that often they cannot rely on their clients for sufficient factual information before a lawsuit is filed, turn instead to their own independent investigation. At the same time, formal discovery devices, such as production of documents and depositions, have escalated in cost. Thus, informal discovery, both before filing and during the life of the lawsuit, is used to meet the needs of the client and satisfy the demands of professional responsibility.

MYTHS AND REALITIES OF THE PRACTICE OF LAW

Before we discuss the various discovery techniques used today, we must understand the mythology and reality of today's law practice.

First, although computer technology has strongly affected the nature of law school curricula, law students and professors still focus primarily on legal theory rather than the basic skills needed in the practice of law. Law school graduates lack adequate preparation for dealing with clients; seldom does a graduate know how to conduct an initial client interview and maintain a proper attorney/client relationship. Many new lawyers embark upon the practice of law without practical knowledge of the court and administrative systems before which they will practice. Typically, a new lawyer relies on a legal secretary or legal assistant to know how and where to file a lawsuit.

Thus, a number of continuing legal education programs have sprung up to bridge the gap between law school and law practice in the real world. Not surprisingly, many older, experienced lawyers attend such programs to refresh their skills and learn the latest procedures from court clerks, records custodians, and administrative agency personnel.

Second, because of the diversity in court procedures, law schools teach discovery and trial methods based upon federal procedural and evidentiary rules. However, many state court systems do not follow the notice pleading concepts of the federal rules, nor are they as liberal in the use of formal discovery techniques. In the real world, most litigation takes place in the state court systems, not the federal courts, and procedures vary from state to state and even district to district, so that the lawyer must know the court rules and procedures of each jurisdiction in which the lawyer practices.

In the same vein, law school professors teach substantive courses such as real estate, estates, and business entities by focusing on uniform laws, but fail to integrate theory with practice by having students prepare essential documents, including deeds, wills, and articles of incorporation.

Law as a Business

While law schools train their students to be professionals, they do not train them to be business people. Depending on whether the lawyer practices in the public or private sector, the nature of the business will vary, but the basic considerations of overhead and accountability will be present everywhere. A county prosecutor's office submits budgets like any other government agency, and the county prosecutor must perform satisfactorily or risk being replaced at the next general election. In the private sector, the pressures of overhead (office expenses before salaries) and accountability can be immense in a large law firm. Generally, overhead should be 40% of gross income generated by fees, but other factors can affect overhead, including the client base.

A law firm with a plaintiff client base, working on a contingency fee basis, tends to manage its overhead more frugally than does a law firm with a defendant client base, where overhead and expenses are billed to the client whether a case is won or lost. A plaintiff attorney's accountability to clients is easily measurable in good settlements or favorable judgments; a successful plaintiff's lawyer must develop a positive reputation for making the best deal for his or her clients. However, they must also deal with overhead, so the plaintiff's lawyer must continually weigh the value of potential cases against associated expenses.

Because of the contingent fee concept, plaintiff's lawyers notoriously do not keep time records. If they did, many would be aghast at the low hourly rate their cases generate.

On the other hand, defense lawyers and law firms enjoy the luxury of retainers and clients who pay on an hourly or flat rate basis. Their client base usually consists of insurance companies, banks and financial institutions, corporations, and governmental entities, all of which exact or expect favorable representation. However, in the changing marketplace, defense lawyers are now more apt to watch their overhead and expenses, as savvy clients (generally businesses themselves) have begun to balk at paying for what they perceive as excessive or unreasonable fees and expenses.

Changes in the Legal Profession

Still, for all the diversity of practice, a commonality exists among lawyers. By training, they are scholars, advocates and advisors. They act on behalf of others by reviewing, interpreting, and applying the law to specific situations. Judicial opinions, treatises, practice materials, and other legal works demonstrate the serious attention they give to their vocation and professional responsibility.

However, the legal system and profession have experienced extraordinary change, including the technological modernization of the courts, administrative systems, and law offices. Lawyers consider a professional support staff as an absolute necessity for the effective delivery of legal services; legal assistants (paralegals) and their managers, law office administrators, legal investigators and other nonlawyer specialists, have become essential in providing lawyers with cost-effective assistance. As the discovery process takes on greater significance with the explosion of information, a competent professional support staff gives a lawyer a powerful advantage over lawyers who choose not to use such personnel. (A discussion of the special relationship between lawyer and legal assistant will follow later in this chapter.)

Finally, trial practice, culminating in the courtroom, has become a lost art for various reasons. First, despite efforts by many judges to clear out their dockets, the time from the filing of a petition/complaint to trial has not been reduced. It still takes years to litigate, and over 90% of all lawsuits are disposed of before trial on the merits.[2]

In response, lawyers and judges have turned to other methods of resolving disputes, such as ADR, including mediation and arbitration. At the federal level, legislation known as Administrative Dispute Resolution Act (ADRA), Public Law 101-552 (104 Stat. 2736), has been enacted to streamline the government judicial system, and many federal courts are requiring potential litigants to utilize such nonjudicial methods before a lawsuit is filed. The act's purpose is to encourage federal agencies to avoid protracted litigation by utilizing mediation, mini-trials, negotiation, and arbitration. In many states, the courts and legislatures are encouraging this conversion of our legal system.

Although many law schools now teach courses in dispute resolution, most practicing lawyers are unfamiliar with its use. Until the legal community has a better understanding of alternate systems to resolving disputes, our court systems will continue to be clogged with unnecessary litigation.

STATUTES OF LIMITATION

Although ADR may be the wave of the future, in the here and now lawyers must deal with the controlling factors of the practice of law in the real world. To the plaintiff's lawyer at the beginning of the lawyer-client relationship in a litigation matter, the most crucial factor is the determination of law governing the plaintiff's dispute and the corresponding statute of limitations. For most plaintiffs, this is a relatively simple process, since statutes of limitations are explicit for traditional torts (negligence, battery, defamation, etc.) and for contract actions.

However, some statutes may be open-ended. With fraud, generally the cause of action is not deemed to have accrued and the statute does not start running until the fraud is discovered, so the key date becomes the date of discovery. Further, statutes have been enacted to deal with "technological torts" that encompass causes of action arising from medical treatment and product liability, and statutes of repose have set time limits on how much time a plaintiff has to file a lawsuit after the occurrence of a specific event.

Further, law firms must perform the applicable time computations to determine the outside date by which a lawsuit can be filed. Even if timely filed, failure without good cause to accomplish service of the summons and complaint/petition within the specified time limits can result in dismissal without prejudice.

In addition, time computations and extensions may vary from jurisdiction to jurisdiction. Generally, time begins to run on the day following the act or event and includes the last day of the statutory period unless it is a Saturday, Sunday, or legal holiday. Because different states celebrate different legal holidays, the lawyer must verify the term "legal holiday" for each jurisdiction.

Statutes containing time computation standards include provisions that grant judges discretionary authority to enlarge or extend the time. However, a wise lawyer will never rely on such discretion, for not all judges will grant extensions. Fortunately, some extensions are specifically set out in statutes of limitations, but again these can vary.

The most common situation of a legally sanctioned extension occurs when the plaintiff has a legal disability. The plaintiff may be a minor child, or may be incapacitated and unable to act on his or her own behalf. For such situations, the law extends the statute of limitations until the disability is removed, and the plaintiff can then file suit for a specified period of time, usually one or two years thereafter. Other extensions apply when the commencement of an action has been stayed by an injunction, there has been a partial payment or acknowledgment of a liability, or the defendant is out of state or has absconded or concealed his or her person.

Beyond the statute of limitations for enforcement of substantive rights, others deal with the procedural aspects of the practice of law. A workers' compensation statute might specify that the worker has 150 days after the injury to file a claim with the employer. A probate statute might give a creditor of an estate six months after the first publication of notice to creditors to file a claim against the estate or be forever barred from collecting the debt. A statute might require timely notice before a lawsuit can be filed to enforce a mechanic's lien.

There has been a significant expansion of court rules relating to time limitations, particularly concerning utilization of discovery methods. Moreover, courts are enforcing these rules by granting requests for sanctions for obvious noncompliance and by refusing to grant motions rectifying time-related errors.

Also, administrative agencies at all levels of government have developed staggering numbers of rules and regulations that affect not only the timeliness of litigation but also disputes and matters that can only be resolved through the administrative process. For example, a taxpayer might be denied access to the Tax Court of the United States because a protest or notice was not timely filed during the administrative process. An unemployment claim might be denied because the claimant failed to file for benefits by the prescribed deadline.

Such rules and deadlines are necessary if more than 260 million people are to live in harmony in our complex and technological society. However, clients focus upon themselves and their needs, and it does little good to applaud the smooth functioning of our system when a client's cause is barred by the statute of limitations or the client is denied relief by some administrative time requirement.

This being the case, how can the lawyer best serve and protect the client's interest with respect to the applicable statutes of limitations and other time factors? This question can be answered by adherence to the following procedures:

1.   As soon as the lawyer-client relationship is established, determine the nature of the cause of action and its beginning event.

2.   Ascertain and review applicable statutes, rules, or regulations.

3.   Determine the time limit or requirement.

4.   Apply the time limit or requirement to the client's situation to decide from what specific action or event the time limit or requirement is computed. This process must be strictly adhered to during the lawyer-client relationship, not only for the client's interest but also for the lawyer's own professional and financial well-being.

Professional malpractice claims against lawyers by clients have increased substantially, and a high proportion have been predicated upon the misapplication of statutes of limitations and failure to comply with time factors. Often, courts are finding that a lawyer-client relationship existed even though there was no formal contract of employment. When a person consults with a lawyer but does not formally retain the lawyer's services, the lawyer must provide or send the person a letter of nonemployment to protect against potential liability. The letter should contain the following:

1.   Identification of the date of and subject matter of the consultation with a statement that the lawyer's services were not retained;

2.   A statement of the facts put forth by the person during the consultation or ascertained by investigation;

3.   A specific reference to the applicable statute of limitations and/or time factors involved;

4.   The last date upon which the action must be commenced and/or time limitation must be complied with;

5.   A recommendation that the person consult with another attorney or take action to protect one's interest before expiration of the identified statute of limitations or time limitation; and

6.   A statement at the end of the letter for the person to sign, acknowledging receipt of the letter and understanding of the contents.

If possible, the letter should be given personally to the person and an executed copy obtained. If this is not possible, it can be sent by certified mail, restricted delivery, with a copy for execution and return envelope enclosed. Where the lawyer has been retained and a decision has been made to terminate the relationship by either party, or the client decides not to pursue the matter, then the letter should be modified appropriately. If a lawsuit has been filed, then court rules will affect the lawyer's withdrawal of representation. In any event, there must be some written communication advising the client of the status of the litigation.

STATUTORY PRIVILEGES AND IMMUNITIES

All jurisdictions have enacted statutes that address privileged communications arising out of relationships. These privileges grant the right to a designated person neither to testify about nor disclose a confidential communication or information about him- or herself. Applicable statutes also give the designated person the right to prevent another person from testifying about or disclosing any confidential communication between them during the course of a specified relationship.

During discovery, applicable statutory privileges must be analyzed to determine areas of evidence exclusion.

Predominant aspects of statutory privileges are reviewed below:

1.   **Lawyer-Client Privilege**. Professional confidences and communications between a lawyer and client during the course of their relationship are privileged. The client has the privilege

- as a witness to refuse to disclose any such communication;
- to prevent the lawyer from disclosing it; and
- to prevent another witness from disclosing the communication if it evolved out of the lawyer-client relationship.

Only the client has the privilege. The privilege extends to consultations for the purpose of retaining the lawyer or obtaining legal advice, even if no contractual relationship has developed.

A communication includes any disclosure by the client made to a representative, associate, or employee of the lawyer, including legal assistants and paralegals employed by the lawyer or retained incidentally to the professional relationship with the client.[3]

2.   **Privilege of Accused and Self-Incrimination**. In criminal actions, the accused has the privilege not to be called as a witness and not to testify, but this does not include the right to refuse, upon order of the court, to be available for identification. A person has the privilege to refuse to disclose in any action, civil or criminal, information that would be incriminating. This privilege includes the right to refuse disclosure to public officials. For example, a murder suspect cannot be compelled to talk to the police investigating the murder.

3.   **Physician-Patient Privilege**. The patient has this privilege against disclosure of confidential communications with the physician necessary for treatment or diagnosis of a medical condition. Some jurisdictions have eroded this privilege by exceptions related to driving while intoxicated or under the influence of drugs, commitment proceedings for the patient, and treatment or medical consultation sought by the patient to avoid detection or apprehension after the commission of a crime or tort.

4.   **Marital Privilege**. Generally, the spouse who transmitted the communication to the other spouse has the privilege to prevent him or her from disclosing the communication. Exceptions exist in an action by one spouse against the other and in certain criminal actions revolving around their marital relationship and children of their marriage.

Other statutory privileges regarding confidential communications include the penitential (religious) communication privilege, privileges against disclosing religious beliefs and trade secrets, and the privilege of the voting booth. (No voter can be compelled to testify for whom or what he or she voted.)

Many states have expanded the privilege to include communications arising out of confidential relationships that involve the treatment of a person in a mental health facility or those arising from the activities of social workers.

ETHICAL CONSIDERATIONS AND THE LEGAL ASSISTANT

In discovery, ethical considerations affect four main transactional areas in the practice of law.[4] The following discussion focuses upon the relationship between the lawyer and the legal assistant employed by the lawyer, particularly the legal assistant's performance of delegated functions.

Statutes, court rules and decisions, and professional associations and their standards of conduct recognize the legal assistant as a member of the lawyer's professional support staff. Nationally, the American Bar Association (ABA) allows qualified legal assistants to maintain an associate membership in that organization. The ABA has been involved in defining the legal and ethical parameters of employment of legal assistants and their professional relationship with lawyers, and it demonstrates its concern with legal assistant education through its ongoing approval of legal assistant education programs.

Legal assistants have formed their own professional organizations, which have developed ethical standards of conduct and professional guidelines for the utilization of legal assistants in the practice of law. Predominantly, these are the National Federation of Paralegal Associations (NFPA) and the National Association of Legal Assistants (NALA).

The NFPA adheres to its Model Code of Ethics and Professional Responsibility, which outlines its positions on paralegals' competence, professionalism, and conflicts of interest, the unauthorized practice of law, and the confidentiality of client communications. NALA has developed its Code of Ethics and Professional Responsibility, containing canons or statements referencing the ABA Model Code of Professional Responsibility (Code); the canons define the parameters of legal assistant conduct in the practice of law.

For many years, the ABA Model Code of Professional Responsibility was considered the hallmark of professional and ethical conduct for lawyers. Many state supreme courts still follow it, with some modification; however, most have now incorporated the ABA's newer Model Rules of Professional Conduct (MRPC) into their rules governing the practice of law and the discipline of attorneys in their respective jurisdictions. The MRPC is more specific and self-contained than the Code and its interpretive disciplinary rules (DR). The Code relies upon Ethical Considerations (EC) outside the Code to guide lawyers in situations where they must decide upon a course of action not controlled by case law or found in a DR.

In some jurisdictions, a lawyer can obtain an advanced ruling or guidance as to ethical conduct from the supreme court's disciplinary administrator or counsel responsible for enforcement of its rules, but most leave lawyers to their own devices and interpretations. In many states, bar associations have ethics advisory committees that issue ethical opinions for given fact situations upon request, but these are not binding upon anyone.

Whatever the approach taken in a particular jurisdiction, the lawyer and legal assistant must recognize situations that threaten a breach of ethical standards. For the lawyer, ethical misconduct may result in disciplinary action in the form of disbarment, suspension, censure, or admonition. Since the lawyer has supervisory responsibility of the work performed by the legal assistant, unethical actions by the legal assistant become those of the lawyer, and the lawyer will be disciplined accordingly. Although legal assistants might escape being disciplined for unethical conduct, the very least consequence will surely be economic (loss of job); prosecution for engaging in the unauthorized practice of law is not unheard of.[5]

Therefore, legal assistants must be aware of the ethical requirements of the jurisdiction in which their employer-lawyers practice law, not only for the protection of the lawyers, but for their own professional and financial well-being. An ethics checkup might be accomplished in the following manner:

1.   Obtain and periodically review the statutes and current rules of discipline and practice of law. If the lawyer is licensed to

practice in more than one jurisdiction, then the statutes and rules of each jurisdiction must be obtained and reviewed.

2.   Recognize situations and instances where an ethical question is involved. If possible, consult with the lawyer as to the appropriate course of action. If not possible, then report what happened to the lawyer for review and determination of further action.

3.   When further action is deemed necessary, obtain and review applicable cases and disciplinary reports of the jurisdiction. Develop materials for the lawyer requesting an ethical opinion by the appropriate authority.

Ethical questions arising in the practice of law are very circumstantial, and it would be impossible to accurately identify every situation. However, ethical considerations can be grouped into the following transactional areas of the practice of law:

- the lawyer-client relationship
- relationships with judicial and nonjudicial systems
- relationships with others
- public contact.

The lawyer-client relationship is an outstanding example of the agency concept in which one person acts in a representative capacity for another. Of importance is the purpose of the agency, the authority granted to the agent (lawyer) by the principal (client), the duties of the parties to each other and to third persons, and the liabilities arising out of the relationship. When employed by a lawyer, who represents and deals with a client, the legal assistant functions as an alter ego of the lawyer. In this respect ethical requirements of the relationship dictate that:

1.   Confidential communications of the client to the lawyer and legal assistant cannot be disclosed, and situations where confidentiality could be breached must be avoided. For example, if a client makes a confidential statement to the legal

assistant with a friend of the client present, then the confidentiality is lost.

2.   The client must be advised of the professional limitations of the legal assistant. A legal assistant cannot establish the lawyer-client employment relationship, cannot determine fee arrangements, and cannot give legal advice or opinions as to the legal consequences of an action of the client in a given matter.

3.   The client must be kept informed of the status of the representation. This, along with fee disputes, is one of the major areas of complaints against lawyers. Many lawyers could avoid grievance complaints by returning their phone calls more promptly.

4.   Lawyers must avoid situations that give rise to a conflict of interest, where the representation of one client will be directly adverse to the interests of another. Where such is discovered after representation has begun, the conflict of interest must be revealed to the client and all other parties affected. (Many legal assistants now carry "baggage" with them when they change jobs because they worked for a law firm that represented an opposing party in a lawsuit with a client of the new law firm.)

5.   A lawyer may have to decline or terminate representation of a client, if:

   • representation will violate professional rules of conduct or of other law;
   • the client persists in a criminal or fraudulent course of action;
   • the client's objectives are repugnant or imprudent to the lawyer; or
   • the lawyer's services are retained to perpetrate a crime or fraud.

Next, relationships with judicial and nonjudicial systems consist of interactions by the lawyer and legal assistant with the courts, administrative agencies, and legislative entities. As the client's advocate, the lawyer has a duty to zealously represent the client's interest even to the extent of subordinating the interests of others.

However, in dealings with judicial and nonjudicial systems, ethical limitations require that:

1. A lawyer shall not institute actions or assert defenses on behalf of a client that would be considered frivolous. The legal assistant must inform the lawyer of information obtained during discovery that may have a bearing on the lawyer's duty to adhere to this requirement.

2. A lawyer must have candor toward the judicial and nonjudicial systems and must avoid knowingly presenting false evidence. During discovery, the legal assistant must verify all evidence and must ensure that all forms of discovery are used and responded to properly.

3. A lawyer must act fairly toward the opposing party and counsel. This entails avoiding the use of improper tactics during discovery, avoiding the destruction or concealment of evidence, and improperly influencing witnesses. Many activities of the legal assistant during discovery focus upon the gathering of evidence and identifying witnesses. All should be done through competitive, fair practices.

4. A lawyer must avoid being a witness at a trial where the lawyer is acting as an advocate. Although exceptional situations might justify this, it still is not a good practice for a lawyer to function in the dual capacity of lawyer and witness. Use of the lawyer's legal assistant may alleviate this problem, but even the legal assistant may be tainted by the employment relationship.

5. Agencies, legislative entities, and other nonjudicial systems are entitled to expect lawyers to deal with them in the same manner that they would deal with courts. Since many government

agencies are allowing legal assistants to appear on behalf of a client in place of lawyers, this expectation applies equally to legal assistants.

Transactions with others during discovery are subject to several ethical considerations that apply equally to the legal assistant and the lawyer. They include:

1.   The requirement that the lawyer or legal assistant be truthful in dealings with others on behalf of the client. Statements of material fact fall into this category, and false statements should not be knowingly made on behalf of the client.

2.   The avoidance of communicating with persons represented by another lawyer in the matter. If, during discovery, the legal assistant interviews a potential defendant and finds that he or she is represented by a lawyer, then the communication must be immediately terminated.

3.   The protection of unrepresented persons from interacting with a lawyer or legal assistant without full disclosure of the role of the lawyer or legal assistant in the matter. Note that only a lawyer can advise unrepresented persons to obtain their own lawyer.

Finally, the legal assistant must be concerned with public contact in its many forms: advertising, written and oral communications. For this area of ethical conduct, the jurisdictions differ greatly as to what is considered proper. The legal assistant must consult the statutes, rules and case law of the jurisdiction. The difference of opinion or diverse application of ethical rules can be best illustrated by the following:

1.   Most jurisdictions allow legal assistants to have and give out business cards, but some are very restrictive as to what may be printed on them. Some allow the name of a legal assistant to appear on the lawyer's letterhead, provided that there is a designation as legal assistant. Others, however, would find such to be a deceptive and unethical practice.

2.   Advertising by lawyers has become very liberalized, and a statement in an advertisement that the lawyer uses legal assistants in the practice of law is commonly found. However, what may be acceptable in one jurisdiction may be grounds for discipline in another. The key is whether or not the advertisement is deceptive to the public.

3.   Increasingly, many lawyers are protesting activities by nonlawyers as constituting the unauthorized practice of law. In some jurisdictions, correspondence signed by legal assistants was found to be such. While everyone agrees that a legal assistant cannot sign a pleading, nothing prevents a lawyer from delegating to the legal assistant the preparation of the pleading, provided that the lawyer supervises the delegated work and retains responsibility for it. Here, the violation might be in the eyes of the beholder, particularly where the lawyer's legal assistant deals directly with the opposing lawyer. Unfortunately, to be safe, the position of the opposing lawyer should be determined to avoid problems during representation.

Obviously, determining the ethics of a situation is no easy task and depends on the relationship and situation involved. To complicate matters, legal ethics are local or jurisdictional. Many jurisdictions now require practicing lawyers to have annual continuing legal education credits in ethics.

Perhaps ethical standards have become too complicated and render enforcement difficult. At the same time, legal issues have become complicated in situations once simple to solve.

Therefore, to apply legal ethics in the day-to-day aspects of the legal practice, legal assistants must understand all ramifications of their actions. As we shall see, this is no small task in the discovery process.

THE PROFESSIONAL RELATIONSHIP OF
THE LAWYER AND LEGAL ASSISTANT

The Lawyer

To comprehend the professional relationship of the lawyer and legal assistant, we must first understand what lawyers are as professionals. First, although public respect for lawyers has declined in the last few decades, college graduates still scramble for entrance into law schools. The number of lawyers in the United States is approaching one million.

However, recent information indicates that many are leaving the profession for various reasons, some of which are explored below.

The explosive increase in legal and factual knowledge and technology has produced practical problems in the practice of law that are beyond the knowledge and training of many lawyers. Many lawyers are unwilling to learn and integrate new technologies into their law practices. For example, a lawyer well-versed in manual access of land records books may resist using a computer terminal to access the same materials.

Many lawyers who thoroughly enjoyed law school find that the practice of law is not what they perceived it to be. Particularly in private practice, the hours are long, the competition for billing and advancement are fierce, and relationships with clients can be difficult.

Education and Training

During the first two years of law school, students study fundamental areas of the law: constitutional law, criminal law, contracts, property law, tort law (personal injury), legal procedures, and legal research and writing. Use of computers for legal research is fairly standard, and the public legal databases are offered free to law students. Specialized courses are offered, predicated upon the location of the law school; oil and gas law, for example, is a standard course offering in states having that industry. Students can gain practical experience from participation in school-sponsored legal aid or legal clinic activities, but these activities do not promote competency in most areas of practice. While in law school, many law students work as law clerks with lawyers and law firms to obtain practice skills.

Competencies

Lawyers primarily deal with the law and facts; their expertise lies in their ability to apply the law to a given fact situation. This requires keen analytical skills and the ability to recognize applicable legal theories, plus the ability to conceptualize legal practices and procedures and fact situations. Lawyers must be able to interact with various personalities and societal entities, so effective communication and interviewing skills are a must in the law practice.

Personality

Lawyers are first and foremost individuals, so it is difficult to write a personality profile of the typical lawyer. According to one occupational study, lawyers are artistic people and have a great need for self-expression through writing and performing. They are independent and nonconforming, intuitive and sensitive, disorganized in their work habits and creative in solving problems. [6]

Functions

A lawyer in our society performs three functions: as a representative of clients, as an officer of the legal system, and as a public citizen with professional responsibility for the quality of justice and service given the public.[7] Most of the time, a lawyer represents clients, and in that capacity wears many hats.

First, the lawyer functions as an advisor for the client, providing competent information about the client's legal rights and obligations and their practical implications. The lawyer is the client's advocate, negotiating to fulfill the client's needs and goals. To carry out these functions, the lawyer must not only demonstrate competence, but must communicate regularly with the client and keep the latter's confidences.

As an officer in the legal system, the lawyer supports the legal process, including proper use of the courts and other legal systems. As a public citizen, the lawyer should educate the public about the law and participate in activities designed to make the legal system available to all.

Concerns and Expectations

Since the practice of law is a professional business or occupation, the lawyer wants to be financially successful. Lawyers associate financial performance with professional success, i.e., the development of a positive reputation among peers and the public.

The lawyer devotes careful attention to professional liability arising out of the relationship with clients and other parties. Increasingly, clients are suing lawyers for professional malpractice, and lawyers are held accountable for failure to represent the clients' interest to the fullest extent possible. Many states require lawyers to contribute to a malpractice claims fund, and lawyer trust accounts are required and monitored extensively. Since the activities of the legal assistant working for the lawyer are legally those of the lawyer, the lawyer expects the legal assistant not to engage in any activity that will give rise to professional liability.

Lawyers are held accountable through court decisions and statutes for frivolous claims or defenses and unscrupulous actions for clients. Sanctions for this include the assessment of legal fees and expenses and recoveries for abuse of the legal process or malicious prosecution. No longer can a lawyer proceed on the "facts" as presented by the client and file a lawsuit; he or she is obligated to make a diligent investigation and give the potential defendants an opportunity to tell their side of the story.

Prudent lawyers are concerned with maintaining their professional license and status in the legal community. Professional ethics affect all aspects of the practice of law. State supreme courts are stringently enforcing the rules of discipline for lawyers licensed in their states. Professional malpractice is now considered a basis for disbarment, and many find the activities of the lawyer's legal assistant, including engaging in the unauthorized practice of law, as those of the lawyer in making such a determination. The lawyer cannot maintain any professional relationship with the legal assistant without expecting the latter to have a well-grounded understanding of the disciplinary and ethical rules applicable to the lawyer. In the final analysis, the lawyer's professional ethics must be those of the legal assistant.

Responsibilities

The responsibilities of lawyers in their professional relationship with legal assistants are well-defined. Beginning with its Formal Opinion 316 in 1967, the ABA has provided substantial guidance for lawyers in their relationship with legal assistants and the supervisory responsibility that entails.

Currently, the ABA Model Rules of Professional Conduct provide in Rule 5.3, "Responsibilities Regarding Nonlawyer Assistants":

With respect to a nonlawyer employed or retained by or associated with a lawyer:

- A partner in a law firm shall make reasonable efforts to ensure that the firm has in effect measures giving reasonable assurance that the person's conduct is compatible with the professional obligations of the lawyer.
- A lawyer having direct supervisory authority over the nonlawyer shall make reasonable efforts to ensure that the person's conduct is compatible with the professional obligations of the lawyer.
- A lawyer shall be responsible for conduct of such a person that would be a violation of the Rules of Professional Conduct if engaged in by a lawyer if:

  (a) the lawyer orders or ratifies the conduct involved; or

  (b) the lawyer is a partner in a law firm in which the person is employed, or has direct supervisory authority over the person, and knows of the conduct at a time when its consequences can be avoided or mitigated but fails to take reasonable remedial action.

Although the above rule does not specifically identify legal assistants, it remains the standard of supervision for lawyers employing and utilizing legal assistants. State bar associations are diverse in their ethical opinions concerning supervisory problems.

Most agree that, in supervising the activities of the legal assistant, the lawyer must maintain a direct relationship with the client. Further, the scope of the legal assistant's role must be established through a detailed position description. The lawyer must provide clear directions for the legal assistant about specific tasks to be performed.

Instructions for the Legal Assistant

One of the worst problems in the lawyer-legal assistant relationship is that lawyers often don't know how to give instructions! Since most lawyers are not trained to be supervisors, they do not easily delegate work. However, in assigning tasks to the legal assistant, particularly in discovery, the lawyer should adhere to the following approach:

1.   Explain the client's situation or problem, i.e., why the client has retained or would like to retain the lawyer's services.

2.   Outline in detail the specific task(s) to be performed and the relationship of those tasks to the overall representation of the client.

3.   Reference or provide applicable legal resources for the legal assistant to utilize or consult in performing the task.

4.   Provide existing factual information in a form that supports performance of the assigned task(s). Alert the legal assistant to any sensitive matters.

5.   Give time deadlines and an estimate of the time to be spent on each task. Always identify crucial time factors such as statute of limitations.

6.   Provide suggested methods of accomplishing the task.

7.   Monitor the assignment through periodic reviews.

Written instructions are preferable, and checklists are very useful. If the lawyer is unable to write out instructions, then the legal assistant should be allowed to use a tape recorder during any consultations with the lawyer about assigned tasks.

The Legal Assistant

The growth of the legal assistant profession has been phenomenal and reflects the acute information needs of our complex society. While individual lawyers may or may not possess technological skills, legal assistants as a professional group are high-tech. Although the ABA has never determined what constitutes the practice of law, it has specifically defined a legal assistant:

"A legal assistant is a person, qualified through education, training, or work experience, who is employed or retained by a lawyer, law office, governmental agency, or other entity in a capacity or function which involves the performance, under the ultimate direction and supervision of an attorney, of specifically delegated substantive legal work, which work, for the most part, requires a sufficient knowledge of legal concepts that, absent such assistant, the attorney would perform the task."

To truly understand legal assistants and their professional relationship with lawyers, we need to examine the ideal personality traits, functions, responsibilities, and other factors associated with the professional identification of legal assistant.

Personality

Several significant personality traits must be present in legal assistants who work successfully in discovery. Above all, they are organized. They methodically identify goals and objectives and how to obtain them. Legal assistants engaged in discovery are curious, almost to a fault, about people and things and are always willing to expand their existing abilities. They are analytical, attentive to details, and persevering when others would stop.

Legal assistants think independently and are outward-directed, unafraid to ask questions. They are intuitive and sensitive to other people, and the best legal assistants are able to persuade others to cooperate.

Education and Training

Although there are no education requirements for employment as a legal assistant, many lawyers seek legal assistants with formal legal assistant education and a college degree. The legal assistant involved in discovery should also have been trained in interviewing and investigation techniques. On-the-job training by the lawyer can be perilous, unless extensive training in ethical considerations is provided.

Competencies

The legal assistant must be able to work independently. Other essential competencies include communication skills, client assistance, the implementation of legal procedures, legal research, assistance in litigation, and the performance of investigative functions.[8] All are a part of discovery.

Functions

The legal assistant performs two dominant functions in assisting the lawyer during discovery: fact gatherer and communicator. As a fact gatherer, the legal assistant develops the factual basis for the client's problem and renders full support of the lawyer in representation of the client. As a communicator, the legal assistant processes information gathered from the client, witnesses, and related fact sources. The legal assistant facilitates communications between the lawyer and the client so that each can make competent decisions affecting their relationship.

Concerns and Expectations

Legal assistants must be concerned with maintaining their professional integrity. Although ethical misconduct will not result in any disciplinary action, most likely there will be job loss and inability to find similar positions.

Legal assistants have a right to expect lawyers to supervise all their activities, to provide specific instructions, and to refrain from using legal assistants in any way that would jeopardize the representation of the client.

Responsibilities

Legal assistants must aid supervising lawyers by keeping them informed about the progress of their work. Also, legal assistants must maintain their professional competence and ethical stance vis-à-vis the client and the lawyer. During discovery, legal assistants must maintain objectivity and protect lawyers from involvement in a matter that could jeopardize the lawyer's professional standing and responsibility.

NOTES

---

[1] J. Kelner and F. McGovern, *Successful Litigation Techniques*, Student Edition, 4-1 (1981).

[2] Id, 1-5.

[3] A. Golec, *Techniques of Legal Investigation*, 33 (2nd Ed 1985).

[4] Materials developed from the American Bar Association's Model Rules of Professional Conduct (1983).

[5] J. McCord, *The Litigation Paralegal*, 27 (1998).

[6] J. Strong & I. Hansen, *Strong-Hansen Occupational Guide*.

[7] Preamble, Model Rules of Professional Conduct (MRPC), American Bar Association, (1983).

[8] Michael A. Pener, *Paralegal/Legal Assistant Occupations, Catalog of Performance Objectives & Performance Guides, Vocational-Technical Education Consortium of States (V-TECS)*, (1988).

Chapter Two

THE NATURE OF EVIDENCE AND
ITS PLACE IN DISCOVERY

In judicial proceedings, evidence is factual information that forms the basis for conclusions as to ultimate facts. Evidence consists of testimony, opinions, hearsay, tangible materials such as writings, documents, objects, demonstrations, and similar information having a bearing on the claim or defense.

When the legal assistant undertakes any task during discovery, applicable rules of evidence must be reviewed and referred to so that evidence obtained will be admissible if adjudication becomes necessary. Because of the complexity of rules of evidence, voluminous materials have been made available as resources. Most state bar associations have prepared continuing legal education manuals on evidentiary rules for their particular jurisdictions.

For evidence to be admissible in a judicial proceeding, the following three basic requirements must be satisfied:

- It must be material.

- It must be relevant.

- It must be competent.[1]

MATERIAL EVIDENCE

To be admissible, material evidence must be necessary for a fair and informed determination of the disputed issues. Although the final decision on admissibility is made by the trial judge, such evidence should not be discounted during discovery. For example, while a shocking photograph of the plaintiff's injury could be excluded on the basis of materiality, it might be advantageous to show it to the insurance claims adjuster for the defendant during settlement negotiations.

Relevance

Relevant evidence is "evidence having any tendency to make the existence of any fact that is of consequence to the determination of the action more probable or less probable than it would be without the evidence." Relevancy revolves around the elements of the present dispute between the parties. Evidence that the defendant in an automobile injury case previously pled guilty to a traffic violation in another case would not be relevant evidence.

Even if evidence is found to have probative value, a court might still exclude it for a number of reasons: danger of unfair prejudice, issue confusion, misleading the jury, undue delay, waste of time, or repetitive presentation of evidence. Whether or not surprise is grounds for excluding evidence will vary from jurisdiction to jurisdiction.

Competence

Each jurisdiction has its own rules regarding competence of evidence. Generally, all evidence is considered competent unless its admissibility is restricted by some rule of evidence.

To determine the applicable rule, the character of the evidence must first be classified as testimony of witnesses or physical evidence. Next, its content must be analyzed for items of identification that can then be correlated to the jurisdiction's rules. In many instances, this will be a simple process.

For example, the federal rules provide that a witness may not be forced to provide testimony or to testify to a matter without the introduction of evidence sufficient to find that he or she had personal knowledge of the matter. This personal or firsthand knowledge must be information perceived by witnesses through their senses of sight, touch, hearing, taste and smell. Also, a confession given under force is not competent testimony.

TESTIMONY OF WITNESSES

Beyond this basic premise, there is some uniformity in the further limitations placed upon the testimony of witnesses, such as:

1.   **Opinion**. For other than experts, opinion may be allowed as to common, everyday observations and observations of a more personal nature. In the case of everyday observations, this includes measurable information regarding speed, weight, height and width, volume, and age. Observations of a personal nature are usually associated with repeated observations of or sufficient contact with another person so that the witness can give an opinion regarding an emotional or mental state, handwriting and voice, and personality traits.

2.   **Expert Opinion**. A witness qualified as an expert by reason of knowledge, skill, experience, training, or education beyond that of an ordinary person, may give an opinion as to scientific, technical or other specialized knowledge. Such opinion must assist in the understanding of the evidence or the final determination of the facts in issue. Two major factors to be considered in dealing with an expert are:

- qualification and

- the facts or information the expert uses to formulate the opinion.

3.   **Character and Conduct of a Witness**. Within certain limitations, the credibility of a witness can be attacked or supported by evidence given in the form of opinion or reputation. Generally, character evidence is not admissible, but will be allowed where the character of the witness has been attacked. Even then, the evidence is limited to the witness' character for truthfulness or credibility. Prior statements by witnesses inconsistent with their testimony could be used to challenge their credibility.

4.   **Capacity of a Witness**. The ability of witnesses to testify, admissibility of all or part of their testimony, or their credibility can be limited or restricted by legal, mental, or physical incapacitation. For instance, a young child may not be competent to testify. Statutory

privileges have many legal restrictions, including court-imposed restraining orders or determinations of mental incapacitation. Personality disorders, severe drug or alcohol abuse, and intellectual dysfunction are limiting factors. Physical characteristics or deficiencies may hamper the witness' ability to communicate or testify and may result in disqualification if the communication restriction cannot be removed by use of a qualified interpreter.

Hearsay

The hearsay rule resides in a category by itself. This rule excludes evidence of a statement made by someone other than the witness but nevertheless used in testimony to prove the truth of the matter stated. Hearsay testimony repeats some communication outside of the hearing which is offered as evidence. Exceptions to the hearsay rule are allowed in circumstances where there is a high probability of truthfulness. Admissibility is not predicated upon the truth of the content of the hearsay, but rather upon the fact that it was made.

Exceptions

There are several important exceptions to the hearsay rule in discovery, including:

1.   *Unavailability of the declarant as a witness*. Former testimony, a statement under a belief of impending death ("dying declaration"), a statement against interest, and a statement of personal or family history do not violate the hearsay rule if the declarant is unavailable to testify. Unavailability may be based upon privilege, refusal to testify despite an order of the court, testimony of lack of memory, death, physical or mental illness, or absence from the hearing if the declarant's attendance has not been procured by process or other reasonable means.

2.   *Declarations against interest*. Statements contrary to the declarant's self-interest may be admitted. Self-interest may include assertions against pecuniary or proprietary interest of the declarant, a statement that subjected the declarant to civil or criminal liability, or a statement that no reasonable person would make unless that person believed it to be true. For example, if a defendant in an automobile

accident case pleads guilty to a violation of a traffic ordinance in municipal court, that guilty plea can be used against him or her in the trial of a civil lawsuit brought by a person injured in the accident.

3.   *Spontaneous Statements*. Testimony of a spontaneous exclamation or utterance made at the time an event occurs is admissible if (1) it was made while the declarant was observing the event; and (2) the declarant was under stress of the excitement caused by the event, or (3) the declarant, unavailable as a witness, made a recollection without incentive to falsify or distort. Example: "Look out! He's going too fast!"

4.   *Business Records*. Records of businesses, including any institution, association, profession, trade, occupation, and similar activities (whether for profit or not), are admissible if

- they were kept in the course of a regularly conducted business activity, and

- it was a regular practice to make the record.

However, such may be excluded if it can be shown that the source of information or the method or circumstances of preparation indicate a lack of trustworthiness.

5.   *Public Records*. Public records in any form from public offices or agencies are admissible under the hearsay rule, even if the declarant is available as a witness.

PHYSICAL EVIDENCE

Although evidentiary requirements affecting the admissibility of testimony are extensive, consideration must also be given to their effect upon physical evidence. This evidence usually consists of tangible items or things that are representative in their nature. Tangible physical evidence can be felt or touched and has meaning unto itself, such as personal items (jewelry and clothing), automobiles, household goods and appliances, machinery, and equipment.

The importance of physical evidence lies in its perception by the court or jury. Experts may interpret the meaning of such evidence and give opinions on the effect of its content, but the court or jury determines its ultimate factual significance when the verdict is rendered.

One key factor affecting admissibility of tangible evidence is the establishment of chain of possession or control of the item until it is presented as evidence, to ensure that it has not been tampered with or altered since the event in controversy.

In some instances, logistics may pose a problem as to the admissibility of such evidence (try getting an automobile into a courtroom). Rules of evidence solve this problem by permitting tangible items to be represented through still photographs, x-ray films, video tapes, and motion pictures, provided that they are properly offered into evidence through appropriate authentication and identification.

DOCUMENTARY EVIDENCE

Such requirements also apply to items or things that are purely representative, such as writings and recordings, photocopies, data, documents, publications, records, and reports. All such evidence is admissible subject to the "best evidence" rule; this requires the production of the original to avoid the admission of false or altered items. In practice, a duplicate may be admitted in the place of an original unless the genuineness of the original is questioned or it would be unfair to admit the original instead of a duplicate. If the original is (1) lost or destroyed (but not in bad faith), (2) not obtainable, or (3) in the possession of the opponent who was forewarned that its contents would be the subject of proof, then the original is not required and other evidence, including a duplicate of its contents, can be admitted.[2]

1.   **Public Records**. The production of originals of public records comes under special consideration. In the past, an unnecessary imposition arose by requiring the production of original public documents in court. In the electronic age, many public records are kept or preserved in electronic form, to be reproduced when needed. Therefore, rules of evidence allow their submission in certified form

whereby the custodian of the records certifies the copies as correct in compliance with the rules or statutes.

2.   **Affidavits and Stipulations**. To alleviate the twin burdens of time and cost, courts are encouraging litigants to expedite discovery through the use of custodian affidavits for private records and stipulation agreements between the parties that admit evidence as true without proof of its authenticity. However, the attorney must still ensure that completeness be verified and that the effect of the evidence is not diminished in its abbreviated presentation.

3.   **Judicial Notice**. For the same reasons, courts may, at their discretion, take judicial notice of federal, state, and foreign law and generally known facts not reasonably subject to dispute, including specific facts and propositions of generalized knowledge that can be immediately and accurately determined by indisputable sources. Such law and knowledge might include a city ordinance, public records, scientific procedures, and matters of common knowledge within the community. In some jurisdictions, statutes require courts to take such judicial notice.

ADMINISTRATIVE EVIDENCE

Evidence that fails the tests of admissibility in court may still be admissible in an administrative process or procedure such as a statutory due process hearing. In some states, statutes and court rules provide for the convening of professional malpractice screening panels in conjunction with the filing of a professional malpractice liability action. Such panels are empowered to hear and receive evidence without strict adherence to rules of procedure and evidence applicable to civil cases. Administrative agencies are generally more liberal in admitting evidence, and most use a probative or contributory approach to admitting evidence that might be found to be incompetent in the courts. Pure hearsay may be allowed if there was no firsthand observation by witnesses — if, for example, in a workers' compensation hearing, the only witness to an accident is the injured claimant who has been in a coma since the accident occurred.

Therefore, inadmissible evidence that violates some rule of evidence should not be discounted completely, but rather should be viewed as significant during the discovery process. Except for privileged matters, the scope of discovery is not limited to admissible evidence. Discovery can include any information, regardless of admissibility, if it appears reasonably calculated to lead to the discovery of admissible evidence.

PLANNING FOR DISCOVERY

Discovery is the gathering of information. Regardless of the nature of a particular matter or dispute, the lawyer and legal assistant must formulate an overall tactical plan for the approach to discovery. This plan will guide them in the development of discovery strategies so that the client's objectives can be accomplished.

Since many methods for discovery exist, any lawyer and experienced legal assistant with extensive discovery experience will develop their own formula for success. A review of a number of methods indicates several common factors for all of them.

1. Identification of the legal theory involved in the problem. Focus here depends upon point of view, i.e., whether representation is of the plaintiff or defendant. For a plaintiff, the elements of proof defined by applicable substantive law of each legal theory are ascertained, and possible defenses are examined. Potential procedural bars, such as a statute of limitations or improper venue, are identified.

2. The factual theory or material facts needed to support each element of proof, defense, or procedural bars. This is usually done in chronological or "story" form. If the dispute evolves into full-fledged litigation through the filing of a lawsuit, then each supporting fact will be categorized and referenced to the elements of proof. Objectivity is essential, since, in the beginning stage of discovery, many fact sources (including the client) may be "tainted" with subjectivity or a one-sided viewpoint.

3.   Review and selection of appropriate forms of formal and informal discovery for optimal effectiveness in the development of the facts. Selection depends on timeliness, ease of use, costs, and satisfaction of evidentiary requirements.

4.   Specific provisions covering methods of gathering and preserving information, whatever its source. During the life of the lawsuit, there must be set procedures for identification of information and its orderly control and retrieval.

5.   A method of evaluation of the discovery plan. Because discovery is fraught with variables, reevaluation is necessary to maintain flexibility. Circumstances may dictate that the plan be changed so that previously unused discovery methods and sources can be considered.

However, before we review the formal discovery techniques provided by statutes and court rules, we need to fully understand that, in some situations, formal discovery will not be considered in planning objectives or developing an investigation plan. For example, where witnesses to a will must be located so that the will can be submitted for probate, formal discovery is not necessary. But what if a witness is terminally ill and initial facts indicate a possible will contest? Then plan reevaluation allows latitude to factor in formal discovery. Where allowed, the testimony of the witness could be recorded before litigation over the will's validity is filed.

Thus, there is a significant connection between formal discovery and informal discovery. Informal discovery cannot be used advantageously unless the lawyer and legal assistant understand the formal discovery techniques available.

FORMAL DISCOVERY

Many consider the discovery process to be the most important phase of a lawsuit. With the liberalization of the Federal Rules of Civil Procedure (FRCP) and corresponding state statutes and court procedural rules, there is very little information that one party to a lawsuit can withhold from the other. Because lawsuits are adversarial, there is no requirement that everything be disclosed unilaterally.

Formal discovery encompasses the methods set out in Rules 26 through 36 of the Federal Rules of Civil Procedure and in the procedural rules of most states. These methods include written interrogatories, production of documents or things or permission to enter upon land or other property for inspection or other purposes, depositions by oral examination or written questions, physical and mental examinations, and requests for admission.

Rule 26 discusses the scope and limitations of formal discovery. Identification of experts and facts known and opinions held by persons with knowledge about the subject matter of the lawsuit is discoverable. Related documents and business records can be obtained, as well as insurance agreements and statements made to an insurance carrier during its investigation.

Privileged information is not discoverable, nor will the court allow one party to obtain the work product of the other. A party may seek the court's protection from discovery via a claim that the discovery is unduly burdensome or expensive; this protection is within the discretion of the court to grant. Where a party has failed to cooperate in discovery, under Rule 37 the other party may request the court to order the dilatory party to comply and order sanctions, including reasonable expenses and attorney's fees. A motion for sanctions is a powerful discovery tool, but its effectiveness depends on the discretion of the court and the time involved, since several steps must be taken before it can be requested.

Effective use of the foregoing formal discovery methods is accomplished by identification of objectives, application of strategies, and adequate preparation. Before any formal discovery method is used, there should be in place a list of objectives. These objectives will include identification and purpose of the information being sought and should allow for preservation of testimony.

Before a lawsuit gets to the point of formal discovery, the lawyer should formulate strategies and consider several important issues. Will this case end up in trial, or is settlement a more realistic outcome? Is the client willing to bear the expenses associated with discovery? Will we unnecessarily disclose material information to the other side by engaging in a "paper war?" How critical is timing to this strategy?

Defining discovery objectives and strategies depends considerably on the situation. Adequate preparation is supported by having knowledge of the "rules of the game" and access to related materials. The Federal Rules of Civil Procedure, state statutes, court rules, and local court rules should always be reviewed for limitations and procedural requirements before formal discovery begins. The attitude of the judge toward formal discovery should be ascertained; one judge may be a former trial lawyer who looks disdainfully on discovery, while another judge may be overly progressive and apt to call repetitive discovery conferences. The reputation and competence of the opposing lawyer and legal assistant should be evaluated.

In conjunction with its use, the lawyer should identify the advantages and disadvantages of each method of formal discovery.

However, knowing the "rules of the game" is not enough; the lawyer must be able to use formal discovery methods effectively. In some jurisdictions, the courts have developed standard interrogatory questions and sample pleadings for other forms of formal discovery. Many law firms have developed their own master forms and formal discovery materials for the use of their staff, making it unnecessary to "reinvent the wheel" for each new case.

Even if master forms are unavailable, excellent form books and litigation materials provide resources to a legal assistant engaged in formal discovery: Bender's *Forms of Discovery, Am. Jur. Pleading and Practice Forms, Trials,* and *Proof of Facts*. In addition, books cover a wide spectrum of specialty areas: Blashfield's *Automobile Law and Practice, Automobile Accident Law and Practice*, and *Product Liability* are very useful. Another excellent resource is *Lawyer's Desk Reference*.

However, there is no substitute for legal assistants' developing their own materials for the preparation of formal discovery. With this in mind, let's examine in detail the forms of formal discovery.

Pre-Discovery Disclosures

To speed up the formal discovery process and promote settlement, the Federal Rules of Civil Procedure (Rule 26a) and similar state statutes and court rules have been changed to specifically require parties to a lawsuit to make disclosures of pertinent information before formal discovery begins. These disclosures include:

1.   Identification of witnesses likely to have discoverable information relevant to disputed facts. This includes names, if known, addresses, and telephone numbers.

2.   Copies or descriptions by category (including the nature and location) of documents, data compilations, and things in a party's possession that are relevant to disputed facts.

3.   Calculations of damages claimed and all documents supporting them (except privileged or work product).

4.   Production of applicable insurance policies for inspection and copying.

Rule 26a further imposes on each party the duty to make reasonable inquiry into the facts of the case before making the required disclosures. And each party has the duty to supplement its disclosures as the investigation and discovery proceed. Failure to comply with the rule can result in monetary sanctions and exclusion of witnesses' and the introduction of exhibits at trial.

Interrogatories

Interrogatories are written questions by one party submitted through their attorney to an opposing party who must answer them in writing and under oath. Compared to other forms of formal discovery, interrogatories are very cost-effective. In preparing interrogatories, a legal assistant should utilize a standardized checklist that sets out planning considerations and drafting techniques.[3] Planning considerations should always include the following:

- specific instructions from the lawyer

- review of the case file, particularly all pleadings and legal theories

- identification of the focus of the interrogatories, i.e., basis of liability, contentions, or fact discovery.

When appropriate:

- identification of the specific individuals to answer the interrogatories

- review of applicable rules and sample or form interrogatories

- avoidance of "paper wars" and overexposing the case to the other side.

When called upon to draft interrogatories, the legal assistant should adhere to the following techniques:

- Begin with instructions, notice of ongoing requirement to update answers, and a reference to the applicable rules and time requirements.

- Provide definitions of terms if complex issues are involved.

- Use plain language.

- Avoid any form of question that would allow evasive answers or a basis for objections.

- Always ask that supporting documents be attached. This will reduce subsequent document requests.

While the information sought varies from case to case, several common areas of inquiry exist for all suits:

- identification interrogatories that seek information covering the other party's personal background or information regarding a business or legal entity

- interrogatories that require the responding party to provide information supporting the fact allegations of the complaint or answer

- interrogatories used to pinpoint the contentions of the other party, making it difficult for the opponent to change position at a later date.

In formal discovery, the legal assistant plays an integral part in the preparation of answers to interrogatories. While not a substitute for the lawyer with the client, the legal assistant can act as a "communicator" between them, especially in answering interrogatories, and can substantially reduce the amount of time those answers will take.

First, the legal assistant should review the interrogatories before they are submitted to the client, analyzing their content to identify strengths and weaknesses of the opposing party's case and the extent of any discovery undertaken previously. Questions can be analyzed for possible objection to answering; objections can be based on irrelevance, work product, privilege, vagueness or broadness, or undue burden. Next, the client must be informed as to what this form of discovery entails. Too often the lawyer will not fill the client in on the legal theories of the case, and clients will attempt to answer questions to which they truly do not know the answers.

Upon receipt of answers to interrogatories, the legal assistant should review them thoroughly for responsiveness to the questions and correlate each one with the legal theories and factual information previously gathered. The lawyer or legal assistant should then determine if supplemental interrogatories should be prepared or if steps should be taken to compel the other side to respond properly.

Requests for Production of Documents, Things, and Inspections

Rule 34, FRCP, allows a party to request that the other produce for inspection and copying documents and records, charts, photographs, and tangible things. This rule also permits a request to inspect or enter upon land or other property in the control or possession of a party for the purpose of inspecting, measuring, testing, photographing or sampling.

The rule, in its broad scope, strongly encourages its use. Some lawyers may not utilize this formal discovery tool, reasoning that documents can be obtained at a deposition through the use of a subpoena duces tecum. Or they may feel that its use is time-consuming. However, in most cases, an initial request for production immediately follows the service and answer of interrogatories, before any depositions are taken. This demonstrates to the other side that the party means business by following up on the information obtained from the interrogatory answers. Document production before depositions allows the lawyer to preview requested key documents and conduct inspections and tests, so that the focus of the questions at the deposition will be more sharply defined.

Like other forms of formal discovery, this method can be wasted if not properly prepared.

Preparation of the document request is fairly routine, and samples are found in the appendices to the FRCP, most state procedure rules, and the form books. In preparing the request, the following should always be considered:

1.   There must be an understanding of the subject area that the documents, etc. pertain to before preparation. This can be developed from information obtained from the client, knowledgeable contacts, and information sources.

2.   The request must be as detailed and specific as possible so that the other side cannot use the excuse of ambiguity to evade compliance. For example, don't ask for "tax records." Specify "the federal income

tax return filed for 1997 and all documents, receipts, ledgers, invoices, notes, records, data, and similar items used in the preparation thereof."

3.   The content of the request should reflect previous discovery but serve as a starting point for future discovery. Information obtained from a request for production serves to confirm past discovery and act as a catalyst for future discovery.

When involved in the actual inspection, particularly without the lawyer's presence, the legal assistant should conduct the inspection in an efficient manner.[4] A method of identification should be used. Descriptions of the documents should be noted. An audio recorder might be used, and in the case of the inspection of land and things, a camera or video camera will be useful equipment.

Word to the wise: When in doubt about the evidentiary significance of a document, always copy it!

The response to a request for production or inspection affords the legal assistant an opportunity to examine the client's case objectively. All too often, a client might fail to disclose important information to the lawyer or legal assistant. Some of that information might fall within the purview of privilege or work product, but the lawyer is to determine that, with assistance from a legal assistant.

In any event, all documents requested and things designated for inspection must be thoroughly reviewed and examined prior to the date of inspection.

Request of Business Records of a Business not a Party

This formal discovery method resembles a request for production and functions the same as a business records deposition without the costs. After contacting a business having records believed to be related to the lawsuit, a party serves a subpoena duces tecum on the custodian of the business records, but the presence of the custodian is not required, and only copies of such records have to be produced. The custodian complies by filing them with the clerk of the court that issued the subpoena. After the clerk has notified the requesting party of receipt of the documents, that party is to give reasonable notice to all other parties to the lawsuit.

Because the subpoenaed business can demand reasonable costs of copying the records, the legal assistant should ascertain the charges before the request is made. Since the business records could be voluminous, the prior contact can help to eliminate unnecessary records from the request or subpoena.

Depositions

In a deposition, the lawyer asks oral or written questions of an opposing party or a witness. Oral depositions are the more common of the two, and many lawyers consider oral depositions of the parties the most significant discovery device and use it readily. It gives them the opportunity to hear firsthand the other party's fact story and to evaluate the opposing lawyer for competence and case strategy. At the same time, the deposing lawyer must take great care not to give the opposing lawyer the impression that a "fishing expedition" is being conducted.

In developing a deposition strategy, the lawyer must first analyze the pleadings and any previous discovery, formal and informal, to determine the remaining legal and fact questions and the specific information needed through deposition. Documents to be used at the deposition must be reviewed and organized. The lawyer or legal assistant should outline the deposition and prepare specific questions for key issues, as well as general information questions for the party-deponent covering personal and work relationships, medical information and history, damages, details of the event, and witnesses.[5]

A review of reference materials, office files, and form books will help the lawyer formulate special questions related to the subject of the litigation. The outline should be flexible so that the deposing lawyer can explore new avenues of information.

The legal assistant is invaluable in deposition preparation. Besides assisting in the development of the deposition outline, the legal assistant can gather and prepare documents and exhibits to be presented for evidentiary purposes at the deposition. The legal assistant can identify potential deponents from the documents produced and can gather background information of the deponent and information for loaded questions. (A "loaded" question is one where the lawyer already knows the substance of the answer and is using the question to check the deponent's veracity.)

If present at the deposition, the legal assistant can keep the questioning organized and help the lawyer avoid "legalese" questions. The legal assistant will be in charge of monitoring the documents and exhibits and can take notes and make observations concerning the deponent's demeanor. Many lawyers maintain that how a question is answered is just as important as the substance of the answer.[6] To this end many lawyers videotape their depositions.

If the deponent is the client or a friendly witness for the client, the lawyer should use various techniques to prepare him or her for deposition, ranging from letters or pamphlets explaining the deposition in detail to a mock deposition, where the client or witness comes to the law office and undergoes mock questioning. Sometimes the client will watch a videotape of a sample deposition that was produced by the lawyer or obtained from a legal vendor. Whatever approach is taken, deponents must understand that they are always to tell the truth and to remember during the deposition that the deposing lawyer is not their friend.

Physical and Mental Examination of Persons

When use of other formal discovery methods does not provide sufficient needed medical information of a party or a person, then, upon a showing of good cause, the court can order a physical or mental examination. Obviously, this form of formal discovery has limited application to personal injury and paternity cases. The legal assistant will be involved in the arrangements for such examinations.

Requests for Admissions

The last form of formal discovery is the request for admissions. Although this discovery device can be used any time from the filing of the lawsuit to the close of discovery, the lawyer often uses it at the end to narrow the issues. The request for admissions requires the other party to admit to the truth of matters covered by formal discovery, including facts, opinions, and application of the law to facts, or admit to the genuineness of documents, photographs, exhibits, and physical evidence. The disadvantage to the request for admissions is the same as the advantage: while the lawyer can use the answers to pinpoint weaknesses in the other side's case, the other side might see them as well and begin to build defenses against them.

The sequence of formal discovery usually begins with interrogatories and ends with requests for admissions. While depositions can be most effective, they are the most expensive, and their use must be thoughtfully considered with the client who bears the expense of litigation. Good informal discovery can supplement and augment depositions and other formal discovery if settlement is not obtained before litigation commences.

INFORMAL DISCOVERY

Informal discovery is all other activity that takes place during discovery, i.e., gathering, organizing, and synthesizing factual information without the direct involvement of a court, governmental entity, or any other authority having the power to resolve the dispute. Informal discovery involves interviews and investigations for the purpose of assembling all pertinent facts.

Definition of Fact

Because informal discovery concerns facts and their relationship to a client's dispute or problem, we should discuss the concept of a fact.

During informal discovery, a fact is anything that has happened: a thing, event, action, occurrence, circumstance, incident, experience, statistic, datum, perception, or similar information.[7] A fact's significance is not related to its admissibility or relevance as evidence, but rather to its ability to help the lawyer develop the true story of the dispute or problem. Any factual information directly associated with the dispute or problem is a "direct fact." Factual information that might relate to, explain, or enhance a direct fact, but which exists regardless of the happening of the direct fact, is a "related fact."

Elements of Informal Discovery

No master plan can cover every conceivable task that might be done
during informal discovery for all situations. However, certain tasks and
applications are germane to the great majority of situations, and can be
used as a basis for informal discovery. Any plan will be subject to
variables including time factors (internal and external), costs, access
limitations (physical and legal), and methods of implementation.

1.   *Contact with or on Behalf of the Client.* While legal assistants
are not usually involved in the initial contact with the client, they will
conduct a substantive interview with the client and subsequent follow-
up contacts as the matter progresses. In the first interview with the
client, the legal assistant should attempt to gather the following:

- background information

- details of the accident, event, or reason for representation

- information pertaining to physical injuries or economic loss,
  where applicable

- information about other parties involved and witnesses

- documentation in the possession of the client

- information about resources that the client may know.

In the course of researching the direct facts, the legal assistant may
need to obtain related facts, i.e., medical records, income tax records,
birth, death, marriage, and divorce records, and employment records.
For example, a standard for a medical test (a related fact) might affect
a direct fact (the medical exam and the client's condition).

2.   *Party or Defendant Profiles.* The legal assistant will assemble a
profile of all available factual information concerning adverse parties.
In initial informal discovery, identification of adverse parties or
potential defendants is of the utmost importance. First, the lawyer must
research any potential previous representation by the lawyer or the

lawyer's partners of the adverse party or potential defendant, to rule out a conflict of interest. Second, statutes and case law have allowed courts to impose liability, including reasonable lawyer's fees, against lawyers who file lawsuits against defendants without ascertaining the extent of their involvement or without reasonable notification. Third, even if the client's legal position is unassailable and the adverse party's position is seriously lacking or the potential defendant's liability is established, research might reveal that the adverse party or potential defendant is without financial resources or other means to satisfy the demands of the client.

3.   *Witness Profiles*. During informal discovery, every witness with pertinent knowledge of the primary facts of the client's problem must be identified and interviewed, as soon as possible after the initial client interview. The following information about each witness should be developed:

- background, personal, and employment information

- specific details as to the basis for their involvement

- identification of other witnesses

- corroboration of the client's facts

- determination of whether he or she is a "friendly" or "hostile" witness.

If an expert witness will be needed, then the plan will include provisions for the identification of possible expert witnesses through the search of appropriate information sources.

4.   *Information Sources*. Another element of informal discovery consists of identifying and gathering information from various information sources other than those already discussed. The legal assistant should review and analyze existing and potential factual information, keeping a sharp eye out for new information sources.

5.   *Fact Control*. As informal discovery takes place, all gathered factual information must be recorded, including all contacts with the client, adverse parties, potential defendants or their representatives, witnesses, and information sources. All information should be recorded so that anyone would understand what took place or what information was obtained. The recording, whether in written or other form of communication, should be in a standardized form, and should be organized to assist the lawyer in determining other fact sources to pursue through further informal discovery or formal discovery.

6.   *Fact Synthesis*. Once substantial factual information is gathered and organized, it can be synthesized. The legal assistant assembles the factual information in a format that allows its complete utilization by the lawyer, whether the lawyer resolves the client's problem through settlement or litigation. If litigation begins, then the factual information can be integrated into formal discovery and trial, through summaries of client information and records, witness interviews and statements, and compilations of all other factual information.[8]

Variables

As any experienced lawyer or legal assistant knows, each client's case is unique. The client, the nature of the problem, parties and witnesses, particular goals of the lawyer — all of these and other variables affect fact investigation. For this reason, any plan for fact development must be flexible enough to meet exigencies when they arise.

However, certain factors must always be considered during the formulation and execution of the fact investigation plan.

1.   *Time (External)*. As with formal discovery, the conducting of informal discovery is affected by external time requirements. The most prominent time requirement is the statute of limitations for the filing of a lawsuit. An administrative agency might require information to be provided by a certain date, or it will take action unfavorable to the client. For example, the collection branch of the Internal Revenue Service commonly levies upon a taxpayer's wages when it is not provided requested information. The client might set a deadline for the gathering of information.

2.   *Time (Internal)*. Internal time is the time made available for informal discovery in a matter or for a particular informal discovery task. The lawyer must make an estimate of the amount of time to be expended on informal discovery at the onset of the matter. In litigation, the plaintiff's lawyer enjoys a false luxury of being able to devote unlimited time to the client's cause; if the lawyer kept time records, the low time-cost-effectiveness in many instances would be startling. Location of witnesses, evidence and information sources also affects internal time.

3.   *Costs*. The great inhibitor for many lawyers is the cost involved in representing a client. Everyone wants to achieve favorable results with minimum expenses. While expenses are the responsibility of the client, in reality the lawyer often "gets stuck with the bills" if litigation is unsuccessful. The client might simply be unable to pay the expenses. The corporate or insurance defense attorney might not be as concerned about expenses, but even corporations and insurance companies have been known to suffer business failures and declare bankruptcy, and legal bills might remain unpaid forever.

4.   *Methods*. The plan should embody how informal discovery is pursued and which methods will be used to locate and obtain factual information. Of course, standard methods such as personal interviews, use of the mail and delivery services, and use of the telephone are utilized to a great extent, but variations of these methods, particularly electronic means, have exploded upon the scene. In some jurisdictions, courts allow lawyers to file petitions or complaints in lawsuits via facsimile (fax) devices and electronically, and court records can be accessed by means of telecommunications. Witness statements are often recorded over the telephone.

The Informal Discovery Plan

The lawyer should begin to formulate the informal discovery plan right after the initial interview with the client, or even before if sufficient information is available. In an automobile accident case, if the location of the accident is known, the legal assistant might visit the scene of the accident, take photographs, and prepare an accident scene diagram for the lawyer's use at the initial interview. In the informal discovery plan, flexibility and adaptability are the key words. The plan should lend itself to easy revision, since it will be revised after the initial and substantive interviews of the client, during informal and formal discovery, and during trial preparation. While lawyers take different approaches in determining what goes into the plan, all good plans are thorough and inquisitive.

Using an automobile accident case as an example, let's prepare initial investigation plans using two popular forms: checklist and topical outline.

Checklist Form

To formulate the initial investigation plan, many lawyers and legal assistants like to brainstorm or engage in critical thinking to help identify important information. The legal assistant records this in checklist form and spotlights the items of factual importance. This approach usually suffices in uncomplicated matters, or in a case similar to many handled in the past where the lawyer and legal assistant do not need to "educate" themselves about an unique fact situation or technical matter. The checklist might include columns to identify the method used and person responsible for gathering the information with an estimate of the cost involved.

Automobile Accident Investigation Plan Checklist [9]

- What kind of vehicles were involved?
- Weather and road conditions.
- Particulars about our client such as driving record, physical disabilities (glasses, etc.), on medication?
- Check with motor vehicle licensing authority on driving records.
- Photographs or videotaping of the accident?
- Newspaper stories?
- Check with governmental department or agency responsible for maintaining the streets, roads, or traffic control devices.
- Get accident report, interview police officer.
- Visit accident scene, make a diagram, take photographs or videotape.
- Check for evidence of accident such as skidmarks, debris.

- Contact and interview all potential defendants; find out about insurance policies and their limits.
- Contact and interview all witnesses, take statements if significant.
- Get client's medical records, past and present.
- Start gathering damages information like lost wages, out-of-pocket expenses, medical bills.
- Contact and interview treating physician.
- Do we need any experts?
- Similar accidents at that location?
- Canvass the neighborhood for possible witnesses.
- Get client's insurance information—do we have a subrogation problem?
- Possible product liability—check with Consumer Product Safety Commission and National Highway Traffic Safety Administration.
- Get vehicle ownership records.
- Particulars about other drivers; driving while on the job?
- Examine and photograph the vehicles involved. Do they need to be preserved as "evidence" or for later examination by expert?
- Obtain books or manuals on this type of accident case.
- Prepare format for client "diary" or daily record of pain and suffering.
- Prepare for substantive interview with client, including medical and other record authorizations.
- Check applicable rules of the road.
- Accident reconstruction?
- Get vehicle maintenance and repair records.
- Get income tax and social security records.
- Obtain information on potential defendants' entity status.
- Obtain birth and death records.
- Obtain background information on witnesses.

Topical Outline Form

Like the checklist, the topical outline form identifies areas of investigation, but uses major topics for a more organized expansion and carryover into formal discovery. The lawyer must first determine the major topics to be explored; then the legal assistant should do some independent brainstorming and categorize the results under the appropriate major topic as set out below:

Automobile Accident Investigation

The Accident

- Weather and road conditions.
- Photographs or videotaping of the accident?
- Newspaper stories?
- Check with governmental department or agency responsible for maintaining the streets, roads, or traffic control devices.
- Get accident report, interview police officer.
- Visit accident scene, make a diagram, take photographs or videotape.
- Similar accidents at that location?
- Obtain books or manuals on this type of accident case.
- Check applicable rules of the road.
- Accident reconstruction?

The Client

- Particulars about our client such as driving record, physical disabilities (glasses, etc.), on medication?
- Check with motor vehicle licensing authority on driving records.
- Get client's insurance information — do we have a subrogation problem?
- Prepare format for client "diary" or daily record of pain and suffering.
- Prepare for substantive interview with client, including medical and other record authorizations.
- Obtain birth and death records.

Potential Defendants

- Check with motor vehicle licensing authority on driving records.
- Contact and interview all potential defendants; find out about insurance policies and their limits. particulars about other drivers, driving while on the job?
- Obtain information on potential defendants' entity status.
- Obtain birth and death records.

Medical/Damages

- Get client's medical records, past and present.
- Start gathering damages information like lost wages, out-of-pocket expenses, medical bills.
- Contact and interview treating physician.
- Get income tax and Social Security records.

Witnesses

- Contact and interview all witnesses, take statements if significant.
- Do we need any experts?
- Canvass the neighborhood for possible witnesses. Background information on witnesses.

Vehicles

- Get vehicle ownership records.
- Examine and photograph the vehicles involved. Do they need to be preserved as "evidence" or for later examination by expert?
- Possible product liability — check with Consumer Product Safety Commission and National Highway Traffic Safety Administration.
- Get vehicle maintenance and repair records.

Non-Dispute Plans

Although informal discovery is part of the litigation process, this procedure can also be used in other situations. Some examples are:

1. The client plans to make a secured business loan to another person and needs to know if any previous Uniform Commercial Code (UCC) financing statements have been filed for the borrower.

2. The client is the administrator or personal representative of an estate and needs to locate one of the heirs of the decedent.

3.   A corporate client is selling a piece of real estate and needs an
          official certification that it is a corporation and is in good
          standing under the laws of the state of its incorporation.

4.   The client plans to revise its employment application for
          prospective employees and needs assistance in identifying
          discriminatory requests for information.

Each situation might demand certain informal discovery, but it will
seldom be as extensive as a legal claim or dispute. A client desiring a
will might tell the attorney that the client owns real estate jointly with a
child but that the deed cannot be located. Through the informal
discovery plan, the legal assistant may verify the ownership through the
land recording records of the county and state where the real estate is
located.

The following is a sample informal discovery plan for incorporation of
a going business:

Existing Business Entity

- sole proprietorship or partnership
- employer identification number
- sales tax identification number
- depository bank
- assets and liabilities
- UCC filings
- present owners and employees
- retirement and medical plans
- trademarks, copyrights, and patents
- lease and franchise agreements

Incorporation

- corporate name, reservation, permission from others?
- specific business purposes
- capitalization, classes of stock and authorized amounts
- stock restrictions
- registered agent and location of registered office

- board of directors, number, how elected, and powers
- incorporators, qualifications
- filing requirements and costs

Organizational Documents

- pre-incorporation agreements
- initial minutes
- bylaws, limitations on powers, amending, duties
- transfer of assets, leases, etc.
- issuance of shares of stock
- shareholders' agreement
- loan agreements

Tax and Financial Matters

- application for employer identification number
- "S" corporation election
- bank accounts and loans
- new stationery and business forms
- tax year and other accounting matters

Informal Plan Effectiveness

Development and execution of informal discovery can take considerable time and effort, and time, of course, has become a very valuable commodity. but when properly done, a plan gives the lawyer tremendous foreknowledge of the viability and settlement potential of a client's claim, as well as a complete understanding of the client's problem and the appropriate method of resolution. Thus, informal discovery is an integral part of the discovery process.

NOTES

---

[1] A. Morrill, *Trial Diplomacy*, 42, (2nd Ed. 1972).

[2] Fed. R. Evid. 1002.

[3] J. McCord, *The Litigation Paralegal,* (3rd Ed. 1997).

[4] Id, 307.

[5] A. Morrill, *Trial Diplomacy*, 200, (2nd Ed. 1972).

[6] P. Lisnek and M. Kaufman, *Depositions, Procedures, Strategy and Technique,* Law School and CLE Edition, 4-1 to 4-5, (1990).

[7] W. Statsky, *Legal Thesaurus/Legal Dictionary*, 309, (1985).

[8] L. Charfoos and D. Christensen, *Personal Injury Practice: Technique and Technology*, 376, (1986).

[9] H. Philo, *Lawyer's Desk Reference*, 7th Ed., 681 to 683, (1987).

Chapter Three

**LEGAL THEORIES AND
FACT ANALYSIS**

DISCOVERY PROCESS

Four fundamental factors affect the discovery process:

1.   the development of legal theories

2.   fact analysis

3.   identification of parties and entities

4.   identification of property interests.

This chapter will focus on the use of legal theories and fact analysis. In discovery, the development of applicable legal theories and fact analysis are essential. Law and facts go hand in hand. Neither can be sustained without the support of the other.

Determination of Applicable Law

In the practice of law, the most fundamental requirement for success is the lawyer's ability to recognize the legal issues of the client's problem. Even when the legal basis for a lawsuit is easily determined, often other factors, such as the identification of parties and interests, procedural rules, and jurisdiction, come into play. The lawyer maintains the primary responsibility for formulation of legal theories applicable to the client's problem.

LEGAL THEORIES

For lawyers, the skill of finding applicable legal theories was developed in law school through analysis of a set statement of facts to determine the legal problem. Typically, law students categorize the given facts into topical areas: persons, subject matter, the legal basis, and defenses. Using this approach, students access appropriate sources of law, principally statutes and cases, and determined applicable legal theories.

While this method works for the law student, it falls short in the real practice of law. Facts are not always complete, particularly in the initial stage of client representation, so the lawyer must be flexible in the identification of legal theories. Further, for many clients, economics render it unfeasible to conduct extensive legal research on the fine points of the law. Rather, practicing lawyers look to legal materials for a quick and thorough analysis of applicable legal theories as the facts are developed.

Development

The development of legal theories is a true example of the cart sometimes traveling in front of the horse. Rarely will the lawyer be able to formulate applicable legal theories until first meeting with the client and conducting a preliminary investigation of the problem; the lawyer usually develops the facts and the legal theories simultaneously. Many experienced lawyers have devised checklists of legal theories of liability pertinent to their areas of practice for reference during the initial stage of client contact. For example, legal theories of strict liability can be organized into the following topics: animals, aviation, blasting, fires, utilities, poison sprays and insecticides, ultrahazardous activities, and unnatural uses of real estate.[1]

Lawyers often substitute or supplement the checklist method with a legal analysis as soon as sufficient facts have been identified.

Legal Analysis

Legal analysis consists of identifying central legal theories that support the client's position, relegating side issues to secondary status. For proper perspective, the lawyer should examine and analyze all facets, especially defenses and opposing positions. The following outline provides a pattern for accomplishing this.[2]

Our Client's Situation

- identification of all possible, supportive legal theories
- identification of most applicable theories, based upon present fact development
- identification of weaknesses
- basic elements of each applicable legal theory
- information needed to support each applicable legal theory
- information sources and limitations
- procedural problems that may be encountered
- affirmative positions that may be raised by the opposition
- strategies

The Opposing Party

- identification of all possible opposing legal theories in conflict with our client's position
- positions based upon legal insufficiency in our legal theories
- identification of strengths
- information under its control
- defensive strategies

Overall Legal Theories

- central legal issues
- final strategies
- core position in support of client's situation

Legal Perspective

In the development and analysis of legal theories, much depends upon the lawyer's legal perspective. Many factors affect the legal perspective: the lawyer's personal and legal philosophies, the nature of the client's problem, and the lawyer's legal practice. It is not uncommon for a client to have one or two lawyers to decline representation of a client before the client finds a lawyer who engineers a successful recovery. Obviously, since the law and facts did not change, the lawyer's legal perspective played a major role in finding the applicable law.

During the beginning stage of discovery, legal perspective is extremely crucial. Here, important questions must be answered, particularly where possible litigation will be involved. Although the client's injuries or damages may be severe and the potential defendant may be financially responsible, the lawyer's initial legal perspective might not support legal liability and may overshadow the process of finding supportive law. The wise lawyer forgoes making inadequate judgments before conducting legal research of the legal theories involved.

Legal Research

Legal research is one of a lawyer's most important tools. Most lawyers today still do their research manually; however, computer-assisted legal research (CALR) through the use of legal databases and Internet legal resources is becoming a significant alternative. Whatever the approach taken, the lawyer must still have a basic understanding of the significance of legal research and the various methods used for successful research. A legal assistant engaged in fact-gathering, interviewing, and investigation must be able to conduct legal research and apply applicable law during discovery.

During discovery, the lawyer's responsibility to develop legal theories and substantiate them through legal research is paralleled by the legal assistant's responsibility of fact development. Often, the lawyer asks the legal assistant to perform legal research before fact development takes place, or the lawyer will instruct the legal assistant to become familiar with the legal aspects of the client's problem before the legal assistant embarks upon fact development. Legal assistants may take the initiative before or during fact development to review the applicable law to be sure that they are taking the correct fact-gathering approach. No matter the reason, legal research is an essential part of discovery, and legal assistants must be prepared for this important task.

Appropriate Legal Research

What constitutes appropriate legal research will depend on several factors: (1) the nature of the client's problem; (2) the degree of familiarity of the lawyer or legal assistant with the legal problem presented; and (3) the goals or objectives to be accomplished through the legal research. Usually, the nature of the client's problem will be easily recognized. However, with the explosion of statutory and case law, the lawyer and legal assistant must guard against becoming myopic in their legal viewpoint when conducting legal research. Legislatures enacting statutes earnestly try to cover related situations that may arise, but they cannot foresee every situation that might occur in our complex society. However, with the arrival of electronic law libraries, even the most obscure law can be located.

A lawyer or legal assistant lacking knowledge about a particular subject may completely overlook the client's legal problem. There is no right way to become knowledgeable about the law. However, an open-minded, common sense approach to legal research becomes invaluable, and the legal assistant may have more insight into a problem than the lawyer in this regard.

Because the law is multifaceted, legal research during discovery is necessarily open-ended. Fact development is a continual process, and any change in the facts naturally affects applicable law. For this reason, legal research should be conducted for a specific purpose that is identified before the research ever begins. The lawyer may ask the legal assistant to conduct initial legal research as a pathfinder, so that the lawyer will be able to quickly access legal materials later. During the course of fact investigation, the plaintiff's lawyer, wanting to interview a potential defendant's employee, needs to know if this is legally possible without the permission of the defendant's lawyer.

Overview of Legal Concepts

In conducting legal research, legal assistants should obtain a thorough understanding of the applicable law so that they can easily access relevant legal materials. Even if they are quite familiar with certain legal concepts, this approach should still be taken, due to the rapid evolution of the law that has taken place. When a legal assistant works for a lawyer who specializes in a specific area of the law, the internal law library at that lawyer's offices will usually contain legal materials related to the particular practice area. A lawyer specializing in bankruptcy law will have *Collier's on Bankruptcy*; a lawyer who handles automobile accident cases will probably possess Blashfield's *Automobile Law and Practice* or similar materials.

Even in such instances, the case may demand more extensive authorities. The lawyer should guide the legal assistant to materials appropriate to the research task: continuing legal education books and presentations in audio or video form, legal databases and Internet resources, and briefs and research projects of similar legal questions in other matters the lawyer has worked on. However, where the lawyer or legal assistant is unfamiliar with the subject matter, the legal assistant should first turn to legal encyclopedias, treatises, legal periodical literature, and annotated materials.[3]

Legal Encyclopedias

Legal encyclopedias contain narrations on cases and statutes pertaining to major legal topics. While some jurisdictions have their own encyclopedias, *American Jurisprudence 2d* and *Corpus Juris Secundum* are considered the two national legal encyclopedias, since they contain complete surveys of all American case and statutory law. In print form, both arrange the law in topics and have extensive index volumes.

If analysis of the legal research problem results in a clear identification of a legal topic, then the legal assistant should review the materials on that topic. However, where there is uncertainty, the legal assistant should turn to the index volumes and research the topic as follows:

1.   Analyze the legal research topic for descriptive terms or words.

2.   From the general index volumes, select section references relevant to each descriptive term or word.

3.   Examine each selected section reference in the topic volumes and pocket parts of the encyclopedia for relevance to the topic

4.   Cite and summarize portions of each section applicable to the legal research topic (correct form of citation is given at the front of each volume).

Treatises

A legal treatise embodies all of the law about a particular legal topic in one work. It usually includes a commentary and extensive annotations to applicable cases and statutory law. Treatises will also provide the user with sample pleadings, documents, and suggested methods of accomplishing related tasks. While treatises can be quite comprehensive (some may contain a number of volumes), their use is of limited value if they are not periodically supplemented or in electronic form.

The format for researching the law in treatises follows:

1.   Identify relevant treatises by using the law library's card catalog or online database.

2.   Select treatises relevant to the legal research topic.

3.   Examine the index of each selected treatise for relevant entries.

4.   Examine each relevant entry in the main body of the treatise and the current supplement.

5.   Cite and summarize relevant parts of each treatise.

Legal Periodical Literature

Because they focus on current legal issues and often discuss applications of particular jurisdictions, one of the best sources of legal research is legal periodical literature. While law reviews published by law schools contain extensive information about specific areas of the law, articles in journals of bar associations are usually written by lawyers with considerable practice experience. Annual indexes are provided. Legal periodical literature can be researched as set out below.

1.   Analyze the legal research topic for descriptive terms or words.

2.   Select a legal periodical index. (The three major ones in print,
        CD-ROM, or online form are *Index to Legal Periodicals*,
        Current Law Index, and *Legal Resource Index*.)

3.   Examine the index for relevant articles.

4.   Examine each article for relevance to the topic.

5.   Cite and summarize relevant portions of each article.

Annotated Materials

Annotated materials are arranged so that, following a complete court
opinion, there is an extensive outline and index of the topic discussed.
The dominant publication is the *American Law Reports (ALR)*. The
ALRs consist of groups of volumes, each with its own index and are
available in CD-ROM format. Annotations are cross-referenced in *Am.
Jur. 2d, Proof of Facts, Pleading and Practice Forms*, and the *ALR
Digest*. Citations are to all jurisdictions. The *ALRs* can be utilized as
follows:

1.   Analyze the legal research topic for descriptive terms or words.

2.   Locate appropriate volumes containing annotated materials.

3.   Review preface or explanatory pages of annotated materials for
        information and examples of use.

4.   Select index volumes.

5.   Locate relevant references in index volumes.

6.   Find each relevant annotation in the main body of the annotated
        materials.

7.   Review each annotation for relevant information, references,
        and case citations.

8.   Cite and summarize.

9.   Update each relevant annotation by reviewing supplements.

Statutes

Some lawyers maintain that statutes should be checked for applicable law before any other legal research is done. Annotated statutes will contain legislative histories, sources of prior law, notes, references to related statutes, practice aids such as pertinent legal periodical literature, and case annotations, along with an extensive index. Some states publish their own statutes in this form, but many are done by private publishers.

Why check statutes first? Obviously, an applicable statute may support the client's problem or work against it. A legal researcher familiar with the subject area might access statutes by topic, rather than by use of an index. However, an applicable statute can be easily overlooked if it is not listed under the topic being searched, so the legal assistant is well-advised to use an index. In general, use the following method to research statutes in print form:[4]

1.   Determine the facts and legal issues to be researched.

2.   Select appropriate statute books.

3.   Review their preface, explanatory pages and/or general index. (Many may contain explanatory materials and examples of how they can be used.)

4.   Locate statutory references in the general index.

5.   Locate statutory references in statute books, annual supplements, and session laws, when applicable.

6.   Review each statute and its annotations, if any, for application to the facts and legal issues.

7.   Cite, summarize, and shepardize the relevant provisions of each statute and, if any, its case annotations, etc. (A description of shepardizing is provided later in this chapter.)

Administrative Law

Because statutes cannot cover every conceivable situation that may be affected by their passage, an immense amount of administrative law has developed: rules, regulations, and administrative decisions. No administrative agency can develop and put into force any regulations without an enabling statute. On the federal level, administrative regulations can be found primarily in the *Code of Federal Regulations* (CFR). Current regulations should be checked in the *Federal Register*, the federal government's "daily newspaper" or through Internet access.

Regulations of state agencies usually follow the same publication format as the CFR. However, there may be variations and any unfamiliar, published state regulations should be reviewed thoroughly before being utilized. The CFR in print form can be researched as follows:[5]

1.   Analyze the topic to be researched by identifying its facts and legal issues, if any, in descriptive terms.

2.   Locate the CFR index volume.

3.   Review the preface or explanatory pages of the CFR volumes and the index volume for use information and examples.

4.   Select relevant index volume entries for each descriptive term.

5.   Locate each selected entry in the identified volumes.

6.   Examine each selected entry (regulation) for relevance to the topic.

7.   Cite and summarize relevant provisions.

8.   Check the monthly and annual index of the *Federal Register* for additional entries.

9.   Locate each relevant additional entry in the issues of the *Federal Register*.

10. Cite and summarize the relevant provisions of each additional entry.

Court Rules

State and federal court rules covering litigation procedures, evidentiary requirements, and ethical matters impact any determination of applicable law. While the Federal Rules of Civil Procedure (FRCP) have influenced the rules of many state court systems, any researcher should bear in mind the uniqueness of the particular applicable court rules. In addition, local court rules, depending upon the practice sophistication of the jurisdiction, may have specific requirements that regulate discovery. For example, the rules of the state supreme court may limit the number of interrogatories in formal discovery without approval of the trial court or agreement of the opposing party, and the trial court rules may further limit the format of such to prevent any attempt to bypass the intent of the state supreme court rules.

In researching court rules, the legal assistant must take care to have the latest version of the applicable rules, available from the clerk of the jurisdiction. Many state supreme courts and local courts provide their rules in print form without annotation at a nominal cost. They are also available through the Internet.

Case Law

The heart of legal research is finding relevant case law. Computer-assisted legal research has alleviated this task immensely, but many researchers still adhere to manual methods through the use of case digests. No matter the approach, care must be taken to ascertain the latest controlling case law, if any, and to adequately "brief" relevant cases. (A description of a brief is provided in item 10 below.) The following is suggested when researching case law through the use of law digests:[6]

1. Analyze the research topic by identifying the facts and legal issues in descriptive terms, e.g., parties, places, things, basis of action or issues, defenses, and relief sought.

2.   Select the relevant case digest.

3.   Review its preface or explanatory pages and its general index
        for explanatory materials and examples of how the digest can
        be used.

4.   Locate topics and subtopics in the general index for each
        descriptive term.

5.   Locate topics and subtopics in the digest volumes, annual
        supplements, and update supplements.

6.   Review each topic and subtopic for relevant case summaries.

7.   Record citations of relevant case summaries.

8.   Retrieve each case by using the volume and page number in the
        state reports, regional reporter system, or applicable federal
        reporter system.

9.   Read each case for relevant points of law.

10.   Prepare a "brief" for each relevant case containing:
        • the name, citation, and date
        • the legal topic(s) covered by the case
        • a summary of the material facts
        • the questions or legal issues presented by the case
        • answers to the questions or legal issues presented by the
          case
        • a summary of the court's reasoning
        • a summary of significant concurring and dissenting
          opinions, if any
        • a concise statement of the legal significance of the case.

Citators

Statutes, administrative regulations, court rules, and case law must be
verified for accuracy and validity through the use of a citator. The most
popular is *Shepard's*, available in print, CD-ROM, and electronic form

through WESTLAW or LEXIS. Although *Shepard's* can be utilized for several types of "shepardizing," its two primary functions relate to cited case and statutory law. Explanatory pamphlets entitled *How to Use Shepard's Citations* and *Questions and Answers* can be obtained from Shepard's, 1275 Broadway, Albany, NY 12204, 1-800-899-6000. Following are suggested methods for shepardizing a case or statute in print form.[7]

Shepardizing a Case

1.   Identify the statute.

2.   Select the set of *Shepard's* containing the cited case.

3.   Collect all bound volumes and paperbound supplements available for the selected citator set.

4.   Check the table of contents of the selected citator set for starting pages of the table of citations and illustrative examples.

5.   Locate the volume number of the cited case in the citator table of the bound volumes. (Note: The latest citing authority may be obtained by reversing the process and starting first with the most recent paperbound supplement.)

6.   Locate the page number (boldface type) of the cited case on the citator page.

7.   Examine each entry (citing authority) following the page number (boldface type) of the cited case.

8.   Identify the parallel citation, history of the cited case, citing cases, citing legal periodical literature, citing annotations, and citing opinions of attorney general, if any, for each entry.

9.   Use the preface pages and abbreviations tables of the table of contents of the citator to ascertain the meaning of abbreviations to the left and right of each entry and the small raised number (superscript), if any, contained in each entry.

10.   Record each relevant entry (citing authority).

11.   Repeat steps 5 through 10 using the remaining bound volumes
        and paperbound supplements of the citator.

Shepardizing a Statute

1.   Identify the statute. (Note: Use the codified citation before the
        session law citation.)

2.   Select the set of *Shepard's* containing the cited statute.

3.   Collect all necessary bound volumes and paperbound
        supplements available for the selected citator set.

4.   Check the table of contents of the selected citator for
        illustrative examples.

5.   Locate the cited statute (boldface type) in the citator table of the
        first, bound volume. (Note: The latest citing authority may be
        obtained by reversing the process and starting first with the
        most recent paperbound supplement.)

6.   Review each entry (citing authority) following the boldface type
        of the cited statute.

7.   Identify parallel citations, the history of the statute in the
        legislature and courts, citing administrative decisions, citing
        legal periodical literature, citing annotations, and citing
        opinions of the attorney general, if any, for each entry.

8.   Use the preface pages and abbreviations tables of the table of
        contents of the citator to ascertain the meaning of the
        abbreviations for each entry.

9.   Record each relevant entry (citing authority).

10 .   Repeat steps 5 through 9 using the remaining bound volumes
        and paperbound supplements of the citator.

COMPUTERIZED (ELECTRONIC) LEGAL RESEARCH

In the brief time since this book was first written, computerized or electronic legal research has become an impressive reality and portends substantial changes in the practice of law. Presently, many laborious legal researching tasks have been lessened or eliminated by this new instant access to the law. Experienced lawyers and legal assistants are scrambling to take courses and seminars that explain how to use this phenomenal legal research tool. Judges now commonly have computer terminals in their courtrooms with access to online or CD-ROM legal databases such as WESTLAW, LEXIS, and LOIS. Legal resources and virtual law libraries are available on the Internet at uncountable sites. What this all means is that any identification of basic legal skills must include the ability to competently access legal databases and Internet resources. Practicing legal assistants, as well as those entering the profession, must possess these competencies.

FACT ANALYSIS

Legal assistants play a very important role in fact analysis during discovery, since they will most likely be directly involved in gathering any factual information essential to the dispute or matter. The lawyer and legal assistant must take care to communicate during all phases of fact analysis. Further, although objectivity is the standard to be achieved, several subjective factors will influence the techniques employed and results obtained.

The lawyer and legal assistant employ fact analysis in much the same way as they do in their private lives. We all formulate questions or responses as we encounter various situations and use our previous experiences to answer or act. In some instances, we alter our normal approach because the circumstances require us to develop specific conclusions based upon general facts or assumptions. In either case, we break down information about people, things, activities, assumptions, ideas, and facts to determine their nature, function, and interrelationship.

In the legal setting, the lawyer and legal assistant use this analytical process for specific legal tasks necessary for client representation. In discovery, they take into consideration several factors:

- the final objective of the analysis
- the nature of the resources available
- the purpose of the results of the analysis
- the parameters of the analysis.[8]

Analytical Methods

When we analyze, we use two kinds of formal reasoning or critical thinking: the inductive and the deductive. Both are used in fact analysis during discovery.

Inductive Thinking

A legal assistant assigned the task of finding out additional information about the financial status of a potential defendant will probably use inductive thinking. Inductive thinking is a method of gathering related information so that a fact-based conclusion can be drawn and tested or applied to the case circumstances.

The gathering of factual information is the first step. Sometimes it can be extremely simple; for example, the client maintains he or she is old enough to qualify for Social Security retirement benefits, but has no evidence to substantiate this. To do such, the legal assistant would obtain a certified copy of the client's birth certificate.

The second step consists of taking the gathered evidence and drawing a conclusion or making an assumption if the information is inadequate. In the above example, suppose the client brought in a copy of his or her birth certificate showing a qualifying age? Here our gathered evidence would be that document, but we would make an assumption based upon its contents as to the client's age, since it was not certified.

Deductive Thinking

With deductive thinking, a conclusion is drawn from a fact premise or assumption through syllogism. A syllogism is the process of drawing a conclusion based on major and minor premises.

For example, take the statement that "he doesn't have any symptoms of a cold, so he can't have a cold." The major premise: People with colds have recognized symptoms. The minor premise: The person does not have any such symptoms. The conclusion: The person does not have a cold.

Of course, a major problem with deductive thinking is that, while the conclusion may be correct as to its major and minor premises, one or both of them may not be true. Thus, for deductive reasoning to have any impact in fact analysis, it is imperative that every attempt be made to ascertain correct fact premises before any syllogism take place.

No matter how the fact premises were obtained, either by the inductive or deductive methods, all terms must be defined as precisely as possible. Generalizations should be avoided but, if used, must be retained along with any other qualifying premises in the conclusion. Any conclusion that is essentially identical with the basic premise is useless.

Analytical Process

While it is difficult to describe the process of inductive or deductive reasoning, each will usually follow certain lines of reasoning. First, we use our powers of observation to identify facts affecting us or the problem. Next, we use our inventive ingenuity to identify possible explanations of the facts. Then, using our experiences and acquired knowledge, we examine each explanation for its validity. Finally, we then verify. While this process is used extensively in scientific investigation, it also applies to fact analysis in discovery. In both instances, problems can arise from the limitations, background, and knowledge of the person performing the fact analysis.

Limitations

Those knowledgeable in psychological behavior maintain that our personalities have two major components: genetic and environmental. The former consists of our inherent ability to use words and concepts, our physical and biological characteristics, temperament, and skills. The latter involves our development of tastes, standards, values, beliefs, and social identification. Personality traits are recognized as "limitations" only in the sense that they affect the ability of a lawyer or legal assistant to analyze successfully during discovery. Simply stated, we all carry our own baggage.

Some personality traits support fact analysis: perseverance, attention to detail, curiosity, and communication skills. Conversely, a deficiency in any of these will detract, and extremes in other personality traits can have an adverse effect. Prejudices and bias opinions based on past experiences or teachings may limit the ability of the lawyer or legal assistant to conduct fact analysis, even though they possess other more positive personality traits. A legal assistant well-skilled in fact analysis, but whose childhood friend was killed by a drunk driver, may not approach fact analysis for a client accused of killing someone while driving drunk with the necessary impartiality.

Background and Knowledge

Legal assistants bring to fact analysis all of their education, knowledge, and background, and all these factors affect the outcome of the analysis. For this reason, many lawyers engaged in medical malpractice cases hire nurses without any previous legal training to work as "legal assistants." Ideally, a sufficient background or experience along with accompanying knowledge should enable a legal assistant to recognize necessary fact information or make correct fact premises in any situation, but there are few such Renaissance individuals. Most of us tend to "see only what we know."

Legal assistants should recognize the extent of their background and knowledge and gauge their effect on their ability to conduct fact analysis. When their knowledge is lacking, they should take steps to educate themselves about the subject matter of the client's problem before they undertake any fact analysis.

Legal Methods

In the legal environment, how one goes about conducting fact analysis can be crucial. One advantage, however, is that the fact premises that are obtained, particularly in litigation matters, often turn out to be the ultimate facts necessary to sustain or support the legal theories applicable to the client's problem. Thus, once the facts are identified, the legal assistant can move through fact analysis with a specific purpose. However, any identification of the fact elements of a legal theory should not restrict a full development of the fact story of the client's problem.

Fact analysis can be accomplished by different methods, but success is predicated upon certain elementary factors.

Recording

Any good fact investigator will either say "write it down" or "make a record." The problem may stretch over several years, and information can get stale or lost. While ideally the lawyer and legal assistant work as a team, substitutions of either of them can occur as a matter progresses.

Trivial facts discovered at the beginning of a lawsuit should always be recorded. As issues develop, an initially unimportant fact may grow in importance.

Time Sequencing

Whenever possible, all results of fact analysis should be set forth sequentially or within a chronological framework to put the facts in their proper perspective. Time sequencing can be done by inserting the time of events in a story outline or by preparing a chronological chart of times and corresponding facts outlined in detail.

Story Outline

The client's file should contain a detailed story outline of the facts of the problem, and the story should be updated continuously as fact analysis proceeds. Some lawyers not only develop a general story outline, but also outline the affirmative existing evidence of the client and the opposing party and the client's potential affirmative and rebuttal evidence.[9]

A good rule to follow in preparing a story outline is to know the answers to the following questions affirmatively:

1.   Would anyone reading this story outline understand what the client's problem is about?

2.   Would anyone reading this story outline understand what facts have been developed and what facts need to be developed?

Cyclical Process

Legal fact analysis is, by its nature, a cyclical process. The analysis consists of gathering and confirming existing facts, but any confirmed fact raises new questions to be answered, analyzed, and added to the existing facts. Every new fact changes the existing factual information and prompts analysis and re-evaluation, which might lead in turn to more fact identification. This cycle continues until the matter is either closed or settled or ends with a trial. It does not stop with the end of formal discovery.

Method Selection

One can take different approaches to fact analysis. One method is to identify essential fact elements to a matter, identify their sources, and then obtain the fact information. Another analyzes the facts from the different perspectives of the client and the opposing party. A third method analyzes fact information chronologically.

Whether to choose from these methods or to develop some hybrid method depends upon the case at hand and the abilities and personality of the legal assistant. In any event, unless the legal assistant performs a thorough and objective fact analysis, the legal theories applicable to the client's problem may not find firm and reliable support.

NOTES

---

[1] H. Philo, *Lawyer's Desk Reference* (LDR), 7th ed., 1342 (1987).

[2] Utilized materials in *Pretrial Advocacy, Planning, Analysis, and Strategy*, M. Berger, J. Mitchell & R. Clark, 31-33, (1988).

[3] Michael A. Pener, *Paralegal/Legal Assistant Occupations, Catalog of Performance Objectives & Performance Guides, Vocational-Technical Education Consortium of States* (V-TECS), 39 & 40 (1988)

[4] Id., 42.

[5] Id., 43.

[6] Id., 45.

[7] Id., 47 & 48.

[8] The National Association of Legal Assistants, *Manual for Legal Assistants*, 72-75 (2nd Ed. 1992).

[9] D. Binder & P. Bergman, *Fact Investigation*, 40 (1984).

Chapter Four

IDENTIFICATION OF PARTIES, ENTITIES, AND PROPERTY INTERESTS

During discovery, the lawyer and legal assistant must understand and identify the individuals and entities in a legal matter and the nature and extent of their property interests. Plaintiffs' lawyers must specifically identify potential defendants; indeed, failing to do so can cause severe financial repercussions. Defense lawyers must explore all avenues of defense, including identification and involvement of other parties as defendants.

IDENTIFICATION OF PARTIES AND ENTITIES

In simple litigation, "parties" will usually mean a plaintiff and a defendant. Since litigation is not always simple, other persons or entities who are not plaintiff or defendant may have a substantial interest in the outcome of litigation. An employer of a worker, having paid workers' compensation benefits, may have a statutory right of subrogation for such payments when the worker seeks additional recovery from a third party deemed responsible for the worker's injuries. Even where litigation is not involved, the respective rights and interests of persons other than plaintiff and defendant must be identified.

Identification of parties involved in a legal matter and their capacities and respective interests constitutes one of the most important tasks during initial discovery. By identifying all potential defendants, the plaintiff proceeds against them all in one action and precludes the possibility of a defendant avoiding liability because he or she was left out of the lawsuit. Since comparative negligence statutes affect determination of damage awards, the potential defendant will want all persons who may have been responsible joined in the lawsuit.

During discovery, the legal assistant must help the lawyer determine the parties involved, their relationships, and their capacities. The nature of business, government, and other entities must also be clarified, since they may affect the course of discovery.

Pleading Requirements

Rule 17 of the Federal Rules of Civil Procedure (FRCP) and similar rules of state jurisdictions make it quite clear that any civil action must be maintained in the name of the real party in interest. If a minor child is injured by a defendant in an automobile accident, any lawsuit against the defendant by the minor child must be in his or her own name through a legally designated person, e.g., a parent as a next friend or a guardian or conservator appointed by a court. The rule specifically identifies persons with special interests or rights who may sue and be sued: bailees, beneficiaries and subrogees under contracts, statutory plaintiffs, and fiduciaries such as executors, administrators, guardians, and trustees. Rule 17 liberally allows joinder, ratification, and substitution when the identification of the proper parties is difficult or an understandable mistake is made, but errors will not be rectified if other parties will be prejudiced by a correction.

Capacity of the Parties

Generally, the capacity of an individual to sue and be sued is determined by the laws of one's domicile (usually one's home). The capacity of corporate entities is determined under the law of the jurisdiction in which they were organized. In all other instances, with the exception of partnerships, other unincorporated associations, and certain statutory entities, capacity to sue and be sued is determined by the laws of the jurisdiction where the litigation takes place or where the cause of action arose.

Special Situations

Rule 17 specifically identifies representatives such as guardians, conservators or similar fiduciaries who may file or defend a lawsuit on behalf of an infant or incompetent person. (The more modern terms are "minor" and "disabled person"; however, the terms used in the statutes and court rules of the applicable jurisdiction should be followed.) Where an infant or incompetent person does not have an appointed legal representative, Rule 17 allows the lawsuit to be brought by a next friend or by a guardian ad litem. The court will appoint a guardian ad litem or make other protective orders, if there is no legal representative. As a safeguard, experienced litigation lawyers will seek appointment of a legal representative prior to filing of a lawsuit; many will even create a guardianship or conservatorship estate with a legal representative for an infant or incompetent person.

The Client

The lawyer and legal assistant work in peril if they make assumptions about the identity of their client or fail to fully investigate the extent of the client's legal relationships and interests. Even law firms retained by insurance companies to represent defendant policy holders must guard against the potential conflicts that can arise from the legal relationship between the two because of inadequate identification.

With any client, the lawyer must consider ethical questions and possible liability claims. Many law firms now have a "conflicts legal assistant" or "client coordinator" who reviews every matter initially and periodically to determine any problem with representing the client. Identification of the client should be made through the use of a Client Profile similar to the following:

Client Profile
(Individual)

A. Name

_____

[Present Name, Previous Names, Including Fictitious Names]

B. Residence

_____

[Present And Previous Residences]

C. Identifying Numbers

_____

[Social Security Number, Tax Identification Numbers]

D. Legal Status_____

              [Adult/Minor, Single/Married/Divorced, Citizen/Alien, Etc.]

E. Legal Relationships _____

              [Parent/Child, Statutory, Contractual, Etc.]

F. Work Status_____

              [Employer/Employee, Previous Employment, Etc.]

G. Family And Social Relationships

_____

_____

[Including the Lawyer and the Legal Assistant]

H. Previous Litigation or Legal Matters

_____

_____

Opposing and Other Parties

The lawyer and legal assistant must identify all opposing parties and parties with interests in the matter. Their relationships, legal and otherwise, may give rise to responsibility or liability. With the rising costs associated with various forms of insurance, subrogation plays a large part in the handling of legal matters, particularly personal injury claims. Accordingly, the plaintiff's lawyer must coordinate legal activities with anyone claiming subrogation rights in the claims of the client.

The lawyer must clearly identify opposing parties, not only for the client's interest, but to protect the lawyer against court-imposed sanctions or malicious prosecution accusations by a defendant improperly included in a client's lawsuit. Bearing this in mind, we will examine the relationships and identifying factors pertaining to individual and entity identification.

Individuals

The status of an individual has substantive and procedural importance. For example, the doctrine of negligent entrustment imposes liability upon an automobile owner who entrusts it to another if the owner knew or should have known that the borrower would drive it unsafely. Procedurally, service of process upon a legally incompetent individual is ineffective.

Legal Relationships

From birth to death, each individual has a myriad of legal relationships: adult or minor status, residency, citizenship, marriage, divorce, the legal relationship between spouses, and the legal duties and rights of parents with respect to their child. One particularly important legal relationship is created by contract. For many clients, one or more of these legal relationships may compel the client to seek the lawyer's services, and may indeed be crucial to the client's case.

Statutory Relationships

Beyond the legal relationships arising out of an individual's status or life activities, statutory relationships may affect one's status, especially when acting in a fiduciary capacity. A fiduciary is any person who acts in a position of trust or for the benefit of another person: a personal representative (executor or administrator) of an estate, a guardian of person (body) of another individual, a conservator of the living estate of another person, and an attorney-in-fact pursuant to a grant of power of attorney.

Sometimes a statute may protect or give preference to an individual or define the limits of an individual's liability as set forth below:

- Veterans may be given statutory preference in job applications.
- A pharmacist who reports medical malpractice may be granted statutory immunity from suit.
- Athletic officials may be granted statutory immunity from suit.
- Individuals who volunteer to assist a nonprofit organization may be immune from liability if the organization carries liability insurance.

- An individual who files a workers' compensation claim against an employer may be protected by statute from being fired.
- At the federal level, the Soldiers and Sailors Civil Relief Act gives individuals in the military protection as to their jobs, property, and interests.
- A teacher may not be fired without cause.

In some instances, a statute or court rule may allow an individual to obtain special status or occupational licensing such as: notary public, certified public accountant, physician, surety, lawyer, surveyor, and real estate broker. Many statutes define the extent of liability or limit the licensee's ability to recover fees or commissions where there is sufficient noncompliance on their part.

Business Entities

Proper identification of business entities will have a substantial effect upon determining the nature, interests, responsibilities, and capacities of the client and other parties involved in the client's dispute. It also will have a bearing upon what investigative methods will be employed and the extent to which information can be obtained without resorting to formal discovery. When a lawsuit must be filed, thorough identification of business entities during informal discovery will prove invaluable. Before we discuss the four main types of business entities — sole proprietorship, general, limited and limited liability partnerships, corporations and limited liability companies — we need to understand certain legal relationships that significantly affect these entities.

Agency

Agency is a legal relationship, determined factually, whereby one person is authorized to act for or represent the interests of another.[1] Anyone can be an agent, including minors and legally incompetent persons, but the principal (the person or entity authorizing the agent to act) must be legally competent. Therefore, a minor normally cannot be a principal. In an agency relationship, respective rights and liabilities of the agent and principal to each other and third parties will depend upon their duties to each other and the authority given or exercised by the agent.

The most important duty that an agent has to the principal is to act as a fiduciary at all times. This duty includes loyalty, trust, and confidentiality. Much of a principal's liability, particularly to third parties, will depend upon the type of authority an agent has. There are four types of authority: actual, which can be expressed or implied, apparent, inherent, and authority, which is created by the principal's ratification of the agent's acts.

A lawyer representing a third party will want to establish the correct relationship between the principal and agent, since the option exists of proceeding against either. In many instances, the principal often will be in a better financial position than the agent.

Documents and activities that identify the agency relationship may include the following:

- a written or oral contract between the principal and agent (the Statute of Frauds may require some contracts to be in writing to be enforceable)
- other written documents such as checks, promissory notes, leases, insurance policies, permits and registrations, and similar documents identifying the agency
- promotional activities, including seminars, lectures, and advertisements.

Employer and Employee

An employee functions at the will of an employer to the extent that the employer supervises or controls the employee's activities, while an agent usually has discretion to determine what activities will be done to accomplish the goals of the principal.

The nature and extent of an employment relationship will affect liability because of the legal principal of respondeat superior. Under this concept, an employer may be held liable for the negligent acts of the employee through imputation.

Closely associated with the employment relationship is the question of whether one has been retained by another to perform services or work independent of the control of the latter as an "independent contractor." Independent contractors will only be held liable for their negligent or tortious acts unless such were done at the request or authorized by the other party. Factors used to differentiate between an employment and an independent contract are listed below:

- the extent of control, which, by the agreement, the principal may exercise over the details of the work
- whether or not the one employed is engaged in a distinct occupation or business
- the kind of occupation and whether it is one traditionally done without supervision by the employer or principal
- the competencies or skills required for the work
- who supplied the tools or equipment needed to perform the work
- the length of time of employment
- method of payment — by time or job
- whether the work performed is part of the regular business of the employer or principal
- the parties' intent (note: courts will ignore self-serving declarations of independent contractor status in an agreement).
- whether the employer or principal is an established entity

Sole Proprietorship

A sole proprietorship is the simplest form of business organization. The business has no existence apart from its individual owner. Its liabilities are the individual owner's liabilities, and his or her proprietary interest ends upon death.

For tax purposes, the sole proprietorship reports all income and deductions on Schedule C (Form 1040). Other identifying documents and information pertaining to a sole proprietorship are:

- fictitious name registration with the secretary of state
- licenses, permits, and professional registrations
- financial statements, including accounts receivable and inventories, balance sheets, and profit and loss statements

- Uniform Commercial Code (UCC) financing statements and security agreements
- Internal Revenue Service (IRS) taxpayer identification number (can be the Social Security number of the individual owner, but must be an employer identification number [EIN] in certain situations)
- state tax reporting records such as sales and use taxes
- general business documents such as leases, insurance policies, employee benefit plans, personnel records, and agreements with other business entities (franchises, authorizations, etc.)

Partnerships

General Partnership

A partnership is the relationship between two or more persons who join together to carry on a trade or business. Each person (individual, corporation, trust, estate, or another partnership) contributes money, property, labor, or skill, and each expects to share in the profits and losses. A partnership can be described as a "sole proprietorship" of two or more persons, since each partner may be held liable for acts and liabilities of the partnership.

Unlike a sole proprietorship, each state, with the exception of Louisiana, has adopted the Uniform Partnership Act, which has specific provisions dealing with the formation, operation, and termination of partnerships.

Usually, a partnership is created by written agreement, setting forth the rights, duties, and liabilities between the partners. Because partnerships are vulnerable to legal termination for various reasons, including the death or bankruptcy of a partner, agreements will provide for the purchase of a partner's interest in such situations. Normally, general partnerships are not required to file the agreement as a public record.

Each partner is considered an agent of the partnership. Generally, a partnership can purchase, own, and transfer property in the name of the partnership, but any financing arrangements will be in the names of the partners. Depending upon the degree of involvement in the partnership's business, a partner can be classified as a general or full partner, a silent partner, a secret partner, a dormant partner, a nominal or ostensible partner, a trading partner, or a nontrading partner.

For tax purposes, a partnership is considered a conduit, with each partner being taxed on his or her respective share of the partnership's income or loss. IRS Form 1065 is the partnership's tax return, and the partnership has its own EIN.

Limited Partnership

With a limited partnership, the partner exchanges a degree of limited liability for exclusion from management or control over the partnership business. If limited partners engage in management or assert control, they become general partners and lose their limited liability status. Limited partners are only liable for partnership obligations up to the amount of their investment in the business.

A limited partnership is created by permission of the state of its domicile. It is required to submit its partnership articles or application to the secretary of state by certification and disclose the names and place of residence of all of its partners and its registered agent. Each limited partnership must have at least one general partner whom creditors and governmental entities may hold responsible for its debts, taxes, and failure to meet statutory requirements. Most states have adopted the Uniform Limited Partnership Act, which embodies all of these requirements and governs partnership activities not covered in the limited partnership agreement.

Because partnerships involve two or more persons, a lawyer representing one must ensure that there is no conflict of interest between the purpose of the representation and the legal needs of the partners. Many of the identifying documents and information regarding a partnership resemble those of a sole proprietorship. Particularly significant are the partnership agreement and amendments, ownership and liability documentation, and persons having information bearing upon the existence of a partnership where specific documentation is lacking.

Limited Liability Partnership

This business entity is similar to the limited partnership; however, with it, each partner has unlimited liability only for his or her own negligence and not that of the other partners. Limited liability partners are still personally liable for the contractual obligations of the partnership. With these features, the limited liability partnership is well-suited for professionals such as lawyers and doctors.

Corporations

The most widely used and regulated business entity form is the corporation. Whether a large, complex business entity or a small operation with one or two shareholders, all corporations are initially created pursuant to state statutory requirements. Thereafter, statutes of the state of incorporation and those states where the corporation is authorized to do business regulate a corporation's business activities and possible termination of existence.

The most important advantage of the corporate business entity is that its shareholders are not personally liable for its contracts, debts, and torts in excess of their investments for its stock. Being a purely statutory or artificial entity, a corporation can only act through its directors, officers, agents, and employees. Corporations are formed for profit purposes, unless they are specifically designated "not for profit." Typically, corporations come into existence with the filing of an application for charter or articles of incorporation. This document must contain specific information concerning the corporation's name, its initial registered agent and location of its registered office, identification of the nature of its business, its capital stock structure, identification of its incorporator(s), provisions as to its directors, and the duration of its existence. Upon issue of a charter by the secretary of state, the corporation comes into existence. Some states require further that the corporate charter be filed with the land records of the county where the corporation's principal office is located.

Corporate Name

While statutes vary from state to state, all require the corporate name to contain a word or an abbreviation of a word that sets the corporation apart: "company," "corporation," "incorporated," or "limited." Not-for-profit corporations may use appropriate words such as "club," "fund," "foundation," "institute," and "society." Not all states will allow a corporation to use a name identical or similar to that of another corporation. When such a conflict arises where a corporation seeks to do business in another state as a foreign corporation, it will be required to use another name or operate with a "doing business as" (d/b/a) designation.

Annual Reports

During their existence, corporations are required to file annual reports with the secretary of state identifying their current officers, directors, and significant shareholders, and containing an annual balance sheet. Failure to file the annual report can result in forfeiture of charter. In some states a corporation's ability to maintain a legal action can be challenged where its charter has been forfeited.

Corporate Status

To maintain the shield of limited liability for shareholders, the corporation must fulfill all statutory requirements. Corporations that have done so obtain *de jure* status, while those that fail to do so may still afford shareholders protection if found to be *de facto* corporations. Even where the corporation is a *de jure* corporation, courts increasingly allow lawsuits to "pierce the corporate veil" against its officers, directors, and shareholders for the corporation's acts if there was fraud, inadequate capitalization, or blatant disregard for the formalities necessary for a *de jure* corporation.

Special Corporate Formats

Many states recognize special types of corporations. Chief among these are the close corporation, sometimes referred to as the closely held corporation, and the professional corporation designed for professionals such as lawyers, doctors, and engineers. Statutes specifically provide for not-for-profit or nonprofit corporations.

Liability of Officers and Directors

Because they occupy a fiduciary relationship to the corporation and its shareholders, officers and directors may be liable for acts where they put their interests above those of the corporation or where they fail to disclose conflicts of interests. In this vein, the lawyer should exercise great care when representing corporations to avoid liability arising out of conflicting representations.

Significant corporate documents, forms, and records pertaining to a corporation's identity may include the following:

- articles of incorporation and amendments thereto as filed with the secretary of state
- bylaws
- annual and franchise reports
- the corporate minute book
- stock certificates and the stock transfer book
- shareholder agreements
- the corporate documents record book
- tax forms, including income tax forms such as the 1120 and 1120S (for S corporations)
- general business documents such as leases, insurance policies, employee benefit plans, personnel records, and agreements with other entities (franchises, authorizations, etc.).

Limited Liability Company

A limited liability company (LLC) is a statutory business entity similar to both the corporation and partnership. Instead of shareholders or partners, its owners are called members. When an LLC is properly organized and operated, its members are protected from personal liability for its debts and can participate in its management. The LLC is treated as a partnership for federal income tax purposes.

Principal documents for an LLC include the articles of organization, which are filed with the secretary of the state where the LLC is organized, and the operating agreement between the members.

Governmental Entities

Identification of governmental entities is important not only when their activities subject them to legal actions, but also because many of their functions make them an excellent source of factual information.

Where a governmental entity engages in a proprietary function that can be carried on by a private enterprise, no sovereign immunity from legal action exists. Because the "sovereign immunity" barrier has weakened in many states, it is now easier to make claims against and sue governmental entities, but sovereign immunity" still applies to purely governmental functions. Thus, identification of a particular governmental agency having critical information can be tantamount to success in litigation.

Federal Government

With some exceptions and qualifications as set forth in 28 U.S.C. Sec 1346 *et seq.*, all civil actions against the United States must be brought in the United States District Courts or in the United States Claims Court. These include claims for negligent acts or omissions of government employees or agents where the United States, if a private person, would be liable to the claimant under the law of the place where the negligent act or omission occurred.

Liability does not exist for all claims situations. For example, the federal government is still immune from tort liability where there was an intentional tort by one of its employees or agents according to 28 U.S.C. Sec. 2680. Certain federal agencies enjoy specific immunity from suit with regard to their activities.

State and Local Governments

Most state jurisdictions follow the federal sovereign immunity concept and maintain immunity from legal actions for torts unless they have enacted legislation authorizing such. Usually these statutes will be specific. Therefore, it is absolutely essential that they be identified and reviewed for applicability to the client's situation. In some instances, certain state agencies will be identified as the defendant where a lawsuit will be filed. However, at the local governmental level, identification can be even more crucial because of additional limitations.

In some jurisdictions, statutes may preclude governmental liability unless the plaintiff can show liability predicated on other than the execution of a governmental function. In some states, local governments may defend by claiming a plaintiff's noncompliance with statutory notice requirements. Further, in an action against a local governmental entity, many states still require that the suit be maintained against all members of its governing body. Statutory confusion may exist as to whether a governmental entity is a separate and legal entity that can be sued, or whether it is a part of another governmental entity.

For example, police, fire, educational, and publicly owned utilities may have a legal existence separate from the city or county in which they operate. In any event, specific identification is absolutely necessary for lawsuit purposes and access to public records.

Other Entities

Other entities have a legal existence, and in some situations their true composition, nature, or activity can have a bearing on liability. One such association is an organization of persons who join together for some common purpose: clubs, fraternal organizations, and leagues. Of course, many incorporate as not-for-profit corporations, but if they do not, then the members may have personal liability.

Another entity of note is a receiver: a person appointed by a court to take some specific action with respect to property of another. For example, during litigation between shareholders of a closely held corporation, the court may appoint a receiver to manage the corporation until the dispute is resolved, or to liquidate assets and distribute the proceeds. A bankruptcy trustee functions in this capacity. A special administrator appointed during probate functions in a similar manner. For all of these, court documents appointing and specifying duties and responsibilities must be thoroughly examined, for there may be personal liability if receivers engage in activities beyond the scope of their authority.

Finally, legal relationships arise out of the creation of a trust. For any trust, there must always be a trustee. All jurisdictions have statutes defining the trustee's duties and responsibilities as a fiduciary. Banks and trust companies will have statutory authorization to act as trustees, but individuals, if legally qualified, may act in such capacity. Information and records of some trusts, such as charitable trusts, must be open for public inspection by law.

IDENTIFICATION OF PROPERTY INTERESTS

The final factor affecting discovery is the identification of property interests. As we have moved from an agrarian society through industrialization and into the technological age, property interests have also evolved. Evidence of ownership has been simplified to accommodate the new methods of electronic identification. For example, major corporations no longer issue stock in certificate form, but now issue a document that identifies the number of shares owned by the stockholder. In identifying property interests, we must investigate not only the nature of the property itself, but also its ownership and documentation evidencing the extent of ownership and interests in the property.

General Property Concepts

Property is anything that a person has the right to possess and own. From this broad definition, the concept of property can be further classified into two main types: real property, which includes land and everything attached to it; and personal property, which is simply everything else. Sometimes personal property is attached to or installed in real property in a more or less permanent manner and becomes a part of the real property. It then becomes a fixture and loses its separate identity as personal property.

Statutory Considerations

In many instances, identification of possessory and ownership rights in property will be based upon documents prepared in compliance with or to take advantage of statutory requirements of the state where the property is located. Applicable state statutes dealing with real and personal property must always be reviewed prior to or in conjunction with any client situation where identification of property interests is an issue. Furthermore, not only will the statutes provide pertinent statutory requirements, but they are a source of substantive and procedural requirements affecting property interests.

Real Property

When it comes to real property, because of its permanent nature, we are most concerned with identifying the specific interest a person has in a piece of real property and how that interest is owned.

The most unrestricted interest is the fee simple, since a person having such can do what he or she wants with the property, subject to legal restrictions. In some instances, a fee simple may be conditional, conditioned upon some use restriction. For example, title to land is transferred to a church only for religious uses. A lesser interest in real property is a life estate, which gives the holder thereof an interest in the property so long as the person on whose life it is based is alive. Other lesser interests in real property include leasehold interests, easements, and licenses.

Forms of Ownership

Ownership of real property must be in a specific, identifiable legal entity. The simplest form is sole ownership, also known as ownership in severalty, where one individual or legal entity is the owner. As such, the individual or legal entity has sole control over the use and possession of the property, as well as sole and unlimited liability for all obligations arising out of the ownership.

The other form is co-ownership, where two or more individuals each have an ownership interest in a piece of real property. Generally, each possesses the right to convey or transfer ownership interest free from the other co-owners, and also has the right to seek partition of the property into respective ownership parts. As to possession of the property, each is deemed to have an undivided right of possession to the entire piece of real property. Except for tenancy in common where the ownership interests may be unequal, the ownership interests are equal. Characteristics of the four types of co-ownerships are set out below.[2]

Tenancy in Common

- Unlimited individual co-owners.
- May be unequal interests.
- Occupation not required by all.
- Interest of a co-owner may be passed on to others by will or to heirs where there is no will.
- Each may encumber his or her interest.
- Each has unlimited liability to third parties with right of reimbursement from other co-owners.

Joint Tenancy

- Right of survivorship, whereby the interest of a deceased co-owner automatically passes to surviving co-owners without legal proceedings, notwithstanding a will of the deceased co-owner.
- Created by will or deed.
- Unlimited liability.

Tenancy by Entireties

- A form of joint tenancy only between a husband and wife when they take their ownership interests.
- Requirements for such vary from state to state.
- Neither has the power to encumber or convey the property without the consent of the other.

Community Property

- Property acquired during marriage other than through inheritance, will, or gift.
- Considered owned equally by spouses.
- Property owned separately before marriage does not become community property.

- Community property states are: Arizona, California, Idaho, Louisiana, Michigan, Nevada, New Mexico, Texas, and Washington.

Identifying Documents

Documents pertaining to ownership of real property fall into two main categories: deeds and mortgages. Both, if properly acknowledged, may be filed for record with a county officer (a recorder of deeds, county recorder, register of deeds, or registrar of deeds) in the county where the real property is located. In any event, any document so filed becomes a public record and is completely accessible.

Deeds. A deed is a written instrument or document used by an owner of or person with an interest in real property to transfer or convey ownership or the interest to another. Several types of deeds may be used, depending upon the nature of the interest transferred. In some states, the format of the deed may be specified by statute. Below is a synopsis of the more commonly used deeds.

Warranty Deed. Sometimes called a general warranty deed, it gives certain assurances or guarantees ("covenants") to the transferee (grantee) of title. Principally, these covenants are that:

- The transferor (grantor) has good title (seizin).

- There are no encumbrances on the real property, except as stated in the deed.

- The transferee will have quiet enjoyment of the real property by not being disturbed or evicted by someone having a better title or lien.

Special Warranty Deed. With this deed the transferor only covenants against lawful claims or encumbrances arising during ownership of the real property.

Quit-Claim Deed. This deed only transfers or conveys the present interest of the transferor in the real property. There are no covenants. It is commonly used when a married couple is divorced and one spouse transfers his or her interest in their real property to the other.

Mortgages

A mortgage, the other principal document used in real property transactions, is a written instrument by which one person (the "mortgagor") transfers or conveys real property to another (the "mortgagee") to secure payment of a debt. Concomitant with the mortgage, the mortgagor will execute a promissory note, but the latter will not be recorded. Although the mortgage form is used in most states, some states direct the use of a three-party instrument called a deed of trust, where a third party acts as a trustee on behalf of the mortgagee. The advantage of the deed of trust is that there is a nonjudicial foreclosure in the event of default in payment of the mortgage debt.

As with deeds, state statutes may define the requirements for a mortgage. Everywhere recording is essential for protection from claims against the real property by other parties.

Mortgage Forms. Mortgage forms are fairly standardized, especially where the financing is backed by the federal government as with loans through the Federal Housing Authority (FHA) and the Veterans Administration (VA). Uniform provisions include the following:

1.   There must be a prepayment privilege that allows the borrower to prepay the mortgage debt without penalty.

2.   An escrow account with the lender must be established to provide for monthly payments of taxes.

3.   The borrower must not commit waste or deterioration of the property.

4.   The borrower must keep the property insured.

5.   There must be provisions related to acceleration of the debt upon sale of the property or assumption of the debt by another with a release of the borrower.

Other Interests in Real Property

Other interests in real property evidenced by documents filed with the county recording officer include easements, installment contracts or contracts for deed, judgment liens, tax liens of the federal government, liens for unpaid real estate taxes, state tax warrants, long-term leases, and mechanic's and materialman's liens. When any are encountered, the lawyer and legal assistant must review applicable federal and state statutes to determine the correct identifying factors and procedures.

Personal Property

Personal property is any thing or item other than real property in which a person has an ownership interest. Generally, personal property as opposed to real property is mobile and susceptible to destruction. Personal property is also classified as tangible and intangible. Tangible personal property includes automobiles, animals, growing crops, clothing, and anything that physically exists. Intangible personal property has no physical existence, but is a right to receive something of value: cash, bank accounts, stocks and bonds, insurance and pension benefits, promissory notes, accounts receivable, good will, patents, trademarks, royalties, copyrights, claims against others, and similar ownership rights granted by statute or recognized in property law.

Documents Identifying Ownership Interests

With variations, all states provide for the public registration of ownership interests in valuable types of tangible personal property such as automobiles, trucks, boats, and airplanes. Mortgage lien interests of a lender will be shown on the face of the registration form (the "title"). As with real property records, all are public records.

Where public registration is not required, ownership interests may be evidenced by a bill of sale, a receipt, a certificate of ownership, negotiable instruments, and various documents of title and financing instruments described and recognized in the Uniform Commercial Code (UCC) which has been adopted with modification by all states.

Article 9 of the Uniform Commercial Code has elaborate provisions dealing with all forms of personal property and the rights of persons who seek to secure their interests therein based on a conditional sale, chattel mortgage, lien, assignment, or any transaction which is intended to create a security interest. Again, with variations, all states provide that they may file a financing statement with the secretary of state or county recording officer where the personal property is located. All such filings are accessible at a nominal cost through the use of an information request in the format set out in the UCC.

Co-Ownership Interests

As with real property, some forms of personal property may be owned by two or more persons. In the case of bank accounts, creation of joint interests will be governed by the account agreement with the bank or financial institution. Stocks, bonds, and similar intangible assets will provide information of ownership interests on the face of the instrument evidencing ownership.

Bailments

A relationship involving the possession of personal property is a bailment. A bailment is created when one person (the bailor) transfers or delivers possession to another (the bailee) temporarily for some specific purpose, with the understanding that the other person will care for and return the personal property when required to do so. In bailment situations, always review state statutes, if any, for requirements. Title and rights of ownership always remain with the bailor. Only possession is given up to the bailee. Documents pertaining to a bailment may include a receipt, ticket, contract, or voucher.

NOTES

---

[1] W. Statsky, *West's Legal Thesaurus/Dictionary*, (1985).

[2] C. Jacobus, *Real Estate Law*, 39-43, (1986).

Chapter Five

COMMUNICATION TECHNIQUES

GENERAL CONCEPTS

In the practice of law, effective communication is a required skill. To assist the lawyer, the legal assistant uses communication skills beyond those required for everyday living.

Definition of Communication

Communication is the process by which one person transmits information or messages to be received by another. Three factors present in this definition are transmission, the form of the message or information, and reception. Problems arise when any one of the three is less than adequate.

In discovery, we are concerned with communication by and between the legal assistant and the lawyer, the client, and other persons possessing information bearing on the client's situation. Whenever possible, before communicating with any one of them, the legal assistant should evaluate the other person's comprehension level and ability to communicate.

Preparation

No matter the form of communication, proper preparation is necessary. This entails several steps:

1.   reviewing existing materials

2.   determining the most effective form of communication in the circumstances (Should contact be made by telephone or by letter?)

3.   formulating the objective of the communication

4.   determining equipment needs.

Language

Language is the communication of thought or information by the use of spoken or written words or by gestures. Someone may speak a different language because he or she is from another country; yet, an American, speaking English, may not speak it in the same way as the legal assistant. In some instances, a physical or mental handicap, such as blindness, deafness, stuttering, retardation, dyslexia, or illiteracy, will create a language barrier. Communication will not be impossible, but may be limited by the affliction.

Trauma

Often the legal assistant deals with individuals who have lived through or witnessed a traumatic experience. Such experiences produce emotional upset and can inhibit recollection.

Trauma is subjective and manifests itself in various intensities. What produces trauma in one person may leave another completely unaffected. Trauma can manifest itself physiologically, with effects delayed for days, months, or years. Communication with a traumatized person calls for caution, thorough preparation, and coordination with the lawyer.

PSYCHOSOCIAL ASPECTS

H. Allen Smith wrote a humorous book entitled *The Age of the Tail* in which all children were born with tails. The ramifications were overwhelming. Interpersonal relationships were grossly affected, particularly as to physical expressions of emotion. In their education, the children were taught how to control their tails to avoid expressing their true feelings in various situations.

Of course, this is imaginary, and there is no basis for such a premise in our society. Or is there? If people truly expressed their thoughts and information to each other, their interactions with each other would change beyond recognition. But such is not the case; a number of psychological and sociological factors affect communication and render such honesty impossible.

PSYCHOLOGICAL FACTORS

Psychologists generally accept that each individual functions with three ego states: parent, child, and adult. The parent ego state incorporates attitudes, values, and behavior of significant persons. The child ego state embodies the individual's inner feelings, experiences, and adaptation to the environment. The adult ego state is the individual's contact with reality, which can be distorted by contamination from the other two ego states. Each of us interacts with others from these ego states.

Transactions

Interactions between two individuals can be from and to any one of the three ego states. For example, in one adult/adult transaction, a legal assistant interviewing for a position asks about the starting salary of the position, and the lawyer responds that it is $20,000. If the lawyer instead responds that the salary is not disclosed until the employee is selected, then the lawyer is communicating from the lawyer's parent ego state to the child ego state of the legal assistant. When individuals engage in truncations like these that prevent honest and open relationships, they are engaged in psychological games.

Games and Positions

Games have different names, but each has a "payoff," which is avoidance of positive interactions. Usually, a game starts with an opening statement like "I can't do anything right." Games are repetitious, and often individuals will ultimately adopt steadfast personality positions and label themselves. For example, one person might think of himself as "not too bright" and adopt this position in all dealings with others.

Scripts

When an individual repeats positions, then he or she may be playing
out a script or life plan created during childhood. A lifelong script can
influence behavior. If a person chooses a script that requires antisocial
behavior, then interactions with others will be based on that premise.[1]

PSYCHOLOGICAL AND PHYSIOLOGICAL NEEDS — MASLOW'S HIERARCHY

No matter what one's life plan is, each individual while going through
life has psychological and physiological needs.

Abraham Maslow identified these as a hierarchy of human needs that
each individual seeks to satisfy. The most basic is the physiological
need to satisfy bodily needs such as hunger, thirst, and sex. The next
higher need is the need for safety — to avoid and protect against
physical harm, illness, and financial problems. The third need is to be
loved and to feel that one belongs, accomplished through friendship,
affection, acceptance, and expression of positive feelings. The fourth
need is to have esteem through self-respect and through respect and
recognition from others. Lastly, each individual seeks self-
actualization, to do what he or she can do best.

Effect on Communication

Communication is a two-way street, and these psychological factors
and needs apply to the legal assistant as well as to the person with
whom the legal assistant is communicating.

Often these factors and needs will manifest themselves by inhibiting
communication. An individual may be threatened by the legal
assistant's demeanor or parental attitude because it reawakens
memories of a past negative transaction. He or she may be leery of
disclosing extremely crucial information out of fear that it may be
disclosed to others. An individual may suffer from low self-esteem,
reflected in lack of response to the legal assistant's questions.

SOCIOLOGICAL FACTORS

Interwoven with psychological factors and needs is the effect of sociological factors. Individuals bring to any situation where they communicate with another the components of their societal existence, reflected in their values, attitudes, ethics, prejudices, and perceptions of their role and status in society. Many of these attitudes are stereotypical and are easy to recognize during a communication; others are latent and will not readily surface. Often, they are predicated upon the person's educational background, occupation, social status, and gender.

Educational Background

In our society, we place great emphasis upon a person's education. Our expectations of others regarding comprehension, literacy, and ability to interact are directly related to the amount of their education. Yet we frequently encounter college graduates who cannot effectively read or write. An expert in one subject area may be "functionally illiterate" in other fields. Thus, for effective communication, the legal assistant should make an ongoing assessment of the extent of the other party's knowledge and understanding of the subject matter under discussion.

Occupation

Closely related to educational background is occupation or employment. Professions like the practice of law or medicine require specialized education. Other occupations may not require such, but may still necessitate extensive training for their practice. A person in one occupation or employment may become myopic and have limited views on matters beyond the realm of what he or she does, and that occupation may create unwarranted social patterns during leisure time. In other words, they "can't turn off."

Social Status

Another important sociological factor in communication is social status: a person's position in the various strata of society. While position is determined by birth, income, education, etc., most important is people's perception of their position in the socioeconomic groups of which they are members. Here, routine prejudices toward outsiders can become a form of social xenophobia. For example, picture a legal assistant from a large metropolitan area going to a small town to find witnesses to an accident.

Gender

There are significant differences between men and women with respect to how they interact with and perceive members of the opposite sex and the societal expectations and limitations placed upon them. Great strides have been made in recent decades to discard discriminatory activities and attitudes, but much remains to be done to undo old restrictions. Gender stereotyping continues to exist and can hamper effective communication.

TYPES OF COMMUNICATION

While there may be variations, the three identifiable types of communication are:

1. nonverbal: gestures, body positions and movements, facial expressions, and imaging through apparel and adornments

2. verbal: spoken words and listening

3. written: words, letters, or symbols put in a form to be read by another.

Although each person possesses varying skills in the use of these types of communications, certain factors are common to each:

- the extent of one's active and passive vocabulary
- commonality of many expressions and ideas transmitted through the media, with regional influences.

Often, a communication combines two or all three types of communication. For example, a person making a speech (reading written text) will make gestures and facial expressions while speaking.

NONVERBAL COMMUNICATION

We send messages to each other through our actions and through the environment we create. Problems arise when another person gets the wrong message or a mixed signal. A legal assistant who interviews a client in an office with numerous case files may think that the message to the client is "look how busy I am." Yet the client, due to background and personality, may receive a message that the legal assistant is very disorganized. Thus, with nonverbal communications, the psychosocial aspects are very important, since a nonverbal communication can be interpreted differently.

Appearance and Apparel

How individuals look and what they are wearing are very important nonverbal communications since, in normal circumstances, very little of their body can be seen. So when we "read" a person, much is based upon appearance and clothing.

Hair length, physical features, and other indicators of appearance help us determine what a person is about. Excesses are not well-taken, nor is a bizarre appearance tolerated. Generally, lawyers are conservative in their clothing taste, primarily because of their working environment. Since legal assistants are a part of that environment, they too have similar clothing standards, especially within the framework of the law office and judicial systems. But lawyers and legal assistants must be flexible, particularly during discovery, since at times other apparel may be more appropriate. For example, wearing a business suit to a construction site for an interview might prevent the witness from fully communicating.

Environment

Where communication takes place can have a tremendous impact upon its substance. In the law office, legal assistants communicate nonverbally through their surroundings. Office furniture arrangement can set the tone of an interview. Chairs on opposite sides of a desk are standard, but other positions, like side by side, may promote greater openness. Neatness, too, is requisite and indicates that the legal assistant is organized and detail-oriented.

The nature of other office and working environments also communicates information about their functioning and inhabitants. Government offices such as the Internal Revenue Service that have frequent contact with the public are usually Spartan in their appearance, while agencies like the Food and Drug Administration will have plush surroundings. A public library with an inordinate amount of misshelved books tells its users that it is not functioning properly. A legal assistant asked to sit in a chair obviously lower than that of another person should consider this an attempt by the latter to achieve environmental dominance.

Facial Expressions

In our working environments, our faces and hands are "bare" to the world. Everyone communicates information through facial expressions, which often are coordinated with hand movements and touching of the face. Placing one's chin upon the thumb with the forefinger on the cheek may indicate evaluative thinking, especially when coupled with note taking.[2] Because facial expressions are so important in communication, some legal assistants practice making appropriate ones so that they can be used in real circumstances. This should be done most cautiously, lest others suspect that the legal assistant is feigning attitudes and emotions.

The face is divided into three major zones: the mouth, cheeks and nose, and the eyes and forehead. Space does not permit a lengthy discussion of each of these; however, the following summarizes a number of specific expressions and their meanings. In several situations, more than one zone will be used to convey an expression.

The Mouth. The smile and frown are dominant here, with the latter more obvious. The smile can take different forms. A simple smile is used when a person carries on simple activities. An upper smile with teeth showing indicates friendliness. A broad smile (often accompanying laughter) indicates a jovial person. An oblong smile is used for politeness when the circumstances (like the taking of a deposition) would indicate otherwise. The baring of teeth with eyes glaring indicates an emotionally charged person. While adults do not openly stick their tongues out like children, doing so in a subdued manner can indicate hostility.[3]

Cheeks and Nose. Blushing of the cheeks is a human characteristic and may indicate embarrassment or sensitivity to the subject under discussion. Flaring nostrils and deep furrowing of the forehead signal aggressiveness. Touching the nose with a finger may indicate hostility. An upturned nose may mean disdain.

Eyes and Forehead. In normal communication, people look at each other 30 to 60 percent of the time; more or less can indicate greater or lesser interest in what another is saying. Eye contact is greater when listening than when talking. An averted gaze indicates that a person has been asked to respond to questions that create discomfort. Eyeglasses are a part of eye expressions and are marketed for the image that they project. Looking over the top of eyeglasses is authoritarian.[4]

The lack of blinking or rapid blinking are associated with credibility. People in television commercials seldom blink. Raised eyebrows show astonishment, and when down signal conflict.

Gestures and Body Movements

We all use numerous gestures and body movements to communicate. One significant gesture is the handshake. A person who shakes hands with too much force communicates defensiveness and hostility, while a person with a light handshake conveys weakness. Sweaty palms during a handshake may mean nervousness. Not letting go of another's hand after an appropriate period of time connotes possessiveness and dominance. However, any handshake should be "read" with other nonverbal communications given at the same time.

Other gestures and body movements can be classified into areas of emotions and attitudes. [5]

Sincerity: open hands; unbuttoning a suit coat.

Defensiveness: arms crossed on the chest (baseball umpires use it when a manager is questioning a play decision); legs crossed away from another.

Evaluation: a hand-to-cheek gesture; taking off eyeglasses after another's verbal statement (negative evaluation); pinching the bridge of the nose.

Suspicion and Secretiveness: holding a hand over the mouth while talking (holding back information); body movements away from a speaker (discomfort with what is being said); eye rubbing (negative attitude).

Readiness: sitting on the edge of the chair with the body leaning forward.

Reassurance: repeatedly touching one's hair or some personal object.

Frustration and Discomfort: clenched hands; rubbing the back of the neck; hand-wringing.

Confidence: steepling the fingertips; hands coupled together behind the head (also shows vulnerability).

Nervousness: repeatedly clearing the throat; lip biting.

Self-Control: clenched hands; locked ankles.

Boredom: table drumming; foot tapping; blank stare; doodling; the head in the palm of the hand position with drooping eyes (often seen in juries).

Because there is much latitude for interpreting the meaning of nonverbal gestures and body movements, they should always be "read" in conjunction with coincident verbal communications. For example, arms crossed at the chest may indicate defensiveness, but such may also indicate the person is cold. An itch may cause eye rubbing and nose touching.

When nonverbal communications do not agree with the context of verbal communications, the legal assistant should ask a question that requires some confirmation. Techniques include asking the other person to repeat what was said and identifying specific signals that negate the verbal response.

VERBAL COMMUNICATIONS

Verbal communication is an interactive process involving two or more people: conversation, interrogation, interview, and formal and informal speaking before a group of people. In simple terms, it is talking and listening.

However, with the advent of telecommunications, verbal communication has become the dominant type of communication and so has evolved in complexity. This is particularly true in the practice of law, and legal assistants involved in discovery must possess excellent verbal skills to carry out their assigned tasks.

Fortunately, every form of verbal communication includes several basic concepts: vocabulary, voice, linguistics, and listening. While the characteristics of each can be identified, verbal communication is holistic. No characteristic has any greater weight than the others.

Vocabulary

Vocabulary represents the words spoken during verbal communication. Verbal communication is enhanced by a vocabulary above that necessary for everyday conversation; this becomes essential when a person engages in communication with people whose professions and occupations require a specialized or technical vocabulary. A police officer must learn and speak a "language" created for accident investigations. Employees of various governmental agencies have developed technical slang to identify their tasks and functions. Legal assistants regularly performing investigative assignments will, as a matter of course, increase their specialized or technical vocabulary. However, it can be counterproductive to utilize a specialized vocabulary when communicating with a person not versed in that vocabulary.

In this vein, a legal assistant should avoid using legal jargon — words, often in Latin form, which mask or cover up the message. Of course, an understanding of legal terminology is necessary, but the legal assistant should focus on communicating complex legal terms and concepts in plain English. Everyday slang, shoptalk, and colloquial words should also be avoided unless used by the other party. Profanity is unacceptable.

Verbal communication can be furthered hampered by mis-pronunciation. Mispronunciation by legal assistants may cause them to lose professional stature; correction of a mispronounced word used by the other person may destroy an effective level of communication. Excessive mispronunciations by another with no apparent reason (ethnic background, English as a second language, speech impediment, etc.) may indicate a limited understanding of the subject.

Voice

Voice represents the sound of words we make when talking. Various factors affect the quality and effectiveness of our voices. Some of the more significant ones are:

- *Tone or Pitch*. Generally, a low tone or pitch is best. A high pitch may indicate anxiety or nervousness. A monotonous tone should be avoided or replaced with modulation and inflections.
- *Resonance*. The sound of the voice should come from the chest. Talking from the nose sometimes produces an irritating nasal twang.
- *Speed*. The speed with which words are spoken is based on environment, subject matter, and the listener's comprehension level. The legal assistant should avoid choppy phrasing and excessive speed or slowness.
- *Pauses and Throat Clearing*. Meaningless pauses such as "er," "you know," "you know what I mean," and "uh" detract from effective communication. Throat clearing shows nervousness and irritates the ear of the listener.[6]

Linguistics

Linguistics is the scientific study of language, but on a practical level a legal assistant must be concerned with nuances that illustrate better the verbal communications of others. Speech patterns, such as always starting a conversation with a certain phrase, and accents provide the legal assistant insight into the geographical background of another person. Use of sayings and adages may indicate ethics and attitudes.

At present, the most interesting nuance is the linguistic difference between men and women. Linguists have found that men and women have different speech patterns and language usages, and each talks differently with members of the opposite sex. Whether this is genetic or environmental is being examined, but no matter the outcome, the legal assistant must be aware of these dissimilarities during verbal communications.

Listening

Legal assistants' most essential talent is the ability to listen effectively. They must recognize when others are not listening to them and take verbal and nonverbal action to rectify the situation. The ability to listen does not come naturally, but comes through the experience of understanding and using recognized listening techniques.

The listener always has the advantage over the speaker; the listener can listen to almost 700 words per minute while the talker at best speaks around 150 words per minute.[7] Thus, the listener has a lot of time to do other things while another person is talking.

However, listening effectively requires effort and utilization of several standard techniques. These techniques are especially useful to the legal assistant in high-stress situations such as an emotional client interview or an interview with a hostile witness.

Nonverbal Listening. With nonverbal listening, legal assistants send signals that they are listening through gestures, body movements, and eye contact. Legal assistants show others that they are receptive or open to the verbal communication through facial expressions (smile) and body positions (uncrossed arms and legs, sitting up straight). Increased eye contact can be used, but staring should be avoided.

The best listener pays attention quietly and avoids interruptions. If an interruption is necessary, one approach is to employ a raised-hand gesture, usually to the ear or hair.

Verbal Listening. Sometimes it is necessary to speak or make sounds of acknowledgment to facilitate listening. Verbal sounds such as "uhuh," "humm," and "OK" are used, usually with head nodding and other nonverbal gestures, but excessiveness should be avoided. One excellent form of verbal listening is to summarize the essence of what the other person said through expressions like "Let me see if I understand what you said..." or "What you're saying is..."

COMMUNICATION BEHAVIOR

Except for the telephone, a verbal communication to another is punctuated by gestures. Certain verbal and nonverbal gestures create an "attitude" or "appearance" when dealing with others. A knowledge of mastery of these gestures allows the legal assistant to evaluate the personality and behavior of others during a verbal communication.

The differences between a nonassertive and assertive person are as follows:[8]

Nonassertive Person

1.   Nonverbal Communication.
   • Downcast, averted, or teary eyes
   • Weight shifting, slumped body, head down, shuffling walk
   • Hand wringing, lip biting, clothing adjustments
   • Poor posture overall

2.   Verbal Communication.
   • Rambling statements
   • Use of qualifiers such as "maybe" and "I wonder if you could"
   • Use of fillers such as "uh," "well," and "you know"

- Use of negatives such as "don't bother" and "it's not really important"
- Voice in monotone, whining, hesitant, or giggly

Assertive Person

1. Nonverbal Communication.
   - Open, direct eye contact, without staring
   - Standing comfortably, firmly on two feet, steady, straight
   - Hands loosely at sides, relaxed
   - Posture indicates independent person

2. Verbal Communication.
   - Speaks in concise statements
   - Use of "I" statements such as "I want" or "I need"
   - Use of cooperative words such as "How can we resolve this?" or "Let's work together."
   - Empathic statement such as "What do you think?" or "What do you see as the problem?"

All this is extremely important to legal assistants when they deal with "bureaucrats" who possess necessary information. If legal assistants exude nonassertive behavior to such a person, they may fail to obtain the needed information.

WRITTEN COMMUNICATIONS

During discovery, written communications by the legal assistant will take many forms. These include a "memo to file" to memorialize a telephone conversation, letters to the client and other persons, an investigation report, interview notes, or electronic mail. Depending on their working relationship, sometimes the lawyer will have the legal assistant prepare legal research memoranda, briefs, draft pleadings, and formal discovery documents. Since the legal assistant can locate the form and format of these documents in form books, treatises, and continuing legal education publications, they will not be addressed here. Note that many of the following written communication principles still apply.

Common Characteristics

The basic purpose of a communication is to send a message that will be received by another. Communication does not occur when the message is not in an understandable form. Many a client has received a letter from a lawyer only to call and ask the lawyer to explain what was written. Lawyers have been severely criticized for their failure to write in plain English. Many states now require insurers with high public contact such as automobile and casualty insurance companies to write their policies in plain language.

To write plain English in the law office, the legal assistant should follow these guidelines:[9]

1.   Omit of surplus words. Eliminate long, meaningless phrases.

2.   Use the active voice. "Margot broke the pencil," rather than "The pencil was broken by Margot."

3.   Use short sentences. Remember to take into account the reader's comprehension level.

4.   Avoid lawyerisms. Cut all Latin terms and long-winded phrases such as "Notwithstanding anything to the contrary in this agreement heretofore mentioned."

5.   Avoid language quirks. Do not use words that detract from the message.

6.   Avoid inadequate grammar and misspelled words. These signal competency limitations.

7.   Identify the recipient's abilities and disabilities. Is this a recurring communication (i.e., a request to a state agency)? Does the recipient have poor eyesight?

Internal Written Communications

In a law office, written communications during discovery take place between the legal assistant, the lawyer, and other personnel, including the legal secretary.

Some communications are indirect: a telephone message for the recipient or a memo to a case file. The most common is the memorandum. Memos take many forms, such as a format that includes an introduction, body, and conclusion. This format sets out the reason for the memo, the subject matter that gave rise to it, and a recommendation and time references.[10] Another method is to use journalist's questions in the preparation: who, what, when, where, why, and how.

Most law offices will have their own style of memoranda and will prefer that the legal assistant follow their format. However, any memorandum, no matter how brief, should contain the following identifiers:

INTER-OFFICE MEMORANDUM

DATE:
TO:
FROM:
FILE REFERENCE:
SUBJECT:

A second type of internal written communication is the case report. Case reports are written for many reasons: to evaluate a client following an interview; to evaluate a witness; to report the gathering or review of written documents or other physical evidence.

In preparing a report, the legal assistant should always select a form and format that will communicate all information, no matter how unimportant or trivial. While a narrative conveys more information, an outline may be used as long as the legal assistant avoids incomplete statements and phrasing.

The legal assistant should attempt to write the main body of the report as objectively as possible. All statements of fact should be verifiable through attached documentation or through referenced sources. Objectivity in the body of the report can be maintained if the legal assistant avoids an inference. (An inference is a statement "about the unknown made on the basis of the known.")[11] However, inferences can be freely made in the concluding remarks. One example of an inference is "The witness acted hostilely toward me," rather than an objective reporting of "The witness crossed her arms and refused to answer my questions."

Two other nonobjective forms of reporting to be saved for the conclusion are judgments and slanting. Judgments express the writer's approval or disapproval of the occurrences, persons, or objects the writer is describing. "Obviously, he was a crooked lawyer" is judgmental. Words of judgment, also called "buzz words," destroy objectivity and bare the personality of the writer in a negative manner.

Slanting can be used for or against the subject matter of the report. For example, the legal assistant might describe a person in positive terms such as having clean clothes, white teeth, and being helpful to others. Yet the same "facts" could be slanted against that person with statements that the person had torn clothing, crooked teeth, and others avoided seeking his help because he was inept.

However, the report should not be so devoid of subjectivity that the lawyer has no input from the legal assistant. Inferences, judgments, and slanting can be incorporated in the conclusion, as long as the report contains specific recommendations as to how to proceed. If the legal assistant labels a witness as uncooperative or hostile, a recommendation should be made as to how to deal with that person.

External Written Communications

Written communications to persons outside the law office play an important part during discovery. The letter is a primary format, but other forms such as e-mail and faxes have taken on greater significance.

While each law office may have its own standards for letters, certain provisions are universal: the salutation, case reference, and signature block. In the signature block, legal assistants must always indicate their status, i.e. "legal assistant" or "paralegal," even in jurisdictions where the lawyer can put the legal assistant's name and position on the letterhead.

Every external written communication should fulfill one or more of the following functions:[12]

1.   *Requesting Action by the Recipient*. The correspondence should contain a specific statement as to what the recipient must do or the consequences if he or she fails to take the requested action. Sometimes this correspondence will have an affidavit or other document attached that the recipient (usually the client or a witness) needs to execute.

2.   *Giving Notice*. During discovery, there will be times when a person or entity will have to be formally notified of an impending action. Notices may inform a witness that his or her deposition will be taken; statutes and court rules may require an employer to be notified of a worker's compensation claim. Often this type of correspondence must be sent by certified mail. If so, the return receipt number affixed to the envelope should be put on every page of the correspondence and attached documents.

3.   *Providing or Obtaining Information*. A correspondence may provide information or request information. In both cases, style and the identity of the recipient are very important. If the correspondence is a letter to a client explaining what will happen when the deposition is taken, it should be in brief form with numbered paragraphs. If the correspondence is to a governmental agency, the typist should leave an extra-wide left margin or other space for a response, since many have time restraints on making formal responses.

4.   *Making a Record*. A record must be made of any telephone conversations involving case docketing, procedures, offers, and other pertinent information, usually through a follow-up or confirming letter. Sometimes the recipient is requested to sign a statement at the end of

the letter confirming receipt. For example, for protection from malpractice liability, any offer of settlement must be "memorialized" by letter with a statement of receipt.

SPECIAL COMMUNICATION AREAS

Before we move on to communications with and for the client, we need to discuss in detail some major areas of communication: use of the telephone, dictation for transcription, and e-mail and fax. During discovery, the legal assistant uses the telephone more than any other tool of the trade of the legal profession. Yet, because "everyone knows how to use the telephone," the supervising lawyer will give very little training, if any, on effective telephone techniques and procedures. No one gives any training on effective dictation, although the legal assistant's ability to clearly and competently dictate the results of factual investigation for later transcription can be crucial to the successful outcome of the client's matter. And, a lack of understanding of the "dos" and "don'ts" of electronic transmissions can result in disastrous consequences.

TELEPHONE

The telephone is the most unique of communication devices, since its use allows verbal communication without the usual accompaniment of nonverbal communication. It is pure speaking and listening. However, certain telephone techniques can enhance the speaking and listening abilities of the legal assistant.

When we first answer a telephone call, we are briefly a "captive audience." What is said to us and how it is said in those initial moments profoundly affect the rest of the conversation. Of course, the listener is a factor, but we are concerned primarily with telephone conversations with persons with whom the legal assistant has had no previous contact. While this may include the client, for the most part it consists of persons who are directly involved in the client's matter or who have related information. With this in mind, let's examine telephone speaking techniques.

Initial Contact. Legal assistants should always be up-front by identifying themselves to the listener and briefly explaining the purpose of the call.

Voice. The sound of one's voice to the listener is very important. Depending on the listener, legal assistants must be cognizant of the "personality" they project. If in a telephone call to public officials their voices indicate persistency and confidence, legal assistants will not go away with incomplete information.

Nervousness Avoidance. Sometimes the legal assistant will feel nervous about the subject matter of the telephone conversation or about the personality or position of the listener. Many people lessen or eliminate this problem by rehearsing the telephone conversation or by outlining the conversation. In some situations, legal assistants might write out what they plan to say, but they should take pains to avoid a deadpan voice.

Open-Ended Questions. Questions to the listener should be open-ended so that answers are given in narrative form rather than as simple "yes" and "no" responses.

Telephone Listening. For effective listening, the speaking techniques discussed above can be reversed. However, certain listening techniques can help the legal assistant make the most of any telephone communication.

Notetaking. During the telephone conversation, the legal assistant should take substantive notes. All notes should include the name and telephone number of the other party as well as their position, the date, time of call, and subject area discussed.

Referrals. Legal assistants should always note information referrals made by the other party and should actively seek such when they are not freely given.

Silence. One telephone listening technique is to fail to respond when the other party talks about substantive matters. Most speakers will feel the need to fill in the silence by explaining what they said in greater detail.

DICTATION FOR TRANSCRIPTION

During the earlier years of the legal assistant profession, many legal assistants were concerned about any job description that required typing skills, for fear that the legal assistant would be considered a "glorified legal secretary" by the employing lawyer or law firm. Times change. Now the legal assistant must have typing or keyboarding skills to effectively utilize computers, databases, and word processing programs. One consistent competency that has become even more important to the legal assistant job performance is effective use of dictating equipment.

Dictating Equipment. Dictation saves both time and money. In discovery, the legal assistant can use it to write correspondence, reports, client and witness evaluations, and internal memos, and to customize pleadings and discovery requests. Because of the competitive nature of the market for dictating equipment, all suppliers usually provide comprehensive manuals on how to use their dictating machines. With computerized word processing, many law firms have turned to using transcribers for dictation. Centralized equipment has facilitated off-site dictation by the use of a touch-tone telephone.

Experienced lawyers and legal assistants know that true effectiveness results from the development of a good working relationship with the legal secretary or transcriber.

Dictation Techniques. Before dictating, the legal assistant should prepare a mental or short written outline of the dictation. At the start of the dictation, the legal assistant should provide a short identification for the transcriber, including who is dictating, the client and case, the supervising lawyer, what the dictation is, whether the dictated material is to be saved in computer storage, and any other appropriate information. If the case file or other sources will be used, then all should be physically present during dictation and subsequently given to the transcriber for reference. The legal assistant should spell all proper names, all technical and Latin terms, and any unusual words. Providing zip codes during dictation saves time. Beginnings of paragraphs should be identified as well as the beginnings and endings of quotations, indentations, and changes to single or double spacing.[13]

Voice. Once the legal assistant and the transcriber establish a rapport and each becomes familiar with the communication abilities of the other, they can move to a higher level in their relationship. Then, the legal assistant can give "voice cues" for punctuation and special instructions; the transcriber will know that the drop of a tone signals the end of a sentence. Until that time, the legal assistant must focus on diction and correct pronunciation, and avoid slurring or stuttering.

ELECTRONIC TRANSMISSIONS

In the last few years in the law office, the use of e-mail and fax has moved from novelty to necessity. Coupled with the expanded use of the Internet, the practice of law has become dangerously "instant" in form, but remains substantive in effect. For example, in some jurisdictions, a confidential electronic communication to a client loses its confidentiality when it is sent to the wrong electronic address or fax number and received by a third party.

E-mail. Basic components of e-mail include a message header, field (the addressee), subject, identification of the sender, and message body. While there is no privacy or confidentiality with e-mail, many problems can be avoided by verifying the receiving electronic address before transmission of any important information. Messages should be of reasonable length and print copies should be made for future transmission validation.

Fax. The safest approach to the use of fax for confidential communications is "Don't Do It!" But if it is absolutely necessary, do the following: Transmit only to a private (one-user) fax number; put a statement of confidentiality on the cover sheet; and send a nonconfidential transmission to the fax number and get a verifying response before the confidential information is sent.

NOTES

[1] Utilized materials in *Born to Win* by Muriel James, Ph.D., & Dorothy Jongeward, Ph.D. (1971).

[2] Gerald I. Nierenberg & Henry H. Calero, *How to Read a Person Like a Book*, 148 (1971).

[3] Id., 32 & 33.

[4] Id., 34.

[5] Id., summarized 43 to 134.

[6] D. Sarnoff, *Speech Can Change Your Life* (1970).

[7] Nierenberg & Calero, 113.

[8] Based upon "Assertion Theory" by C. Kelley in the 1976 *Annual Handbook for Group Facilitators*.

[9] Utilized materials of Richard Wydick, *Plain English for Lawyers*, 2nd Edition (1985).

[10] The National Association of Legal Assistants, *Manual for Legal Assistants*, 23 (2nd Ed. 1992), hereinafter cited as *NALA MANUAL*.

[11] S.I. Hayakawa, "The Language of Reports," *Language in Thought and Action* (1949).

[12] *NALA MANUAL*, 36 & 37.

[13] L. Charfoos & D. Christensen, *Personal Injury Practice: Technique and Technology*, 300 (1986).

Chapter Six

CLIENT COMMUNICATIONS

DEALING WITH CLIENTS

Because our legal system is adversarial, people must have genuine disputes for it to function. When people engage the services of a lawyer to represent them, a unique relationship is established in which they become a client. Generally, ethical rules of conduct for the lawyer afford the client a great deal of protection during the relationship. Clients should expect lawyers to represent them competently and diligently, to keep all their communications confidential, and to avoid situations where there may be a conflict of interest.

As the principal in this agency relationship, the client retains final authority to determine the objectives of the representation and to decide whether to accept an offer of settlement of a matter. Before discussing the various forms of communication with and for the client, we must understand the client's motivations and concerns.

Client's Expectations

Most people do not consult a lawyer unless they feel it is absolutely necessary. When they do, they view the encounter with greater trepidation than when they see a healthcare professional.[1]

Clients view lawyers as powerful and authoritarian persons, the "movers and shakers" of the legal system. Because of popular television shows about lawyers, many potential clients believe wrongly that their cases will be settled for a substantial amount of money or will be tried very quickly, with the jury awarding an astronomical sum for their injuries.

Clients come to a lawyer with different types of baggage. Some seek to profit; others want revenge. Some seek to right a wrong. Whatever the reason, the lawyer must work with the client to identify mutually acceptable objectives of the representation. Occasionally, for self-preservation the lawyer must reject a potential client bent on revenge, and whose claim has no basis in fact. Unfortunately, many lawyers do not realize the necessity for screening clients or conducting a preliminary investigation, particularly for claims involving a contingent fee arrangement.

Experienced lawyers will thoroughly review the potential client's situation before they take the case. Review is accomplished through interviews with the potential client, contact with persons having important factual information, and collection of initial documentation affecting the matter. The lawyer must believe that the client's claim or defense has merit over and beyond the client's expectations.

Client's Concerns

Although clients rarely show their true concerns at the initial conference with the lawyer, an experienced lawyer will know what the concerns are. First, a client will be concerned about the lawyer's fees and expenses associated with the matter. The client must understand the potential costs, especially if litigation will be involved, because the lawyer cannot control the costs of support services such as depositions and investigators. The possibility always exists that the lawyer will be unsuccessful, so the client must be prepared to bear the ultimate burden of case expenses.

The lawyer must be up-front with the client about fees. Fee rates should be put in writing at the beginning of the representation. When the lawyer charges a per-hour rate and the client asks for an "estimate," the lawyer must make it absolutely clear to the client that the estimated fee can change as the case progresses.

If the lawyer's fee is contingent on the outcome of the matter, legal ethics dictate that the lawyer put the contingent fee agreement in writing, with an executed copy to the client. The legal assistant should not present the fee agreement to the client for execution unless the lawyer has previously discussed its provisions with the client. If the client asks the legal assistant questions about the lawyer's fee before execution, execution should be postponed until the lawyer answers them.

Clients are usually concerned that their case is weak or that it relies on facts that could be detrimental. While clients will not purposefully hide factual information from the lawyer, they will often present those facts in their best light. Sometimes clients will alter their version to accommodate the lawyer's interpretation and application of the law. Thus, to avoid liability to potential defendants, the lawyer must always conduct an independent investigation to substantiate the facts as presented by clients.

Finally, clients may be concerned with the effect the matter will have on their life. Where litigation may be involved, the lawyer should ascertain whether or not the client is prepared to go trial, if necessary. With potential litigation, the lawyer and the client should discuss the economic impact of having a lawsuit hanging over the client's life.

The Legal Assistant-Client Relationship

The lawyer must always make the initial contact with potential clients, whether by telephone, personal conference, or interview. This protects both potential client and lawyer from any question as to when the lawyer-client relationship arose and as to confidentiality of communications. While this seems restrictive, over the years a number of cases have revolved around these questions, and the lawyer does not need collateral issues to decide whether to take the client's case.

Next, clients must be made aware that their primary relationship is with the lawyer, that the lawyer supervises and is responsible for the activities of the legal assistant, and that clients should not put legal assistants "on the spot" by asking them questions that would call for a legal opinion. The lawyer should discuss these points with clients at the initial interview, particularly if legal assistants intend to conduct a substantive interview with the client immediately thereafter. Otherwise, they should be set out in the lawyer's first letter to the client.

The Lawyer-Client Relationship

It is the lawyer's responsibility to establish the lawyer-client relationship. The legal assistant must avoid any communications that will negatively affect the "bonding" process between lawyer and client.

Many advocates of the use of legal assistants promote thorough preparation by legal assistants for a substantive interview with the client, including review of the client's file, available documentation, and the lawyer's initial interview notes and instructions. In reality, the file often will be nonexistent, there will be no documentation, and the lawyer's notes and instructions will consist of a piece of paper with the client's name and telephone number on it with instructions to call and set up an appointment. Legal assistants must not communicate to the client any frustration with the sparse information and documentation provided by the lawyer.

Unavailability of the Lawyer

Although communication between the lawyer and client may start off well, it will often deteriorate. Clients, seeking to maintain the initial level of communications, may turn to legal assistants and may even come to rely on them more than on the lawyer for information about their case. While there is nothing inherently wrong with this, the legal assistant must not act independently from the supervision of the lawyer and must avoid giving any opinions about the progress of the case.

A note of caution: Clients can be quite literal as to communications and so may not ask clarifying questions about instructions and procedures. In dealing with less sophisticated clients, the legal assistant must take all necessary steps to assure that they fully understand what is being done on their behalf.

The Defense Lawyer's Perspective

Most materials available to legal assistants concerning client interviewing and investigation are prepared from the point of view of the plaintiff or injured party. With modification, these can be adapted for use by a legal assistant working for a defense lawyer or law firm.

Defense lawyers face unique challenges in representing defense clients, and the legal assistant must always keep these in mind. First, defense clients are sometimes not covered by insurance. Usually these clients may have tried to resolve the dispute with the claimant or the claimant's lawyer on their own, but now seek representation after receiving a demand letter or being served with the summons and complaint. Because time often lapses between the event and the first consultation with the lawyer, the client may have stale facts, and the substantive interview may not be as productive as one conducted with a claimant.

Next, many, if not most, defense clients come to the defense lawyer or law firm because their insurance carrier has a contractual obligation to provide legal representation when they are sued. The lawyer or law firm is retained and paid by the insurance carrier on a retainer agreement. Thus, unlike the plaintiff's lawyer who can refrain from taking a case, the lawyer has little leeway in defending the insurance-based client; the insurance carrier may expect "miracles" even when a client lacks qualities supportive of the case. If the legal assistant has problems in dealing with such a client, it may be difficult to resolve the conflicts encountered.

Many insurance carriers, except in large or obvious liability cases, initially use adjusters to attempt to settle the claim against their insureds. These negotiations can spread over a considerable length of time after the event, giving rise to liability, and resulting in stale facts by the time the lawyer or law firm enters the case. The adjuster's experience has a great bearing on the amount of information that has been gathered prior to representation. However, a lack of information may not signal the adjuster's dilatoriness, but might indicate that the plaintiff's lawyer refused to provide anything during pre-suit negotiations.

Bad Faith Liability

Most states recognize the right of an insured to sue the insurance carrier for failing to negotiate and settle a claim in good faith. Once claimants identify the insurance carrier of the potential defendant, their lawyer will make a written demand for settlement, often for the insurance policy limits. If the insurance carrier does not accept or fails to act upon the offer to settle for the policy limits in good faith, it could be held liable for any judgment in excess of the policy limits. Once the lawyer is involved, the lawyer must document that the client was made aware of his or her potential liability to the plaintiff for any judgment rendered in excess of the policy limits if there was no bad faith by the insurance carrier. Once aware of their liability, many clients will urge the insurance carrier to settle for the policy limits, which creates a conflict of interest on the part of the lawyer. Both the client and the insurance carrier must be apprised of the situation once it arises.

Tunnel Vision

If a lawyer handles an immense amount of insurance defense work, the lawyer may tend to structure case management and procedures into set patterns. A legal assistant working in this environment can end up slotted into a singular task in multiple cases, summarizing depositions or obtaining medical records. Such an approach, while cost-effective, can lead to career stagnation and loss of interest in the client's case. A bored legal assistant might inadvertently jeopardize the client's defense by overlooking key information and facts that were not part of the routine.

THE SUBSTANTIVE INTERVIEW

Because clients' matters have become increasingly complex, client interviewing has developed into a two-phase process. The first phase lays the groundwork for the case.[2] Under optimum conditions, the lawyer will have some substantive information about the client and the case. Using this information, the lawyer can generally review applicable law and seek out helpful legal materials. Before the first interview, the lawyer may also be able to verify some facts. For example, the potential client may be a minority shareholder of a closely held corporation, so, before the first interview, the lawyer could obtain from the secretary of state the corporation's latest annual report. Usually, the lawyer uses the first interview with the client to identify and evaluate the client's legal problem.

The legal assistant conducts the second, more substantive interview to obtain in-depth information from the client. Although ideally all this information can be gathered in one meeting, in reality the substantive interview may involve more than one meeting with the client and will include other communication means such as the telephone or letters.

The Interview Concept

An interview is a face-to-face process, wherein one person questions another to elicit information. While an exchange of information may take place, the exchange is secondary to the primary purpose. For example, a job applicant asks about working conditions, but the primary purpose of the interview is to determine whether he or she will be hired.

Control

While not an interrogation, an interview is a situation with defined roles of interviewer and interviewee. The interviewer dominates the relationship and must assure control or take charge if the objectives of the interview are to be accomplished. When clients meander in answering a question, the legal assistant must tactfully steer them back to the subject.

Interview Objectives

During any interview with the client, whether it is the lawyer's initial interview or the legal assistant's substantive interview, certain objectives must be accomplished:[3]

1. Development and evaluation of information about:

- applicable law, including witnesses and documents
- the client's background
- the client's personality
- client's desires
- time limitations

2. Imparting information to the client about:

- the legal process
- the lawyer-client relationship
- the functions of the legal assistant
- specific procedures such as answering interrogatories and the taking of depositions

Pre-Interview Planning

Conducting an interview with a client is a challenging task, and can be extremely frustrating and time-consuming without adequate preparation. For maximum effectiveness during the interview, several steps need to be taken beforehand.

File Review

The legal assistant should review documents and materials obtained from the client, plus the lawyer's notes and instructions. In accident cases, if possible, the accident site should be visited and photos taken for use at the interview.

Review of Law

Legal assistants should familiarize themselves with applicable legal concepts through a review of jury instructions, form books, legal encyclopedias, etc.

Preparation of Interview Format

This will always include a client profile and questions in topical form. Questions should be specific, but not so detailed as to prevent openness by the client during the interview.

Figure 6:1 is an example of an interview form.

```
FIGURE 6:1
          INTERVIEW FORM - MEDICAL MALPRACTICE⁴

CLIENT BACKGROUND INFORMATION

    •   name and address
    •   telephone numbers (home, work, mobile)
    •   age and birth date
    •   Social Security number (military service number where applicable)
    •   family data (spouse, children, other relatives)
    •   prior addresses
    •   employment history (present and past employment)
    •   earnings and income sources

MEDICAL INFORMATION

    •   prior medical history, excluding any related to medical malpractice
        (include name and address of family doctor for last ten years and
        details for all hospital stays)
    •   medical history related to alleged malpractice, including symptoms,
        treatment dates, specific claimed act(s) of malpractice, and basis for
        malpractice
    •   present medical treatment, including current condition and prognosis

DAMAGES

    •   estimated and actual medical expenses related to claim
    •   insurance coverage
    •   lost wages
    •   loss of consortium

LITIGATION EXPERIENCE

    •   prior litigation
    •   criminal record
```

Determination of Interview Site

The interview usually takes place in the legal assistant's office, but occasionally the legal assistant may need to meet the client somewhere else.

Scheduling

When the substantive interview does not take place immediately after the initial interview by the lawyer, the legal assistant should schedule a mutually convenient time with the client. Normally the scheduling will be done by telephone, followed up by a confirmation letter.

The legal assistant should send a business card with the confirmation letter in a form similar to Figure 6:2.

FIGURE 6:2

CONFIRMATION LETTER

(Letterhead of Lawyer or Law Firm)

Date

Client Name
1524 Anywhere Street
City, State Zip Code

Re: Case File Number XXXXXXX

Dear Client:

This letter is to confirm our appointment here at our office on Friday, May 28,_____, at 2:00 p.m. You should plan to spend a couple of hours with me. If available, please bring with you the following information and documents:

(Here list specific information and documents)

I look forward to meeting you. If you have any questions, please call me.

Very truly yours,

Pat Smith
Legal Assistant

MAXIMIZE THE INTERVIEW

Books and voluminous amounts of legal materials address the conduct of a client interview, advocating several different effective methods. All maintain that to achieve the objectives of the interview the interviewer must be flexible, avoiding "canned" or rigid interview formats. For the legal assistant, the main objective of a substantive client interview is to obtain as much factual information as possible about the client's problem. For this endeavor, certain time-honored techniques stand out.

Rapport or Ice Breaking

At the beginning of the interview, the legal assistant and the client must establish a mutuality of interest or trust. One method is to convey to the client the legal assistant's empathy and sincere interest in the client's situation. To do this, avoid activities that detract from the client: answering phone calls from other persons in front of the client, conversing with office staff and lawyers about unrelated matters, and using negative verbal and nonverbal communications. Legal assistants should strive to project a positive personal and environmental image, maintain formality until they establish rapport with the client, and treat the client as if he or she were the lawyer's only client.

Notetaking

While effective notetaking is not considered a part of the educational process, it is an integral aspect of interviewing and serves a twofold purpose:

1. The substantive interview will focus on details of factual information; these details must be verified later through contact with witnesses and examination of physical evidence. Correct information from the client concerning details will expedite the verification process.

2. Notetaking demonstrates to clients that what they say is important. However, the legal assistant should avoid engaging in

excessive notetaking, because it diminishes interaction with the client and can lessen rapport.

Questioning

The legal assistant must extract from the client a complete fact picture for communication to the lawyer. Good questioning to elicit information can take different forms.

The legal assistant can use directive questioning, pinpointing for the client specific areas for discussion. However, leading questions should be avoided, because they tend to encourage the client to make responses perceived as the right answers and not necessarily the truth. The legal assistant's questions should promote narrative responses that result in clients telling their "story." Questions should be objective and not judgmental. While questions should be designed to gather as many details from the client as possible, "nitpicking" should be avoided.

Effective questioning often summarizes previous responses to a question. For example, in an automobile accident case, the legal assistant might ask, "What happened after you looked for opposing traffic?"

Client Participation

Although clients participate in the interview by responding to the legal assistant's questions, they are still passive participants. Legal assistants can use certain techniques to involve clients more actively in the interview, such as asking clients to execute authorizations for the lawyer to act or obtain information or documents on clients' behalf. Depending upon the nature of the case, several authorizations can be explained by the legal assistant and executed by the client at the substantive interview, although none should be used until the client has executed a fee agreement with the lawyer. They include:

Medical Records Authorization

When medical records are involved, a general or standardized authorization form can be executed, and the client's signature should be notarized. The client should execute several forms, since each medical services provider will want to retain one for its records. Many healthcare providers, particularly hospitals, will have their own forms, and the clients may have to execute their forms after the substantive interview, particularly when the medical records contain alcohol or drug abuse information. Some healthcare providers will not accept an authorization executed more than one or two months prior to its use.

An example of the medical records authorization is found in Figure 6:3.

FIGURE 6:3
MEDICAL AUTHORIZATION FORM

Patient Name: _____

Address: _____

As the above-named patient I authorize and request:

Name of medical organization or program: _____

Address:_____

_____

to release and furnish to: _____

my lawyer, or his or her designated representative, the following information: (Here indicate the nature and extent of the information to be disclosed. This may include all medical records, x-rays, physician and nurse reports, notes, tests and their results, and bills). This authorization includes the right to examine my medical records before any copies are made.

State of _____ §

County of _____ §

Authorization date: _____

Signature of patient: _____
or
Signature of parent, guardian or authorized representative: _____

_____

Nature of relationship: _____

Subscribed and sworn to before me on _____ .
Notary Public: _____

Employment Records Authorization

In matters involving personal injury and employment-related claims, the lawyer must obtain all employment records of the client. It is helpful if clients turn over all copies of employment records in their possession. Figure 6:4 demonstrates an employment records authorization form for execution by the client.

FIGURE 6:4
EMPLOYMENT RECORDS AUTHORIZATION FORM

Name of Employer: _____
Address: _____

Attention: Director of Human Resources

Name of Employee: _____
Address: _____
Employee Number: _____
Social Security Number: _____

I hereby authorize and request that you allow my lawyer, _____, to examine my employment file and that you furnish and release to him or her, or their designated representative, any and all information and records that they may request concerning my employment with you.

Very truly yours,

(Signature) _____
(Name of Client)

Educational Records Authorization

The nature of the legal matter may require access to the client's educational records, ranging from primary and secondary school records to academic records at colleges, universities, and trade and vocational schools. If legal assistants know the access requirements of the educational institution before the client interview, they can tailor the authorization to meet the school's specifications. An educational records authorization form is found in Figure 6:5. Many educational institutions will require strict compliance with the Privacy Act (discussed in a later chapter).

FIGURE 6:5
EDUCATIONAL RECORDS AUTHORIZATION

Name of Institution _____
Address: _____

Name of Student (Client): _____
Address:_____
Student Number: _____
Social Security Number: _____

I hereby authorize and permit you to allow my lawyer,
_____, or his or her designated representative, to
examine, make or furnish copies of any records or information, academic or otherwise, pertaining to my having been or being a student at your institution.

(When the authorization is by a parent of a minor child, add language requesting access to all psychological and psychiatric tests, reports, and evaluations as well as academic and achievement tests and evaluations.)

Very truly yours,

(Signature) _____
(Name of Client)

Fee Agreement

If the lawyer instructs the legal assistant to have the client execute the fee agreement or contract, the agreement should be signed in duplicate with a copy for the client. (This scenario assumes that the lawyer had already executed the fee agreement). Because the form and jurisdictional requirements for fee agreements vary, no sample form has been provided.

Most lawyers and law firms have standardized their fee agreements. In the event the lawyer has no standardized forms, then use the suggested fee agreements of the American Bar Association or similar materials. If, during the course of the interview, the legal assistant identifies additional information or documents in the client's possession or to which the client has access, the legal assistant should list these items and give the list to the client. Some legal assistants will encourage clients to make their own list during the interview for a review at the conclusion.

Concluding the Interview

Once the legal assistant has accomplished the objectives of the substantive interview, it is time to conclude the interview.

Several steps need to be taken at the conclusion. First, legal assistants should review their notes and the documents the client has provided one final time to be sure that additional information and documents have been identified. Secondly, legal assistants should summarize the interview with the client. Next, legal assistants should ask the client if there are any questions about the case or office procedures, or questions that must be directed to the lawyer. If there are any take-home questionnaires for completion by the client and information sheets and written instructions concerning tasks that he or she will be performing, these should be thoroughly discussed. Finally, if possible, the lawyer should be informed that the interview is finished, so that lawyer and client can meet briefly.

Figure 6:6 is a sample information sheet in a personal injury case.[5] Some lawyers give the client a letter explaining how they process the client's case, similar to the one set out in Figure 6:7.

FIGURE 6:6

**CLIENT INFORMATION SHEET
(PERSONAL INJURY CASE)**

1. Do not speak to anyone about your accident other than me or my legal assistant. You may have contact with your own insurance carriers, but refrain from making any statements about the accident without contacting us first.

---

2. Keep all bills for property damage and your injuries, including medical prescriptions. If possible, pay your bills promptly. (Medical people are usually more cooperative if they are paid.)

3. If you receive a summons to appear in municipal or traffic court with regard to this accident, notify us immediately.

4. Take photographs of your property and personal injuries.

5. Keep a daily log or diary of events since the accident, including treatment dates, days and times of pain from your injuries, etc.

6. Always advise us of any change in your address and telephone number.

7. Prepare a record of your lost work days and the amount of earnings you have lost.

8. If you become aware of any witnesses to the accident other than those previously given, contact us immediately.

FIGURE 6:7
CLIENT INFORMATION LETTER

Dear _____:

Since you are not familiar with the litigation process for personal injury claims, we want to explain how we handle cases of this type. It is helpful that you understand in advance what will happen.

Obtaining Information

Once you have retained us as your attorneys, we will notify the other party's insurance carrier by letter advising it of our representation. We will also request that we be provided with a copy of any statements you may have given to them. Using your authorizations, we will contact and send letters to all physicians and medical service providers. We will send letters to all persons with whom you have incurred bills for related services. The police officer will be interviewed, witnesses will be contacted, and land photographs of the accident scene will be taken.

Evaluation

It is important that no case is settled until the exact nature of the client's medical condition has been determined and all investigation has been completed. This can take several months from the date of the accident, particularly obtaining a prognosis from treating physicians. Once all medical and investigative information is gathered, we will meet with you to evaluate your case. A settlement figure will be determined. No settlement is ever made without your consent.

Lawsuit

If settlement cannot be made with the other party's insurance carrier, we will consider the advisability of filing a lawsuit. The lawsuit will be filed only with your approval. The lawsuit is started by our filing a petition or complaint on your behalf as plaintiff with the appropriate court. A copy with a summons will be served on the other party as the defendant in the lawsuit. The defendant will take these papers to his or her insurance carrier, which turns them over to their lawyers. They will then file an answer with the court and provide us with a copy. Note that even though the litigation process has formally started, settlement is always possible.

Formal Discovery

Once the lawsuit has started, both sides have the right to obtain information about the case. First each may serve the other interrogatories. These are written questions that must be answered in writing under oath so many days after they are received. Second, depositions of the parties and witnesses may be taken. During a deposition, the witness is asked questions by an attorney and the answers, under oath, are recorded by a court reporter. Another key discovery device is to request the other side to produce for our inspection documents and things pertaining to the lawsuit.

Trial

Almost all cases are settled before trial. But if not, a trial date is selected and we will proceed to trial. Right before trial there will be intense case preparation for which we must have your utmost cooperation.

Conclusion

For your case to be successfully concluded, we must have your complete cooperation and absolute disclosure of all information to us. During the course of our representation, we will keep you informed by sending you copies of correspondence and other papers, but it would be impossible for us to give you a weekly status report. But if you have any questions about your case, do not hesitate to call me or my legal assistant. Please review the enclosed information sheet carefully and keep us informed of any material changes in your condition.

Very truly yours,

(Signature)_____

POST-INTERVIEW COMMUNICATIONS

As soon as possible after the substantive interview, legal assistants must prepare a summary of the substantive interview and an evaluation of the client. Next, they should prepare correspondence to medical service providers to obtain medical records if the client has suffered personal injury. Accident reports and other pertinent records will have to be requested. A lien letter for the lawyer's execution will be prepared and sent to the potential defendants and/or their insurance carriers, but it might be wise to delay this procedure until informal discovery has been completed. (A further description of lien letter is provided later in this chapter.) The legal assistant and the lawyer both have the ongoing duty always to keep the client informed about the status of the case.

Interview Summary

The legal assistant should prepare a summary of the client interview as a report. At minimum, the preamble of the summary should identify the client, the office file number, and the nature of the case. If applicable and available, the expiration date of the statute of limitations should be stated. The body of the summary, whether in narrative or outline form, should be objective; legal assistants should save their thoughts and viewpoints for the conclusion. All notes taken by legal assistants at the interview should be transcribed and attached to the summary.

An example of an interview summary is found in Figure 6:8.

FIGURE 6:8

INTERVIEW SUMMARY

Client: John Basil   File No. PI-0123
Date of Birth: 8-1-69
Social Security Number: 000-00-0000

Type of matter: Personal Injury, Auto-Pedestrian Accident

Date of Interview:_____

Facts of Accident: John Basil was interviewed at our offices. He was injured
on January 8, ___, when struck by an automobile driven by Fred Barker. The
accident occurred at 5:48 p.m., while our client was crossing University
Avenue at its intersection with 18th Street. Traffic at this intersection is
controlled by a traffic light. University Avenue at this point has five lanes; two
westbound lanes, two eastbound lanes and one left-turn lane for both eastbound
and westbound traffic.

Prior to stepping from the northwest curb, Basil and a friend, Jack Jones,
determined the traffic light was red for vehicles traveling on University
Avenue and green for pedestrians and traffic traveling on 18th Street. Basil
said he and Jones both looked to their left and saw no vehicles approaching. To
their right they saw only Barker's eastbound vehicle, a _____, at the
next intersection, estimated to be about 500-600 feet away from them.

After beginning to cross the street, they got to the left-turn lane where they
looked to their right and saw Barker's car about 300 feet away in the inside
eastbound lane. Client said that, when he next saw Barker's car, it was
"bearing down" on him, about two car lengths away. He was struck in the
inside eastbound lane by the front of Barker's car, knocked into the air and
thrown across the intersection.

Witnesses: Jack Jones; the police officer who investigated the accident (see
accident report attached); and Ralph and Wilma Crankston (a couple who were
walking their dog and were on opposite side of street).

Injuries: Fracture of right distal tibia and fibula (pins used); contusions and
concussion. Slow healing; kept on non-weight bearing. Emergency treatment at
Hargrove Hospital; taken there by Speedy Ambulance.

Physicians: Primary treatment by Lawrence Johnson, M.D., orthopedic surgeon, 111 Midwest Place, Center City; telephone: 555-5555.

Medical Bills: Client failed to bring with him; will drop them by.

Occupation: Client is a student at City University and is unemployed.

Fact Questions:

- Was driver maintaining proper lookout? Obstructions?
- What was speed of vehicle?
- What were activities of driver while driving? Radio? Telephone?
- Where was our client going?
- Was our client maintaining lookout?
- What were weather conditions? Street lights?
- Was signal device functioning?
- Were pictures taken when investigated by police officer?
- Were medical records provided, including ambulance service?

Conclusions and Recommendations: I believe this is a viable case, but I'm concerned with comparative negligence defense. Recommend that we do the following fact development:

- Have contact with client regarding bills and treatment.
- Interview all witnesses.
- Obtain information on the signal device and previous accidents at this intersection.
- Obtain all medical records; interview ambulance people.
- Obtain college records.

Evaluation of Client

Legal assistants should tell lawyers their impressions, concerns, and judgments of the client. All facets of the client's demeanor and personality must be discussed. Several components make up the evaluation.

First, the legal assistant should prepare a physical description of the client, including both objective and subjective details. Objective details include race, ethnic background, height, weight, complexion, hair (amount and color), and physical handicaps, if any. Subjective details are appearance, clothing, and adornments.

Next, the client's personality and mental traits should be reviewed. At this point in time, this will be subjective since the legal assistant has not yet become familiar with the client. The evaluation should cover the client's interaction with the legal assistant during the interview. Was he talkative, or did the legal assistant have to pull the answers out of him? Was he shy or withdrawn? Did he try to control the interview? Many lawyers are leery of difficult clients whose representation can result in long hours, stressful conferences, excessive telephone calls, very little money, and often a malpractice lawsuit or disciplinary complaint. If the legal assistant believes the client to be such a person, the lawyer should be informed immediately and given specific reasons for this determination. The client's exaggeration of the facts, references to all the governmental agencies and politicians already contacted, and previous consultation with other lawyers are all good signals that this client is a potential malpractice claimant.

Finally, specific nonverbal and verbal factors should be discussed. What was the client's body language during the interview? Did his face gestures match his responses to questions? Did his responses indicate bias or prejudices?

The ultimate question must be answered: what impression would this client make on a judge or jury, or a regulatory board if the case went to other final adjudication?

Figure 6:9 contains an evaluation of the client interviewed in the automobile-pedestrian case summarized in Figure 6:8.

FIGURE 6:9

CLIENT EVALUATION

Evaluation of John Basil
Date:_____

John Basil will be 22 years old in August. He is Caucasian, weighs approximately 180 lbs., and is 6'2" tall. He has a full head of dark brown hair which he wears shoulder length, and he was clean-shaven. He had a tattoo of a rose on his left forearm. He uses a cane when he walks due to his injuries in the accident. His dress was typical of a college student, T-shirt and jeans, but he wore sandals.

He was cooperative during the interview and was very responsive to my questions. However, he only brought in a copy of the accident report, although we had requested his medical bills, etc. He repeatedly asked me how long the case would take and mentioned his "large bills" from the accident several times. He does not have any kind of insurance! Whenever I asked him specifically about his looking for vehicles when crossing the street, he looked away while answering.

I found him to be a nice-looking young man. He was articulate, but talked a little loudly. I think he would make a good impression on a judge or jury, provided he "dresses up" (we must cover the tattoo) and gets his hair cut to a shorter length.

Post-Interview Communications with the Client

Sometimes it may be better to send the Client Information Sheet (Figure 6:6) to the client rather than provide it at the interview, if the client appears nervous or unable to remember important details. In that case, the Client Information Sheet should be sent along with the post-interview questionnaire. The post-interview questionnaire follows up on the information obtained from the client at the interview and contains questions requesting any additional information about the client's claim, corrective information, and a verification request as to key information such as date of birth, employment, etc.

The follow-up letter should be in form similar to Figure 6:10.

FIGURE 6:10

CLIENT FOLLOW-UP LETTER

Date

Mr. John Basil
Address

File No. PI-0123

Dear Mr. Basil:

Thank you for meeting with me last week to discuss your personal injury claim. We covered a lot of ground at the interview. However, from experience in these matters, our office has found that clients recall many important facts and related information after initial contact with us. In this regard, please review the enclosed post-interview questionnaire and return it to us within the next two weeks.

If you have any questions or information that can best be discussed by telephone, please call at your earliest convenience.

 Sincerely,

(Signature)_____
Legal Assistant

Legal assistants will usually communicate with the client by telephone. When calling, legal assistants should always have the file present. They should avoid making inappropriate or demeaning "filler" comments: "This file is a mess" or "Now what was I calling you about?" When the client calls the legal assistant to find out about his case, all calls must be answered! One of the main complaints against lawyers is their failure to communicate with the client. The legal assistant must avoid contributing to this problem.

The communication of confidential or privileged information by telephone should be avoided if the possibility exists that a third party may have access to the conversation. This applies equally to the use of fax and e-mail.

Medical Information and Records

Once the legal assistant identifies all medical service providers from the client's information, the providers must be contacted. Telephone contact works best initially, since the legal assistant needs specific instructions on how to obtain the desired information and records. Except for hospitals, most are not that strict in their authorization requirements, but telephone contact will cut down on duplication of effort. If possible, the legal assistant should review the records in person before authorizing any copies to reduce unnecessary expenses of copying. This review will also assure that all of the records are correctly copied with no material records left out. The legal assistant should utilize a medical/legal dictionary or similar resource materials for understanding medical charts and abbreviations.

The typical hospital or treatment facility medical records will contain standard information covering the following:[6]

- fact sheet and admission summary/emergency room records
- patient consents
- patient history and physical data
- physician orders and progress notes
- consultation information
- nurses' notes
- operative reports
- anesthesia record
- radiology records
- laboratory reports
- medications
- therapy records
- death certificate, autopsy, or discharge records.

Unless the client's medical information and records are detailed, voluminous, or highly sensitive (client's prognosis is not good), the request letters to the physicians, hospitals, and other medical service providers, should be in general form. A copy of all such correspondence should be sent to the client to keep the client informed.

Typical letters for this task are found in Figures 6:11 and 6:12.

FIGURE 6:11
MEDICAL INFORMATION AND RECORDS
REQUEST TO PHYSICIAN

Date

(Name of Physician)
(Address)

Re: John Basil
Patient Number

Date of Birth:

Dear Dr. _____:

This office represents the above person with regard to personal injuries he sustained in an accident on January 8, ____.

Please forward copies of any and all medical records, x-rays, reports, tests, etc. for all medical services you rendered to him. If there is a charge for these records please advise, and our office will make prompt payment. Enclosed is a consent from Mr. Basil has signed authorizing you to release these records.

Also, please provide us with your diagnosis and treatment of Mr. Basil's injuries along with your prognosis of future medical conditions and treatment. If you have any questions, please do not hesitate to call me. Your help in this matter is greatly appreciated.

Sincerely,

(Signature)
Legal Assistant

cc: John Basil

FIGURE 6:12
MEDICAL RECORDS REQUEST TO HOSPITAL

Date

(Name of Hospital)
(Address)

Re: John Basil
Patient Number
Date of Birth:

Dear Medical Records Custodian:

This office represents the above person with regard to personal injuries he sustained in an accident on January 8, ___. We understand that the patient received treatment for these injuries at your hospital. We request copies of all records pertaining to this treatment, including, but not limited to, admission records, graphic charts, physicians' orders, medical history and progress notes, laboratory reports, nurses' notes, and miscellaneous documents.

Enclosed is Mr. Basil's authorization for the release of his records to us. Please advise our office of the charges for the requested records, and we will make prompt payment.

If you have any questions, please contact us immediately. Thank you for your assistance in this matter.

Sincerely,

(Signature)
Legal Assistant

cc: John Basil

Accident Reports and Other Records

In any accident in which a law enforcement officer was called to investigate, an accident report will be filed. If the client has not already obtained a copy of the accident report, the legal assistant should immediately contact the appropriate law enforcement agency either in person or by letter. Most reports are electronically filed by names of parties involved, date of accident, or place of accident, so the legal assistant should have or provide this information when requesting the accident report. A word of caution about accident reports: They may not be accurate and may not be detailed. Thus, the legal assistant should visit the accident scene to expand on the report.

Figure 6:13 is an example of a request for an accident report.

FIGURE 6:13

REQUEST FOR ACCIDENT REPORT

Date

Name of Law Enforcement Agency
Address

Dear Gentlemen:

Please send me a copy of the accident report filed for the vehicle-pedestrian
accident that occurred on January 8, ___ at approximately 5:48 p.m. The
accident was at the intersection of University Avenue and 18th Street. The
driver of the vehicle was Fred Barker, and the pedestrian was John Basil.

Please advise if there is a charge for the report and payment will be made
promptly. Also, a stamped, self-addressed envelope is enclosed for your
convenience. Thank you for your assistance.

Sincerely,

(Signature)
Legal Assistant

cc: John Basil

The Lien Letter and Insurance Notifications

To protect the lawyer's interest in the claims of the client against
another person, the lawyer must send the opposing party a letter
asserting a lien upon the claims. If, after receipt of the lien letter, the
other person or a representative deals and settles with the client without
the involvement of the lawyer, the lawyer can recover the agreed fee
from the other person.

The lien letter should be sent by certified and regular mail to the other
person with a copy to the client, and should contain a demand for
resolution of the client's claims. If the other person is known to have an
insurance carrier, the letter should also be sent to the carrier to fully
protect the lawyer's interest and to protect the client from entering into
an unfavorable settlement. Once the lien letter is sent, however,

productive contact with the other person will probably be extinguished. In some states, the lien letter must state the percentage of the recovery that the lawyer is entitled to receive. While the legal assistant may prepare the lien letter, the lawyer must always execute it before it is sent.

An example of a lien letter is found in Figure 6:14.

FIGURE 6:14

THE LIEN LETTER

Date

RE: OUR CLIENT: John Basil
DATE OF LOSS: January 8, ____
OUR FILE NO.: PI-0123

Mr. Fred Barker
Address

Dear Mr. Barker:

This letter is to advise you that our office represents the above-named client in his claims against you for damages arising out of an accident that occurred on the above date of loss. The facts represented to us and substantiated by our investigation indicate that you are responsible for the damages sustained by our client, and we are, therefore, looking to you for payment of his claim.

Since we have been advised that you carry insurance covering the loss with the Insurance Company, we are sending them a copy of this letter and advising them to contact us immediately for resolution of this matter.

Further, you and the Insurance Company are notified that, pursuant to our fee agreement, our client has agreed to pay us for our services a sum equal to 25% to 40% of any amount recovered. We hereby claim a lien for such amount upon the claims of Mr. Basil against you.

If we do not receive a reply from you within 10 days of the date of this letter, we shall proceed to take whatever legal action is necessary to protect our client's interest.

Very truly yours,

(Signature)_____
Lawyer

cc: Insurance Company
John Basil

Many states have adopted statutes requiring that automobile and other types of insurance carriers provide their insureds with personal injury protection (PIP) and uninsured/underinsured motorist protection. These statutes allow injured insureds to obtain the maximum benefits available to them, be it from the responsible party or their own insurance carrier. Because of subrogation rights and specific statutory procedures, unless the insurance carrier is properly notified, the lawyer could incur liability by failing to notify the client's insurance carrier as soon as the question of uninsurance or underinsurance arises. Usually no settlement should be made without the full participation of the client's insurance carrier.

A sample of a notification is given in Figure 6:15.

FIGURE 6:15
NOTIFICATION OF UNINSURED/UNDERINSURED MOTORIST CLAIM

Date

Name of Insurance Company
Address

Re: Policy No. _____
Insured: John Basil

Dear Gentlemen:

Our office represents John Basil. Mr. Basil as the pedestrian was injured in an automobile/pedestrian accident on January 8, ___. A copy of the accident report is enclosed.

On behalf of our client, we have made a demand upon the insurance carrier of the driver of the automobile. Because the driver of the automobile may be an underinsured motorist, this letter shall serve as notification to you that our client may make a claim under the uninsured/underinsured provisions of his insurance policy with you.

If you have any questions or desire further information, please contact us.

Very truly yours,

(Signature)_____
Lawyer

cc: John Basil

NOTES

[1] L. Charfoos & D. Christensen, *Personal Injury Practice: Technique and Technology*, 435 (1986).

[2] Id., 429.

[3] M. Berger, J. Mitchell & R. Clark, *Pretrial Advocacy, Planning, Analysis, and Strategy*, 68 (1988).

[4] Charfoos & Christensen, 1121 to 1123.

[5] J. Kelner and F. McGovern, *Successful Litigation Techniques,* Student Edition, 2-10, & 2-11 (1981).

[6] Charfoos & Christensen, 533, 534.

Chapter Seven

INVESTIGATING THE CASE:
WITNESSES

INTRODUCTION TO INVESTIGATION TECHNIQUES

After substantive interviews with clients, the legal assistant will have sufficient factual information to prepare or revise the informal investigation plan. By now, the plan should have far more detail, since the legal assistant will be able to identify specific facts for development and verification. Key elements will be witnesses, both expert and those who have personal knowledge of the actual facts of the client's case, and the identification and gathering of documentary and physical evidence.

In all instances, the legal assistant should employ common investigative techniques to complete this part of the discovery process successfully.

Timeliness

Time is of the essence in conducting the investigation of the client's case. Invariably, essential physical evidence will disappear, the memory of a known witness will fade, or a witness will become impossible to locate once his or her identity is known.[1] The automobile in which the injured client was a passenger might be removed to the salvage lot of the driver's insurance carrier or repaired before the legal assistant examines and photographs it or arranges for its examination by an accident reconstructionist. Of course, this may have occurred before the lawyer was retained by the client but, if not, then the lawyer may face a malpractice charge for failure to act in a timely manner with respect to the automobile. The lawyer must immediately contact all known witnesses and take steps to locate all potential witnesses.

Assumptions

When conducting an investigation, the legal assistant must remain objective and avoid all preconceptions. While the legal assistant can assume that there are witnesses and that information pertaining to the client's case exists, it should never be assumed that any witness will discuss the case or that the information obtained is correct without proper verification.

Perseverance and Diligence

A main problem often confronting the legal assistant is finding witnesses and information. However, this obstacle can be overcome through persistence and single-mindedness of effort.

Generally, people want to be liked and want to help, but most do not want to get involved if helping will disrupt their own life pattern. Legal assistants must use all of their powers of persuasion to get the witnesses' cooperation and involvement in the client's case. Even after a key witness or essential factual information is discovered, the legal assistant must verify that all witnesses have been located and that no informational stone has been left unturned.

Case Management

Although most of the investigation should be completed as soon as possible, the legal assistant must not accomplish this haphazardly. The legal assistant should report to the lawyer and record for the case file all investigative activities, whether or not they are productive. A good rule of thumb is an affirmative answer to the following question: Would anyone unfamiliar with the case, after reviewing the reports, records, and notes in the case file, understand what investigation has taken place and what investigation still needs to be done?

Preliminary Investigation

To reduce costs and use time effectively, the legal assistant should conduct as much of the case investigation as possible within the office. The telephone, fax machine, or computer can be used to:

1. Make appointments where appropriate with witnesses to be interviewed.

2. Conduct a telephone interview with known witnesses to determine in advance whether they can be helpful to the client's case.

3. Obtain directions to locations.

4. Obtain information that may lead to witnesses and factual information.

5. Make preliminary contact to find out about unknown witnesses.

6. Send questionnaires and inquiries.

7. Receive responses to questionnaires and requests for information.

8. Obtain documents and relevant information.

9. Enter computer data bases to extract relevant information.[2]

Use of a Professional Investigator

Legal assistants may not be able to conduct the entire investigation, or they may need help in locating a witness or certain information.

Even when an investigator is used, legal assistants should not relinquish the reins of the investigation, and they should remain cognizant of the investigator's activities. The lawyer should not lose supervisory control of the investigator, since the latter is considered an agent of the lawyer. In some cases, the lawyer has been held liable for the tortious acts of retained independent investigators, particularly when their activities involved an invasion of privacy.

Even if legal assistants feel competent to conduct the investigation, they should not do so if it appears that the person doing the investigating might have to testify at trial. Here, the person testifying should be as disinterested as possible.[3]

IDENTIFYING AND LOCATING WITNESSES

In many instances, information about witnesses will be readily accessible to the legal assistant. Obviously, the client will be a primary source. Friendly witnesses (people who voluntarily come forth with information about the client's case) and even people believed to be hostile to the client's interests should always be asked to identify other persons who may be eyewitnesses or who possess information. Accident and other reports, as well as public records, may contain identifying information about witnesses.

However, problems arise when the legal assistant seeks to identify witnesses for whom there is no known information such as name, address, or telephone number.

IDENTIFICATION TECHNIQUES

The legal assistant can employ several methods to identify potential witnesses. Identifying the unknown witness can be most challenging, requiring excellent investigative skills. The following techniques should be used when seeking to identify unknown witnesses or gain additional information about known witnesses.

Neighborhood Canvass

This is a standard identification technique, particularly in vehicular accident cases. The legal assistant should visit the accident scene and canvass the surrounding neighborhood at approximately the same time and day of week when the accident occurred. (Of course, if the accident happened at an odd time of day, the neighborhood should be visited when there is more activity.) It should be determined if photographs or videotape were taken of the accident scene. The legal assistant should seek out not only residents of the area, but also persons who routinely pass through: mail carriers, salespeople, utility workers, and public carriers. Nearby merchants, dry cleaners, pharmacy, etc., hould be contacted. If the accident scene was in a rural area or a quiet city street, the legal assistant should carry on activities that will invite curiosity: photographing the accident scene, measuring skid marks, gathering debris, etc. Names of witnesses are the target information, but even physical descriptions can help.

Emergency Personnel

In any accident investigation, emergency personnel are an excellent source for witnesses and information. Emergency personnel includes ambulance drivers, providers of medical treatment, emergency room personnel, tow truck drivers, fire and emergency preparedness personnel, and all investigating police.

In addition to obtaining names of witnesses from these people, the legal assistant should always obtain their written records and photographs. The investigating police officer should be thoroughly interviewed after a written report is filed, since he or she may leave out information considered at the time to be unimportant.

News Media

Television, radio, and print journalists cover and report major and interesting accidents, fires, catastrophes and other matters in the public interest, so they should be contacted as soon as possible for copies of pertinent videotapes and audio recordings. Copies of newspaper articles can be obtained from the publisher or examined at the local library. Some libraries maintain clipping files on local businesses and organizations and prominent persons in their community. The reporter should be contacted for names of potential witnesses and other information that may not have been included in the news article.

Advertisement

In situations where there are no known witnesses or where known witnesses are adverse to the client's case, an advertisement may be an effective way to find witnesses to an accident or occurrence. A display advertisement may be more effective than an ad in the classified section of a newspaper, and the legal assistant should consider using alternatives such as radio, television, or selective mailings. The ad should be eye-catching and appeal to the reader's desire to help. Figure 7:1 is an example.

> **FIGURE 7:1**
>
> ### WITNESS ADVERTISEMENT
>
> HELP!!!!!!!!!!!
>
> If you saw the accident involving an automobile and a pedestrian at the
> intersection of University Avenue and 18th Street on Wednesday,
> (date) at about 6 p.m., please contact Michael A. Pener at
> 913-555-5555. Call collect.

Public Records

Public records are useful when the legal assistant has no names of
potential witnesses, but has access to other information that may lead to
their identification. For example, the owners of parked vehicles where
an accident took place can be identified through motor vehicle
registration by the license plate numbers. Names of present and
previous owners of real property can be obtained from the county land
records.

City Directories

The legal assistant can use city and county directories published by
R.L. Polk & Company and Cole when there is information other than
the name of a potential witness. While the telephone directory lists by
name, the city directories list by name, address and telephone number,
giving the name of the latest occupant of a particular address. Most
public libraries subscribe to these directories for their circulation area
and retain directories for previous years.

Internet Resources

Search engines and numerous Internet directories can provide the legal
assistant with extensive information about a person. For example, your
author was listed at several sites.

LOCATING TECHNIQUES

When the name, address, and other pertinent information about a
witness is known, and the investigation is conducted soon after the

event, the legal assistant will usually not experience much difficulty in making contact with the witness. However, delays may constitute a disadvantage — people move, change jobs, get married and divorced, and it becomes more difficult to find them. Many times, an unknown witness is identified by name, but the whereabouts of the witness remains unknown.

To locate witnesses, the legal assistant can employ the following methods. The chances of locating a person increase with each item of information discovered about that person.

Telephone Book

A person's residence is a basic starting point, and telephone directories should not be discounted. If the person is listed, there will be an address; even if there is no address, the legal assistant can use the telephone number to access information in a city or county directory. If the person moved and has a new telephone number, the telephone company will provide the new number for a limited time after the move. Public libraries and telephone companies keep telephone books from prior years and for other cities, and current editions for any area can be purchased. Depending on the locale and how common the witness's last name is, names, addresses, and telephone numbers of relatives can be identified, and the legal assistant can contact them for leads and information as to the whereabouts of the witness.

Tax Assessor and Property Records

In many urban areas, the city or county tax assessor's office needs only a name to access information about that person or entity, including the current address. When property is involved, index and ownership books are available, often on computer.

Voter Registration Records

A voter's registration record contains information about the person's age, date of birth, address, present and previous, and possibly his or her occupation.

Court Records

Court records will have a great deal of information about a witness, i.e., whether or not he or she was a party to a lawsuit. Many courts require extensive information affidavits containing financial and personal facts, including the parties' Social Security numbers, to be filed in divorce cases. Probate records will contain information about heirs and beneficiaries of the estate.

Drivers' License Records

Unless restricted by law, given a person's name and date of birth, state departments of motor vehicles will provide information about a person's driving license, including citations. Many states now use Social Security numbers as license numbers.

United States Postal Service

If a person has moved and filed a forwarding address with the Postal Service, for six months to one year after the filing date, it will provide the new address to the sender if the following is done:

On the envelope sent to the old address, write or type the following below the return address — Address Correction Requested. With this instruction, the Postal Service will return the envelope to the sender with the new address on it.

Employment Sources

If a person's occupation or employment history is known, the legal assistant can often ascertain his or her whereabouts through a previous employer, co-workers, trade unions, competitors, professional organizations, and state licensing boards and agencies.

Social Security Administration (SSA) Don't Do It

In addition to complying with disclosure requirements under the Freedom of Information Act (FOIA), the SSA provides a letter forwarding service pursuant to internal regulations (GN 03308.001 through GN 03308.999). Without disclosing to the sender the address of the proposed recipient (missing person), for a nominal fee a letter will be forwarded, provided there are strongly compelling reasons for wanting to get in touch with the missing person:

1. The missing person would want to know about the contents of the letter.
2. The SSA could reasonably expect to have a usable mailing address.
3. All other possibilities for contacting the missing person have been exhausted.

Although the SSA considers having the missing person's name and Social Security number (SSN) adequate for this service, when only the name is known, it will still attempt to identify the missing person's SSN when provided with the date and place of birth and name of parents, or the name and address of the last known employer and when the employment occurred. For complete details about this service, the local SSA office can be contacted.

Locating Companies

What should legal assistants do when they have used all of these techniques, and the witness still cannot be found? In this situation, they should consider using a locator, sometimes called a "skip-tracer." Such companies often have business access to credit information.

When used, they will request specific information as set out in Figure 7:2.

FIGURE 7:2

LOCATION INFORMATION

Information on subject to be located:

Name _____

Spouse (if any) _____

Last address _____

Approx. date _____

Marital status _____

Number/ages of children _____

Previous addresses _____

Dates _____

Date of birth _____

Social Security Number _____

Last known employer _____

Occupation_____

Address/last known employer _____

Date _____

Relatives, friends, credit references, contacts, etc.:

Name _____

Relationship_____

Address _____

Telephone _____

Name _____

Relationship_____

Address _____

Telephone _____

Name _____

Relationship_____

Address _____

Telephone _____

Additional information _____

_____

WITNESS INTERVIEWING

Once a witness has been identified and located, the legal assistant
should contact him or her immediately. First contact is usually done by
telephone unless the legal assistant believes that the witness has been
evasive, might be hostile, or might not be favorable to the client's case.
With a hostile witness, the legal assistant should attempt personal
contact so that the witness is not forewarned.

In accident cases, the legal assistant will find that most witnesses have
already been contacted and interviewed by insurance claims adjusters,

often by telephone. Even though the results of such interviews can be obtained during formal discovery, if suit is filed the legal assistant must still interview these witnesses.

CONTACT WITH WITNESSES

Unlike the client, witnesses may have no motivation to speak to legal assistants about what they saw or to divulge information that may have a bearing on the client's case. Witnesses are people, and legal assistants must gain their confidence and motivate them to share their information by finding the switch that turns on a witness.

In this regard, a number of motivating factors have been identified:[4]

1. **Ego Satisfaction**. Many people derive a great deal of satisfaction from positive public recognition of their involvement.

2. **Desire to Be Liked**. Most people want others to like them; want to be a part of the group. Be wary, however, of the person who overcompensates for this need.

3. **Altruism**. A person motivated by altruism not only wants to get involved, this person wants to right a wrong. An expert witness so motivated can be highly effective.

4. **Novelty and Excitement**. Some witnesses may get involved for the novelty of the matter and excitement of being a part of the litigation process.

5. **Catharsis**. Trauma, post-stress syndrome, guilt, or other psychological reasons can motivate witnesses to relieve themselves of the "burden" they have been carrying.

6. **Loyalty and Friendships**. Many witnesses are motivated by their personal friendship with the client or the other party.

7. **Animosity**. A witness may be motivated by animosity and wants to "get" a party. Such testimony is voluntary and may be counter-productive.

8. **Extrinsic Reward**. Occasionally the legal assistant will come in contact with witnesses motivated by some extrinsic reward. Of course, the expert witness is compensated. But what of the witness who seeks to gain by testifying? Be alert to this need. A further discussion on expert witnesses appears at the end of this chapter.

SPECIAL CONSIDERATIONS

When the legal assistant discovers that a witness is represented by a lawyer in connection with the investigation, legal ethics dictate that all contact with that person be terminated. The situation should be reported to the supervisory lawyer immediately, who in turn can communicate with the witness' lawyer to obtain permission to continue the contact. If a witness may be a potential defendant, he or she should be asked for information about insurance coverage, preferably at the end of an interview.

When measurements and distances or a particular observation are critical, the witness should be interviewed at the accident scene to enhance his or her recollection.[5]

The legal assistant should avoid interviewing witnesses in groups so that one witness will not "pick up" testimony and recollections from another witness.

SPECIAL PROBLEMS

Do not interview witness who has a lawyer.
Attorneys permission in writing

Information previously obtained may alert the legal assistant to special problems involved in contact with a witness. Legal assistants can eliminate many such problems or lessen their impact before contacting the witness for an interview, but some problems will unavoidably develop at the interview.

Chain of Command

When a witness is in another's employ and the purpose of the interview is to obtain information within the scope of employment, the legal assistant must obtain the consent of the witness's responsible supervisor before the interview takes place. This becomes critical when the employer has a law firm on retainer or employs a lawyer as in-house counsel. Failure to observe the chain of command could force the witness's testimony to be excluded.

Children and the Aged

Interviewing minors and older persons can present interesting challenges to the legal assistant. To respect the legal rights and responsibilities of parents to their minor children, minors should not be interviewed without the consent of their parents or legal guardians. When minors are small children, the legal assistant should conduct interviews with parents or legal guardians present. If their presence is obstructive or inappropriate, another adult should take the parents' place. If an older minor feels uncomfortable being interviewed in the presence of a parent, the legal assistant should arrange the interview at the office or outside the home of the family.

Older people may need special treatment. For health or physical reasons, they may not be able to handle long interviews, nor may they have the interest in the subject matter of the interview that a younger person would have.

Usually the best interview site for an older person is at home. Since in a retirement facility privacy may be a problem, the legal assistant should arrange with the director for a private interview site in the building or on its grounds.

Illiterate Persons

In most cases, the legal assistant will have no problem interviewing an illiterate person who was an eyewitness to an accident or event. However, difficulties can arise when taking a written statement from the witness and asking the witness to read it before signing. Some illiterate people will try to cover up this deficiency. If illiteracy is suspected to be a problem, the legal assistant should look at the witness' eyes when the witness is given any document to read. Usually, the person's eyes will not move across and down the page, but will stay fixed on one spot. When a person admits to being illiterate, the legal assistant should have another person read the statement and certify that such was done.[6]

Perception and Memory

Many factors affect a person's ability to remember an important event: the nature of the event, the witness's physiological and psychological profile, and the method by which information is extracted from the witness during the interview. Memory deteriorates with time and can be affected by suggestion. Witnesses will give the most accurate version of the event the first time they tell the story.[7]

Personality Clash or Lack of Rapport

We are fortunate if half of all the people we meet like us. Legal assistants will encounter witnesses who dislike them for no apparent reason, or the legal assistant may dislike a witness, particularly if the witness is hostile, aggressive, prejudiced, or obnoxious. Obviously, legal assistants' personal feelings should not hamper their professional responsibilities, but sometimes this situation cannot be avoided. If maintaining professional composure does not solve the problem, someone else should deal with the witness.

PREPARING FOR THE INTERVIEW

If time permits and the witness is cooperative, the legal assistant should assemble materials for the interview, such as a witness information form and an interview checklist or question outline appropriate for the case (Figures 7:3 and 7:4).

The purpose of the witness information form is to gather sufficient information about the witness to facilitate locating him or her if the witness is needed for trial. Used at the beginning of the interview, the form promotes rapport with the witness. However, if requesting personal background information appears to alienate witnesses and to diminish their cooperativeness, its use should be restricted appropriately.

By having a prepared checklist or question outline, the legal assistant will be able to concentrate on the witness.

FIGURE 7:3

WITNESS INFORMATION FORM

Client _____

Opposing Party _____

File No. _____

Attorney_____

Date _____

Witness _____

Address _____

City_____State_____Zip_____

Telephone _____

Previous Address _____

Date of Birth_____ Age _____Sex_____

Race _____

Physical Description _____

Spouse _____

Children (Names & Ages) _____

Other Relatives _____

Occupation_____

Employer_____

Employer's Address _____

Work Telephone _____

Immediate Supervisor_____

Previous Employer _____

High School_____

Date Graduated _____

College(s) _____

When attended_____ Degree_____

Other Education _____

Witness for Plaintiff_____ Defendant_____

Type_____

Previously a witness or party in a lawsuit_____

Details _____

FIGURE 7:4

INTERVIEW CHECKLIST
(AUTOMOBILE/PEDESTRIAN ACCIDENT)

WITNESS IDENTIFICATION

Name _____

Address _____

Date of Birth and Age_____

Occupation and Employment _____

Relationship to Persons in Accident _____

Person Conducting Interview_____

Date, Time, and Location of Interview_____

INFORMATION ON EVENTS JUST PRIOR TO ACCIDENT

Location of Witness _____

Time and Date_____

Identification and Location of Other Witnesses _____
_____

The Scene Before the Accident (Other vehicles, pedestrians, animals, objects, obstructions, traffic, traffic signals and controls, weather, special circumstances, etc.) _____
_____

THE ACCIDENT

Time_____

Accident Sequence _____

Measurable Factors (Distances, speed, skid marks, points of contact/impact, physical damages_____

Evasive Action by Pedestrian_____
_____

Evasive Action by Driver of Automobile (Horn, brakes, veering)
_____

Detailed Description of What Happened to Pedestrian
_____

Detailed Description of What Happened to Automobile
_____

EVENTS AFTER THE ACCIDENT

Position of Automobile After Impact_____

Final Position _____

Position of Pedestrian After Impact_____

Diagram_____

_____

Description of Injuries of Persons Involved _____

_____

Description of Comments, Quotations from Statements Made by Persons
Involved_____

_____

Description of Arrival of Emergency Personnel_____

_____

Information on Persons Present After Accident (Reporters, photographers,
investigators, tow truck driver, other witnesses) _____

_____

OPINION AND CONCLUSION
Witness's Opinion as to Who was at Fault _____

Basis and Facts Supporting Witness's Opinion_____

_____

CONDUCTING THE INTERVIEW

While the witness interview is similar in some respects to the client
interview, there are some significant differences. The witness interview
is all-inclusive, since the legal assistant cannot repeatedly contact the
witness without becoming a nuisance. While witnesses may be
sympathetic to the client's situation, they may not believe that the case
has any basis, and this may be reflected in their demeanor during the
interview. If witnesses are obviously uncooperative, legal assistants
might tell them that they can be subpoenaed for deposition by the

lawyer, a time-consuming process without compensation, if it becomes necessary that a lawsuit be filed.

Witness interview conditions may not be optimum. Since witnesses usually cannot take time off from work to go to the legal assistant's office for an interview, they will expect the legal assistant to meet with them at a time and place convenient to them. A law enforcement officer, for example, may ask to meet with the legal assistant either before or after duty hours.

Interview Format

Interviews may take many different formats. In one methodical approach, the legal assistant begins the interview by establishing rapport; then, in the "body" of the interview, encourages the witness to tell his or her "story" in narrative form. During the narrative, the legal assistant poses questions to enhance the completeness of the account and substantiate any factual information needing verification. Then, unless a statement is required from the witness, the legal assistant concludes the interview in a friendly and "open-ended" manner in the event future contact with the witness becomes necessary.[8]

An alternate approach, the "cognitive interview," is effective when an eyewitness has difficulty remembering what happened. With this method, the legal assistant tells the witness to reconstruct the surrounding circumstances of the accident, event, or occurrence before beginning a narrative. It might help the witness to reconstruct what happened out of order or use different perspectives.[9]

Form of Questions

While questions to the witness should not be "leading" or call for "yes" or "no" answers, they should direct the witness's responses toward the identified issues of the case. For example, in an automobile/pedestrian accident case, a key issue will be whether both the driver and pedestrian were maintaining a proper lookout and exercising appropriate caution in the circumstances. Thus, one important question to an eyewitness will be: "What was the driver of the automobile doing right before it struck the pedestrian?"

Interview Summary and Witness Evaluation

As soon as possible after the witness interview, the legal assistant should prepare a summary of the interview. Much of its content will be recorded on the interview checklist or outline, but the lawyer will want significant factual information in summary form.

Even if a statement is taken from the witness, the legal assistant still should prepare a summary. Some witnesses, such as the investigating police officer, as a matter of course will not give the legal assistant a statement, so the summary becomes very significant in those instances. The summary should contain the following: *work product*

1. the purpose and circumstances of the interview;
2. the factual information obtained from the witness, tied to the key issues of the client's case;
3. a brief description of the witness;
4. some indication of the witness's worth;
5. concluding remarks and an evaluation of the witness; and
6. recommendations to the lawyer as to how to proceed with the information obtained.

Figure 7:5 shows an example of a summary of an interview with the police officer in an automobile/pedestrian accident case.

FIGURE 7:5

INTERVIEW SUMMARY
(AUTOMOBILE/PEDESTRIAN ACCIDENT)

INTER-OFFICE MEMORANDUM
DATE: _____

TO: Laura Lawyer
FROM: Paul Paralegal

SUBJECT: Interview of Officer Sam Jones

Traveled to City Police Station on _____ and interviewed Officer Sam Jones, the investigative police officer. Officer Jones found Officer Linda Sandstone at the accident scene when he arrived, but he did the investigation and filed the Accident Report. Reviewed his report with him and verified it was correct as he recalled.

WITNESSES TOLD HIM OUR CLIENT WAS WALKING ON THE NORTH SIDE OF INTERSECTION AT THE TIME HE WAS HIT, and did not recall anyone telling him that client had been walking or crossing on the south side of intersection at the time he was hit. (One witness interviewed previously stated that our client was on the south side.)

Reviewed with him attached photographs taken by him and confirmed that automobile's windshield was cracked on right passenger side. Outside door mirror on right passenger side broken off (see photographs).

Issued citation to driver for careless driving. Said such was apparent in this case because when a YELLOW LIGHT HAS TURNED TO RED, A DRIVER IS SUPPOSED TO BE SURE ALL TRAFFIC HAS CLEARED INTERSECTION AND ALL PEDESTRIANS ARE OUT OF THE CROSSWALK.

His investigation and information provided by witnesses indicated our client had traversed (covered) approximately 49 feet of total width of the street, which was 54 feet at the time he was struck. He would have been on the curb in five more feet.

As to his "points of impact," they are for measuring purposes only. The indication in the diagram of Pedestrian is where our client was struck. The other indications are measurements from that point.

Officer Jones will be in municipal court to testify, and I told him I would probably talk to him again at that time.

He was very friendly, cooperative, and helpful. His testimony, if necessary, will be extremely helpful to substantiate what the traffic laws say as to the responsibility a driver has toward pedestrians when a traffic light has turned from yellow to red.

Officer Jones is a Caucasian male, approximately 6 feet 6 inches, very large build, approximately 275 pounds, wears glasses, full head of hair, about 40 years old, and when he speaks, you listen. His presence definitely commands attention.

> He will be a great witness! I strongly recommend that you make it a point to meet him at the municipal court hearing. Also, recommend that we contact Office Linda Sandstone, since she was the first to arrive at the accident site.

WITNESS STATEMENTS

One of a legal assistant's most important tasks in the interview is obtaining a statement from the witness. Whether this task is performed depends upon several factors.

The lawyer may have directed the legal assistant to obtain a statement from the witness, or may have left the decision up to the legal assistant. A witness, while not hostile, may be unfriendly toward the client or the case. If his or her statement is taken and a lawsuit is filed, it would have to be produced during formal discovery and could support the other side's position.

A statement may be superfluous and may be fraught with favorable exaggeration when the witness is considered "in the corner" of a client. If, for example, the client's best friend witnessed the accident, the other side would most likely take the friend's deposition, and the statement may pin the friend down to an awkward position.

If trial becomes necessary, the nature of the witness's testimony may be important but ancillary to the main issues. An example would be testimony from the client's supervisor about how his or her job performance has decreased substantially after the accident.

Whenever a statement is taken, it is important that the legal assistant understand the purposes for which it is done.

Purposes of Statements

The purpose of a witness statement is to provide factual information to enable the lawyer to focus upon the important issues of the case and determine how substantial the evidence will be in support or opposed to those issues. The statement serves to record a witness' recollection of the facts; it can be used later to refresh one's memory or to impeach cross-examination testimony if it is inconsistent with the statement. A statement obtained from an opposing party might be used to obtain admissions against interest during formal discovery. Inclusion of all or part of a statement can be used to promote settlement of the client's case.

Forms of Statements

No matter what form a witness statement takes, the legal assistant should always seek one that demonstrates the witness's knowledge or lack of knowledge about the event pertaining to the case. It may be handwritten, typed, or recorded, or it may be taken by a court reporter.

Substance is more important than proper form, and the legal assistant should not be unduly concerned with always taking statements in the correct format. Of course, no statement should be taken in any unethical or unlawful manner, but if a problem in this area is foreseen, it should be resolved before the statement is taken, to avoid losing evidentiary materials later on because of an overlooked ethical or legal requirement.

Signed Statement

A signed statement is always preferable to an unsigned statement. It promotes involvement by the witness in its creation, and it effectively summarizes the important facts within the realm of the witness's knowledge. Below are several identified standards for the effective writing of a statement by the legal assistant.[10]

1. When the statement is taken from an eyewitness, take the witness to the scene of the accident, event, or occurrence, or provide diagrams, drawings, or photographs to help in explanations.

2. Encourage the witness to use units of measurement such as 50 to 60 mph, instead of nebulous language ("too fast").

3. Avoid the use of qualifiers such as "maybe," "probably," or "I believe"; they weaken the effect of a favorable statement.

4. Prepare the statement in the best light for the case without being misleading or inaccurate.

5. Use the witness' vocabulary and grammar.

6. Avoid references to other witnesses in the statement, unless the lawyer has already determined that the other witnesses will be used at trial.

Format. The format of the statement must be free of defects and must survive the scrutiny of the opposing party. The best format to accomplish this identifies the witness and describes the accident or event in a logical, chronological sequence, and should have the following physical appearance:

1. The statement should be one continuous paragraph with no excessive spaces between words or sentences.

2. Margins should not be wide.

3. Sentences should not end at the bottom of a page, but should continue on the next page to avoid any claim that a page was substituted.

4. The statement should be typed.

Identification and Execution. The statement should start with identifying information about the witness, including name, address, occupation, date, time, place of the taking of the statement, and other relevant information. Then the statement should set the scene by describing the location or physical aspects, the date, weather, if applicable, the reason for the witness's presence, and other pertinent details. Next follows an account of the accident or event and a description of its aftermath. When significant, the statement should include the witness's opinion as to who was at fault.

After the legal assistant writes the statement, the witness should read it and write the following sentence at the end, followed by signature and date:

"I have read the above statement of _____ pages and it is true and correct to the best of my knowledge."

If the witness cannot read or refuses to write the above sentence, the legal assistant should read the statement to the witness and modify the sentence to reflect this was done before requesting the witness' signature.[11]

It is a good practice to have the witness initial or sign each page of the statement. Also, many legal assistants will purposely make at least one misspelling or incorrect word on each page, so that the witness has to cross it out, write the correct word, and initial the correction. This refutes any later claim by the witness that he or she did not read the statement.

Figure 7:6 shows a statement taken from a witness to an automobile/pedestrian accident.

FIGURE 7:6

HANDWRITTEN WITNESS STATEMENT

I, Elaine Sawyer, live at 1121 Sierra, Overland City, Kansas. This statement is being taken from me in my home by Linda Watchert, a legal assistant. I have reviewed the Accident Report of an accident involving a pedestrian being hit by a car at College Boulevard and Quivira on January 8, ____ and the information shown in the report regarding my statement to the ~~investigation~~ ᴱˢ investigating police officer is true as I recall today. The intersection was well lighted. The diagram of the accident report showing its location when the pedestrian landed against it after being hit by the car is correct.

I recall that prior to being hit by the car, the pedestrian was crossing the intersection in the marked crosswalk on the North side of Quivira with another man on a green light, and that as his light just turned red, he was no more than 3 to 5 feet from stepping up on the curb at the time the car hit him. I also recall that the car that hit him was nowhere in sight at the time he was crossing toward the curb and when I first saw the car approaching toward the man, it was going at such a fast rate of speed, it caused me to stop from making a ~~left~~ right turn South onto Quivira from College Boulevard. I thought it was going to hit my car if I turned in front of it. When the car hit the man, both of its headlights were on, and the driver had to have seen the pedestrian if he had been looking at all. The car hit the ~~woman~~ man so hard that I saw the man fly up in the air in a cartwheel like fashion, hit the car's windshield on the passenger's side, and continue to fly through the air, cartwheeling, and then he landed against the side of my car with a very heavy thud. I saw objects of the man fly through the air when he was hit and later found his books, glasses, and shoes where they landed.

When the driver of the car jumped out of his car afterwards, he started hollering at the man and saying he had not seen him. I could not believe this man was yelling at someone he had hit who was laying there and not knowing how badly he was injured. I told the driver to quit hollering at him and that if he had not been going so fast he would not have hit him. After I got out of my car, the man had raised his head from underneath my car but was not able to get up. He was crying and holding his leg and moaning. He was in shock. I stayed with him until the police and ambulance arrived.

I was at the accident scene that night because I attend classes at the College and pass through this intersection at least ~~two~~ ᵃˢthree times a week and this area always had many pedestrians walking across this intersection. In my opinion this driver who hit the man was going much too fast for an area like this and he should have been able to clearly see this man if he had been watching at all. I have read the above statement of ___ pages and it is true and correct to the best of my knowledge.

      Elaine Sawyer
      (Date)_____

Court Reporter Statement

Don't use to interview cooperative witnesses.

When a witness is adverse or uncooperative, the use of a court reporter is an effective means of memorializing what the witness has to say. Of course, doing such with a cooperative witness can be counter-productive, since the witness may make statements or give answers to questions that adversely affect the case, and all this will be readily accessible by the opposing party if there is formal discovery.

However, a court reporter statement is better than a handwritten statement if the witness is very young, aged, blind, illiterate, or has some disability that might lessen the significance of the handwritten statement.

Court Proceedings

In cases involving adverse parties who (as a result of the accident) have been charged with violation of a municipal or county ordinance, the legal assistant should recommend the court reporter's services to record related court proceedings when the court is not of record. This is an excellent way to obtain a statement from the opposing party that may contain admissions against interest, but the legal assistant should first obtain permission of the court.

Perpetuation of Testimony

The Federal Rules of Civil Procedure and the rules of many states make provision for filing a petition for authority to take an evidentiary deposition of the petitioner or another person. The expected adverse party is given notice of the proceeding and deposition and is allowed to participate. The deposition may be used as evidence in any action subsequently brought in any court, provided the deponent is unavailable to testify at trial. This procedure goes beyond the use of a normal court reporter statement, but the legal assistant should be aware of its availability in situations where the witness is elderly, terminally ill, in the military, or planning to leave the country for an extended period of time.

Recorded Statements

With electronic recorders now so common and simple to use, they are used as substitutes for the handwritten statement. While the use of a recorder allows the legal assistant to obtain a statement that contains more information, notes should always be taken while the statement is being recorded in case the tape is defective or accidentally destroyed before it is transcribed.

While the format for a recorded statement is similar to handwritten statements, the legal assistant should control the statement to avoid long or unresponsive answers.

Procedure

Before the recording, the legal assistant should cover several preliminary details with the witness. First, the witness should understand who the legal assistant is and the extent of his or her role in the investigation. Secondly, the legal assistant should advise the witness to wait until the question is completely asked before answering; the witness should also be instructed to answer each question "yes" or "no" first before providing additional information.

Many witnesses will become nervous or have "stage fright" when recorded, so the legal assistant should make the witness feel comfortable with the recording process. Once the recording has begun, the recorder should not be stopped until the witness has completed the statement. When the recording is done, the legal assistant should replay the statement to give the witness the opportunity to make additions or corrections.[12]

The statement should be typed, and the witness should review it for accuracy and corrections before signing an acknowledgment that he or she has read the statement.

The best policy is to obtain the witness's permission to record the statement, but it is possible to record an interview without the knowledge of the witness. However, many states limit the use of such covert statements for evidentiary purposes. Depending upon a jurisdiction's ethical standards for lawyers, such an action may subject the lawyer to disciplinary action. A witness who discovers that the recording was made covertly may become hostile to the client.

Format

The development of the content of the recorded statement is very important. The legal assistant should begin with a statement identifying him- or herself, the witness, the date, time, and place of the recording. Then the legal assistant should state to the witness that the interview is being recorded and ask for the witness's permission. The body of the recorded statement should contain specific questions about the accident or event. Then the legal assistant should end the recording with a statement that it is completed.

Telephone Statements

Insurance claim adjusters like to make contact with witnesses as soon as possible after an accident, via a telephone statement. Such a statement is inexpensive and less time-consuming than a personal interview.

Figure 7:7 is an example of a telephone statement format for an automobile accident case.

FIGURE 7:7

TELEPHONE STATEMENT FORMAT
(AUTOMOBILE ACCIDENT)

This is a tape recording of a telephone conversation between (name of interviewer, title, and name of law firm) and (witness's name). The date is (date) and the time is (time). (witness's name), you understand that I am recording this conversation and I have your permission to do so, is that correct?

1. Please tell me your full name, home address, and telephone number.

2. What is your date of birth? Social Security number?

3. Who is your employer? Your position and title?

4. Where were you on the date (date of accident) at (time)?

5. Can you tell me specifically where you were situated at the scene?

6. Why were you there at that time?

7. What direction were you facing?

8. How far away from the accident were you?

9. Was there anyone with you at the time?

10. Can you describe the condition of the street?

11. What kind of car were you driving? Speed?

12. Were there any obstructions to your vision of the accident?

13. Please describe in detail what you saw.

14. Was anyone injured?

15. Did you assist in any way?

16. Did you overhear any conversations?

17. Are you aware of other witnesses or persons who may have information?

18. Were you there when the police arrived?

19. Did you give any statement to the police?

20. Have you given any statement about this accident to anyone else

21. Are you aware of similar incidents at this location?

Video Statements

Small, hand-held video/sound cameras have had a powerful impact on our legal system. The courts accept video confessions as a matter of course where proper procedures have been followed, and some courts even allow television cameras to record their proceedings. A cable television channel now features actual court proceedings.

Thus, the legal assistant should consider videotaping a witness statement. It allows the lawyer to see the witness when the statement and the witness are evaluated. The content of the video statement will be similar to other recorded statements, but the legal assistant should avoid any techniques such as zooming in on the face of the witness or other unnecessary movements of the video camera. Many video cameras have built-in time and date indicators that will be seen on the videotape. *motion to compel for unedited version.*

The Negative Statement

impeaching a witness

When people refuse to give statements because they adamantly maintain that they know nothing about the accident or event, and the legal assistant believes otherwise, the legal assistant should attempt to obtain a negative statement to that effect.[13]

The negative statement will be in the same format as a regular handwritten statement, but it should be short (a page or less) and should specifically contain language that the "witness" doesn't know anything at all about the accident or event. If the person subsequently becomes a witness for the opposing party and remembers specific details harmful to the client's case, the negative statement should neutralize his or her testimony.

EXPERT WITNESSES

During informal discovery and sometimes after a lawsuit has been filed or other legal action has been taken for the client, the lawyer may ask the legal assistant to locate and interview a possible expert on the factual information in the case. Consulting an expert may be necessary before the lawyer agrees to represent a client. According to Rule 11 of the Federal Rules of Civil Procedure and similar state court rules, a lawyer may be subjected to sanctions, including reasonable attorney's fees of an opposing party, for filing a complaint, answer, pleading, or motion without reasonable inquiry when it proves to be not well-grounded in fact.

An expert can assist in the following during discovery:[14]

1. Interpretation of factual information so that it can be understood by nonexperts, including the lawyer and legal assistant.

2. Setting up information control and retrieval systems, particularly in complex litigation cases.

3. Identification of areas of substantive factual investigation, witnesses, and potential defendants.

4. Determining whether the client's case is viable and can be successfully tried, if necessary.

Definition of an Expert

For court purposes, an expert possesses the knowledge, skill, experience, training, or education to give testimony in the form of an opinion where scientific, technical, or other specialized knowledge will assist the trier of fact to understand the evidence or determine a particular fact in issue.

During discovery, the expert witness should function as a technical source of information and should provide a guidepost for the investigation of the case. At this time, qualifications of expert witnesses are not as important as their knowledge. Some large law firms retain chemists, engineers, physicians, etc., who function as legal analysts in their fields. Not all lawyers can afford this expertise.

When the legal assistant deals with an expert, certain parameters help to establish a successful relationship:[15]

1. As soon as the need for an expert is recognized, one should be located and contacted immediately thereafter.

2. Whenever possible, the best person in the field of expertise should be located. If a person invented a testing device important to the case, then his or her services should be utilized.

3. The expert must understand all the facts of the case, both favorable and unfavorable, and must understand the theories of liability and claimed defenses.

4. The lawyer, legal assistant, and client must clearly understand the expert's fees and costs.

5. The lawyer should establish a clear understanding of what is expected from the expert, especially concerning literature searches.

Locating Experts

Many practicing lawyers, particularly those involved in personal injury litigation, have established relationships with experts in areas associated with the type of cases they handle. For example, a lawyer with personal injury clients will have one or several physicians who specialize in orthopedics. In many communities, certain physicians become recognized "plaintiff" or "defendant" experts, and a lawyer or legal assistant can locate one appropriate to the case by contacting colleagues who practice in that area of law.

The American Trial Lawyers Association (ATLA) and other national lawyer organizations provides their members with services that identify lawyers working on specific types of cases who can be contacted for information about experts. Other sources of experts include:[16]

Technical Materials Produced by Experts. This includes all literature written on a particular subject, including books, treatises, and articles in journals or trade publications. Reference sections of public libraries may contain these materials, but often they will be more readily found in scientific, technical, or medical libraries. Some associations and companies maintain private libraries in that field. Computer databases such as BRS and DIALOG as well as the Internet provide unlimited access to scientific, technical, and medical literature.

Universities, Colleges, and Trade Schools. Universities operate on the principle of "publish or perish," and their faculty do just that. Many have established professional reputations, but an expert from this source may lack practical experience.

Professional, Technical, and Trade Associations. These associations not only publish materials by and for their members, but many maintain lists of members who are willing to consult in their areas of expertise. One of the best sources of such organizations is the Encyclopedia of Associations, usually found in public libraries.

Expert Publications and Services. One of the most comprehensive sources of experts and materials for areas of expertise is the *Lawyer's Desk Reference* by Harry M. Philo. If this two-volume work is not in the lawyer's library, it may be found in the local law library.

Expert services maintain lists of thousands of experts and provide experts through a referral service. Specific companies can be identified by checking national and local lawyer publications and Internet sources.

Government Agencies. Although experts working for a government agency may not be able to act as expert witnesses, they may be able to act as resource during informal discovery. They will probably be able to refer the legal assistant to outstanding expert colleagues in the private sector.

Telephone Books and Nonspecialized Sources. These may be less effective but they may have information on an expert with extensive knowledge in a little known area.

Contact with Experts

After an expert has been identified, the lawyer may ask the legal assistant to make initial contact and determine whether the expert should be utilized during investigation and possible litigation. Before making the first contact, the legal assistant must become educated about the field of the expert and its terminology, including applicable standards, procedures, codes, and regulations. If possible, the qualifying credentials of the expert should be confirmed to avoid problems with discrepancies later on. The legal assistant should obtain and review any published books, articles, or similar materials written by the expert.

Contact Methods

The form of initial contact with an expert depends on who the expert is and what he or she does. For example, due to class scheduling, college professors may be very difficult to reach by telephone, and the legal assistant may have to camp out on the doorstep of their offices to make contact. If the first contact is by letter, the legal assistant should make the content interesting enough to attract the expert into meeting with the legal assistant to discuss the particulars of the case.

Interview Questionnaire

If the lawyer gives the legal assistant the assignment of meeting with a potential expert, the legal assistant should prepare an interview worksheet to help obtain information about the expert's background and qualifications:

- biographical information
- education
- licenses/certifications
- employment history
- professional memberships
- publications

- particular qualifications for this case
- prior court experience.

Evaluation

After meeting with a potential expert, the legal assistant should submit the completed questionnaire to the lawyer along with an evaluation regarding further contact by the lawyer. Since a consulted expert often becomes an expert witness, this evaluation can be crucial. The questionnaire should discuss the expert's qualifications, but should also focus on subjective factors: the kind of impression conveyed to a jury, the ability to effectively communicate in nontechnical language, and the familiarity with the legal process.

NOTES

[1] A. Golec, *Techniques of Legal Investigation*, 48 (2nd Ed. 1985).

[2] C. Bruno, *Paralegal's Litigation Handbook*, 92 (1980).

[3] L. Charfoos & D. Christensen, *Personal Injury Practice: Technique and Technology*, 509 (1986).

[4] The National Association of Legal Assistants, *Manual for Legal Assistants*, 145 and 146 (2nd Ed. 1992), hereinafter cited as *NALA MANUAL*.

[5] A. Golec, 96.

[6] Id., 98.

[7] E. Loftus & J. Doyle, *Eyewitness Testimony: Civil and Criminal*, 120 (1987).

[8] *NALA MANUAL*, 152 to 153.

[9] E. Loftus & J. Doyle, 120-121.

[10] J. McCord, *The Litigation Paralegal*, 108-109 (1988).

[11] A. Morril, *Trial Diplomacy*, 174 (2nd Ed. 1972).

[12] A. Golec, 91.

[13] Id., 101.

[14] J. Tarantino & D. Oliveira, *Personal Injury Forms: Discovery & Settlement*, 3-2 (1990).

[15] H. Philo, *Lawyer's Desk Reference*, 7th Ed., 2&3 (1987).

[16] L. Charfoos & D. Christensen, 489-493.

Chapter Eight

INVESTIGATING THE CASE:
DOCUMENTARY AND
PHYSICAL EVIDENCE

GENERAL CONCEPTS

While investigating a case, legal assistants often have the responsibility to identify, obtain, and analyze documentary and physical evidence directly connected with the case. Depending upon their working relationship with lawyers and the extent to which they are involved in informal discovery, legal assistants may receive specific instructions about the investigative tasks to be performed in this area, or they may have greater latitude in determining what documentary and physical evidence may exist, how it can be procured, and what significance it bears to the case.

Although the investigative concepts discussed at the beginning of the last chapter are applicable to the investigation of the evidence, legal assistants also should be concerned with other factors: form of evidence, preservation of evidence, and control, storage, and retrieval.

Form of Evidence

Evidence is usually either documentary or physical. Documentary evidence is any physical embodiment of information, communications, thoughts, or ideas. In paper and related forms, it includes writings, typed materials, books, publications, computer printouts, drawings, sketches, maps, blueprints, x-ray plates, and any other objects that fall within the basic definition. The list can include microform (microfiche and microfilm), audiovisual (slides, filmstrips, sound recordings, motion pictures, videotapes, etc.), machine-readable materials (bibliographic, statistical and numeric, textual, properties, and full-text data files), optical and CD disks, and other electronically produced materials such as e-mail. Physical evidence consists of material things, objects, items, substances, etc.

Preservation of Evidence

In our society, we have a mania for putting things back the way they were as soon as possible after an event that causes a material change. Unfortunately, this restoration has often already occurred when the client contacts the lawyer for possible representation days, weeks, or even months after the accident or event occurred.

In an automobile accident case, often all debris is removed quickly or the vehicles are destroyed. In product liability cases, clients have often disposed of the offending product before seeing a lawyer. When evidence is accessible, the legal assistant should always attempt to preserve it in its present form. Failing that, the evidence should be preserved in an alternate form that will be acceptable as a substitute if the original is destroyed or cannot be brought into the court for trial. With the courts now willing to impose sanctions upon lawyers and their clients for lack of good faith, it is incumbent upon a party to litigation to take reasonable steps to properly preserve evidence. Several rules apply, including the following:

1. Before investigating the case for evidence, the lawyer should review all evidentiary statutes and court rules for changes in admissibility standards.

2. No marks or writings should be made on the evidence. A penciled word or sentence in the margin of a letter may destroy its admissibility. However, labeling evidence for evidence control is perfectly proper.

3. No evaluation as to the worth of the evidence should be undertaken in the initial stage of the investigation, lest important evidence be inadvertently discarded.

4. Physical evidence should be preserved to keep it in the same condition as it was at the time of the accident or event.

Control and Retrieval

Once an item of evidence is in a legal assistant's control, it should be handled so that it will not lose its evidentiary value. The form of control will vary with the nature of the evidence.

Documents must be kept in an unaltered state. One method is to place them in a transparent folder or envelope with an identifying label on the outside.[1] Obviously, this method will not be practical in large document cases, but all "hot documents" in a case might be handled in this way, with copies made of the rest. Copies made of original documents should be so designated.

The handling of originals of client-produced documents can be solved by one of several alternative methods. The client might keep all originals, with the lawyer maintaining copies. In this case, if the originals are destroyed or lost before formal discovery or trial, the requirements of the "Best Evidence Rule" will be easier to satisfy. Many lawyers keep the originals if they have adequate control and storage facilities; this assures the lawyer that the documents are maintained in their original state.

With physical objects, the legal assistant should establish the chain of custody as soon as they take control. If this is not properly done, an opposing or adverse party will inevitably claim that the evidence has been altered from its original state because of some act or failure to act on the part of its possessor.

To eliminate this threat, some lawyers and legal assistants will place all physical objects and even some documentary evidence in containers with lead seals; the seals are broken only upon orders of the court. Documentary evidence that could be sealed include motion picture films, audio and video tapes, and computer disks.

Storage

Once a document or physical object is taken into custody, it must be kept in such a manner that the chain of custody is not broken or vitiated, and complete control over access to the evidence must be maintained. In catastrophic events that involve numbers of potential plaintiffs, the courts or administrative agencies usually step in and provide for the orderly storage and access to evidence, particularly physical objects. In most cases, however, such procedures will be left to the parties themselves.

Early in the representation, the lawyer should formulate a formal storage and access plan to protect the documentary and physical evidence from unwarranted removal, damage, or alteration during formal discovery, when all parties have formal access through production requests for documents and things.

From the time a document or object is taken into custody until it is used as evidence, a detailed record should be made and kept of all activity pertaining to it, including the date and time, the person authorizing access, examination, or removal from its storage place, the name and other identification of the individual or entity involved in the activity, the duration of the activity, and the date and time it was returned to its storage place.[2] Figure 8:1 is an example of an evidence storage.

CASE OR DIRECT EVIDENCE

In this chapter we are concerned with documentary and physical evidence that is specifically identified with the client, opposing parties, identified witnesses, and property and things that comprise the subject matter of the case. What the evidence consists of and its importance varies from case to case.

For example, in an automobile personal injury case, documentary and physical evidence will include the accident report, medical records, medical bills, ambulance records, birth, death, marriage, autopsy and coroner records (if a fatality), employment and education records, tax records, Social Security records, vehicle ownership and repair records, driver's license records, the vehicles and their damage reports, photographs, sketches, diagrams, and newspaper accounts of the accident. If a potential defendant is a legal entity such as a corporation, documents pertaining to its existence and operation would be case or direct evidence.

FIGURE 8:1

EVIDENCE STORAGE LOG

Storage Log			
Client	Opposing Party		File No.
Type of Evidence			
Method of Acquisition		Date Acquired By	
Identification Number or Markings			
Storage Location			
Form of Storage			
Custodian	Date	Released To	Date/Purpose

Sources

Legal assistants will obtain case or direct evidence from the client, opposing parties, witnesses, third-party sources, both public and private, and through their own efforts (photographs, diagrams, charts, etc.). However, the investigation should not focus only on the gathering of case or direct evidence to the exclusion of accessing specialized information that may have a substantial bearing on the course of the investigation. This is the case even if its admissibility as evidence may be questionable. For example, in an automobile personal injury case, a city street department probably will have street blueprints and information about traffic signal devices and their operation for the street where the accident occurred.

Source Identification

One of the biggest problems legal assistants encounter in finding case or direct evidence is identifying and accessing its source. Certain factors should guide the legal assistant:

1. At every source, a competent person exists who is responsible for the case or direct evidence that is being sought by reason of that person's situation, position, or scope of authority. The person at the evidentiary source has the skill or ability to help the legal assistant in accessing the evidence. The responsible party may not be the most competent party.

2. The "paper trail" must be followed to its end. Once a legal assistant sets out to seek identified case or direct evidence, he or she must obtain all documents or physical objects that are pertinent. For example, if in an adverse possession case (e.g., a real estate matter), the client's recorded deed is identified and obtained from the recorder's office, then copies of previous deeds, mortgages, anything that may affect the recorded title, or an abstract of title must also be obtained during the investigation.

3. The legal assistant must search for case or direct evidence in a systematic manner, and must inventory the evidence either in manual or database form while it is being gathered. Figure 8:2 is a suggested form for a database inventory of a document.[3] For documents, an optical scanner should be used (if available). An inventory of physical evidence can also be stored in similar form as set out in Figure 8:3.[4]

FIGURE 8:2

DOCUMENT INVENTORY FORM

1. Author:
    Address:
    Telephone Number:

---

2. Recipient of Document:
   Address:
   Telephone Number:

3. Case Issues Associated with Document:

4. Elements of Case Document Proves:

5. Abstract of Contents:

6. Follow-Up Measures Taken:
   Interrogatories:
   Deposition:
   Production:
   Other:

7. Document Rating As Evidence:

FIGURE 8:3
PHYSICAL OBJECT INVENTORY FORM

1. Source
   Name:
   Address:
   Telephone Number:

2. Chain of Custody:
   (Name, Address, Telephone Number of All Entities Having Custody)

3. Case Issues Associated with the Object:

4. Elements of Case Object Proves:

5. Testing & Analysis:

6. Summary of Test & Analysis:

7. Rating as Evidence:

INVESTIGATIVE PROCEDURES

Identification

In searching for documentary and physical evidence, the legal assistant should first identify the evidence likely to be relevant to the case. This process requires the ability to conduct a legal and fact analysis of the case. Legal theories must be supported by fact premises which in turn are grounded in relevant documentary and physical evidence and the testimony of witnesses.

Initially, the identification process should not be so structured that it stymies flexibility as the case progresses. For example, in a typical automobile personal injury case, documents and physical objects can be identified easily using standard checklists, investigative guides, and similar formats. If the legal assistant adheres rigorously to such, and ignores identification of other possible items of evidence, the case may have limited development.

Let us explore an example where complete identification allowed the case to reach its full potential: A family of four was driving on a country road when their car struck a horse in the road. The horse rolled up on the hood and roof of the car. The roof collapsed under the weight of the horse, injuring the husband (the driver) and the two minor children and killing the wife, who was sitting in the front passenger seat.

Standard identification procedures produced evidence to support a claim of negligence against the horse's owner. The bizarre nature of the accident suggested that the car's roof support columns and their ability to sustain weight would serve as possible relevant evidence. Result: a successful product liability claim against the automobile manufacturer substantially based upon evidence that the supporting columns did not meet required minimum weight supporting standards.

Identification Techniques — Case Parameters

As discussed above, initial identification for many cases will be based upon the nature of the case or its "theme." Once the theme is recognized, identification is predicated upon the answers to the following questions:

1. Why will this item of evidence be used?

2. Does this evidence tend to prove or help to prove that the defendant is or is not liable and legally responsible for the plaintiff's claims?

3. Will this evidence persuasively compel others (opposing party, insurance carrier, fact finder, etc.) to the conclusion that there is or is not liability?

Since evidence sometimes "blends" documentary and physical evidence, the legal assistant should not classify evidence. However, there is a distinction between documentary and physical evidence. Documentary evidence is a passive record of factual information. Physical evidence, on the other hand, is "active" in that it pertains to an activity relevant to the case. For example, the speedometer of a vehicle frozen at the speed it was traveling at the time of an accident would be physical evidence, while any records of its repair beforehand would be documentary evidence.

Identification Techniques — Knowledge Parameters

In identifying evidence, legal assistants dealing with an unfamiliar factual area may overlook evidence because they are not aware of its existence. We see only what we know. Legal assistants, recognizing this, should take steps to rectify this limitation on their identification skills. Suggestions for improving identification skills include:

1. Using the client as an information resource.

2. Reviewing office files for similar cases. Many lawyers and law offices will keep a library of materials generated in previous cases.

3. Reviewing similar cases on file with local court systems.

4. Making an inquiry with the American Trial Lawyers Association, the Defense Research Institute, or similar organizations.

5. Networking with other legal assistants who specialize in the area of the case.

6. Contacting persons who are knowledgeable in the subject area of the case.

7. Accessing and reviewing literature and technical materials applicable to the case.

Much of the above can be done while the legal assistant is investigating the case. It would be impractical to delay improving one's skills until satisfied with one's knowledge in the subject area of the case. However, the legal assistant will be tested on this self-education as the case progresses, since it falls to the legal assistant to educate the lawyer through reports and evidentiary explanations.

Procurement

The case substantially determines how the legal assistant goes about obtaining potentially relevant documentary and physical evidence. The documentary evidence for an automobile/pedestrian case focuses on documents relevant to the accident (accident report, vehicle ownership and repair records, driver's license records, photographs, etc.) and the injuries and damages (medical records, medical bills, employment records, etc.). In that case, physical evidence would include the vehicle, skid marks, debris, the traffic signals, etc.

The nature of the evidence itself and the rules regarding its accessibility will affect how it is obtained. Generally, a car is not brought into a courtroom for trial, but photographs can be taken of it so that they will be admitted into evidence. Under federal and state rules of civil procedure, a certified copy of a an official document or record is admissible as an exception to the hearsay rule, thus avoiding the impracticality of having its official custodian testify as to its authenticity.

General Procurement Techniques — Documents

Depending upon the nature of the documentary evidence and its use in the case, the legal assistant can use several methods to obtain such evidence. The effectiveness of each method varies from case to case because of factors beyond the legal assistant's control. A method used in one case may not work at all in another.

1.   *Telephone Requests.* Many public officials and agencies as well as private custodians of documents will send copies of identified documents when requested to do so by telephone. The request should be made as specifically as possible to avoid wasting their time and incurring unnecessary costs. For example, if the request is for the property inventory of a probated estate, the request should include all possible names of the decedent and his or her date of death.

2.   *Mailed Requests.* Often a mailed request is more effective than a telephone request, particularly if the source may not have the personnel or resources to handle the latter effectively. Some governmental offices even limit the times during the working day that they will accept telephone calls. Whenever possible, the legal assistant should utilize any pre-printed request forms available from the source. Many will not reply unless this is done (such as the Uniform Commercial Code (UCC) information searches).

3.   *The Fax Machine.* This device has impacted electronic communications significantly and legal assistants use it extensively. If available, it means that a document requester can get a quick, inexpensive response (unless the response is voluminous). Many governmental agencies are even promoting the use of a fax machine to save costs. Many courts allow pleadings to be filed in this manner.

4.   *The Modem and Computer.* Through a simple telephone connection, the modem allows the legal assistant to access a computer database containing documentary evidence. As a matter of course, government agencies maintain public records databases containing information on corporate filings, UCC filings, bankruptcy information, and local official documents and records information, and with the Internet, there are no access time limitations.

5.   *Personal Contact.* Where documentary evidence is in the possession of a person or entity unfamiliar with its substantive content, the legal assistant should probably go to the location of the evidence.

Time and cost can make this an expensive method, and the legal assistant should attempt to limit its use. However, if the documentary evidence is critical to the case, this should always be done to assure that all necessary documents are obtained. For example, in a medical malpractice case, the legal assistant should personally examine all medical records at their source.

Whenever this method is used, to eliminate duplication of effort and reduce costs, the legal assistant should obtain certified copies of official public documents and records, and ask the custodian of private or business records for an affidavit of authenticity.

6.   *Document Search Services.* National and local companies will access and search official public documents and records, including UCC filings, limited partnership and corporate filings and data, and local data on bankruptcies, judgments, tax liens, and assumed business names. In situations where the evidence is critical to the case, or where the information is needed immediately and lawyers are concerned with their own potential liability if they do not get complete information, this may be a better approach. Some of the companies involved in these searches on a national level include:

- Information America (800-235-4008), which provides online information to locate individuals, to uncover assets and to identify relationships between parties. IA also provides general background information on individuals and businesses;

- Corporate Search Company (800-833-9848), which provides information searches for UCC filings and corporate filings with secretaries of state;

- Parasec (916-441-1001), which provides document retrieval from anywhere in the United States; and

- Prentice Hall ONLINE Public Information Services (800-333-8356).[5]

Lawyers have become concerned about clients providing or obtaining the identified documentary evidence, even in certified form. Unfortunately, while the electronic age has enhanced the ability to access documentary evidence, it has also brought with it the capability to alter, change, and even forge documents and manufacture evidence. Where indications surface that alterations have taken place, the lawyer can be safeguarded from liability and court sanctions by taking certain precautions.

First, if a document is an official public document or record, the legal assistant should obtain another certified copy directly from the governmental entity. Secondly, all other documents obtained from the client or other questionable sources should be subjected to careful scrutiny for authenticity. For example, if a client brings in a will that alters the decedent's disposition of the estate, it should be examined by a forensic expert before it is submitted for probate.

Finally, when a third party turns possession of documentary evidence over to the legal assistant, a receipt should be executed and given to the third party. The receipt should identify the third party and the legal assistant and be signed by the latter, and it should identify in detail the documentary evidence. The legal assistant should verify all of the documents listed in the receipt.

General Procurement Techniques — Physical Objects

Physical evidence should be obtained as soon as possible after the accident or event. This is imperative if the physical evidence is determined to have caused the injury or damages sustained by the client. Because the physical evidence must remain in the same condition as it was at the time of the accident or event, it should not remain in the possession of the client. This applies as well to physical evidence in the hands of third parties, if the evidence can be obtained from them. The client or third parties may not completely understand the significance of preserving such evidence.

Important investigative techniques associated with physical evidence are set out below.

1.   *Demonstrative Evidence.*

Photographs. If they meet the requirements for admissibility, photographs can be substituted for physical evidence that cannot be brought into court or a proceeding. They can capture the extent of injuries or damage to property and premises at the time they were incurred. This becomes particularly important in personal injury cases after the injuries heal. *Date taken, who took pic. type of camera, how far away.*

If the legal assistant takes photographs and if evidentiary requirements were not met, the photographs might not be admitted into evidence. Whatever the camera used, the subject of all photographs should be identified and date and time taken, film and lens used, relative distances, and the photographer's name. If photographs are expected to be an essential part of the case, the services of a professional photographer should be used to minimize the possibility of losing the photographs as evidence on a technicality.

Diagrams, Drawings, and Sketches. While legal assistants will not normally prepare these for courtroom use, they should prepare them for the lawyer's use during discovery. Diagrams, drawings, and sketches are now used extensively at trial, and many companies specialize in providing sophisticated materials for trial. As with professional photographers, their services can be expensive.

Video and Audiotaping. Video cameras are now commonly used in case investigations. A videotape played for the jury can bring an accident scene or other event into the courtroom. When a plaintiff suffers from extensive injuries requiring rehabilitation or has been physically incapacitated, "a day in the life" videotape can demonstrate the devastating effect of the plaintiff's injuries to the jury. As with other forms of demonstrative evidence, a professional should produce the video, but the legal assistant can develop the "script." Audio recordings also may be used as demonstrative evidence but, once made, they must be treated like any other type of physical evidence.

2.   *Secondary Evidence.* With greater acceptance by the courts of elaborate presentations of demonstrative evidence, the legal assistant must be familiar with this form of evidence. Sometimes called secondary evidence, it can be developed by the legal assistant, although

in complicated matters it may be best to use professional support services. Secondary evidence includes charts, graphs, compilations, drawings, illustrations, computer animations, models, experiments, demonstrations, and multimedia presentations.

3.   *Collection of Physical Evidence.* Physical evidence must be collected in such a manner that the procedures used will not invalidate its use as evidence in the case. No breakage, loss, or alteration must occur while it is in the chain of custody. In some instances, it may be advisable to have an expert present to collect the evidence to lessen the possibility of losing its evidentiary value. The legal assistant should issue a receipt for all physical evidence taken into custody to the former possessor. No markings should be made on an item of physical evidence, but an identification label can be attached, if appropriate.

Investigative Tools

When investigating a case for evidence, the legal assistant should have available a number of investigative tools. Following is a list of some basic investigative tools that have been used for 25 years.[6] Now, in the electronic age, basic tools must include laptop computer, scanner, still video or digital camera, and cellular phone for telecommunications and Internet access.

1. *One-Hundred Foot Tape Measure.* Distances are important in many cases, and the legal assistant must be able to measure them properly.

2. *Carpenter's Rule.* This is used to measure short distances and should be used in photographs to emphasize the height and width of spaces and objects.

3. *Flashlight.* A necessity for places without artificial light or night work.

4. *Magnifying Glass.* This is used to study photographs, maps, and serial numbers on objects.

5. *Compass.* This may be needed when the legal assistant draws diagrams and can be used in photographs to indicate direction.

6. *Audio Recorder*. This can be used to tape interviews and to make "notes" of the description of objects.

Use of an Investigator

If the lawyer decides to use the services of an independent investigator to procure case evidence, the legal assistant may have the responsibility to arrange for this service. Later, after the investigator has been retained, the legal assistant may coordinate the investigator's activities and integrate the work-product into the inventory of evidence.

Depending upon state and local statutory requirements, an investigator may need to be licensed as a private investigator. Since licensing requirements may vary, the legal assistant should verify with the investigator that he or she is qualified and competent, through training and experience, to do the work, and should also check the investigator's license through any state or local licensing authority.

If the lawyer does not regularly use an investigator in the community, the legal assistant can locate one just like locating a witness. If an investigator is needed in another community, the National Association of Legal Investigators or similar organizations accessible through the Internet can be contacted for a referral.

Surveillance by an Investigator

Defense lawyers often retain an investigator to follow and observe the activities of a plaintiff or claimant, usually because he or she is suspected of feigning the severity of injuries sustained. The goal of the surveillance is to obtain or produce indisputable evidence contrary to the plaintiff's injury claims. For example, many workers' compensation claimants voluntarily dismiss their claims for back injuries sustained in a work-related accident after they are presented with post-injury videotapes showing them digging in their backyard gardens, engaging in sports activities, or lifting or carrying heavy objects. Surveillance, however, can be dangerous for the lawyer who allows an overzealous investigator to gain the sought-after evidence without regard for the lawyer's liability for illegal or tortious activities.

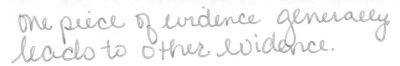
One piece of evidence generally leads to other evidence.

ANALYSIS

As documentary and physical evidence is obtained, it must be analyzed for its evidentiary value. While the legal assistant will do much of this, using the techniques of fact analysis, each document and physical object should first be subjected to an accounting. The accounting for a document involves answering the following questions:

- Who prepared the document?

- What is the purpose of the document?

- Where was it prepared?

- When was it prepared?

- Why was it prepared?

- How was it prepared?

In some instances, the answers to the above questions will be obvious (i.e., the purpose of a birth certificate, automobile title, or minutes of a corporate board of directors meeting). With other documents, the purpose may not be clear. In a product liability case, do promotional materials merely advertise the product, or do the representations contained therein constitute an express warranty?[7]

For physical evidence, the accounting of the object is absolutely necessary, since its evidentiary value may be worthless if it was damaged, altered or allowed to fall outside the established chain of custody, especially after the accident. Legal assistants who have investigated criminal cases know that this is particularly true in cases where the prosecution must show an unbroken chain of custody.

Evidentiary Analysis

After the legal assistant has developed an accounting or history for an item of evidence, it should be subjected to an evidentiary analysis. All evidence should be analyzed for information that may lead to other evidence and witnesses. For example, a death certificate will show the name of the doctor who executed it, and the legal assistant should contact the doctor for further information concerning the cause and circumstances of the death. The analysis should itemize the strengths and weaknesses of the item of evidence, its consistency with other existing evidence and testimony, and its probative value for the material facts of the case. Evidence should not be discounted merely because a question exists as to its eventual admissibility.

Technical Analysis

In many cases, evidential analysis requires competencies beyond the abilities of the legal assistant, and an expert or technical adviser will be needed to conduct testing or analysis before the full evidentiary value is determined. With both documentary and physical evidence, all contacts and activities in this regard must be fully documented in the inventory of the evidence to protect the chain of custody.

The lawyer and legal assistant must clarify before testing whether the evidence will be tested or analyzed by destructive and/or nondestructive procedures. Destructive testing should always be accompanied by notice to and involvement by other interested parties. Once testing or analysis is completed and a report is submitted, the report and any accompanying documentation become evidence. Thus, the expert or technical adviser should be carefully selected. Many areas now have private laboratories that provide testing services similar to those performed by law enforcement criminal laboratories.

Accident Reconstruction

Accident reconstruction is now an established field of expertise. Experts in this area deduce how an accident happened based upon the existing documentary and physical evidence and the statements of witnesses and participants. These experts work most frequently on automobile accident cases where "what happened" is truly difficult to determine. If the lawyer decides to retain an accident reconstructionist, legal assistants should make every effort to be as thorough as possible in their investigative activities.

When given sufficient data, many accident reconstructionists have the technology to provide a computerized simulation of an accident. With such technology being accepted by the courts, it should be seriously considered when the opportunity to use it presents itself.

NOTES

[1] National Association of Legal Assistants, *NALA Manual*, 178 (2nd Ed. 1992).
[2] Id., 179.
[3] L. Charfoos & D. Christensen, *Personal Injury Practice: Technique and Technology*, 524 (1986).
[4] Id.
[5] J. McCord, *The Litigation Paralegal*, 83 (1988).
[6] A. Morrill, *Trial Diplomacy*, 168-169 (2nd Ed. 1972).
[7] L. Charfoos & D. Christensen, 522.

Chapter Nine

INVESTIGATING THE CASE: PUBLIC AND PRIVATE RECORDS

During informal and formal discovery, the legal assistant may need to access public and private records containing specific information about clients, opposing parties, witnesses, and the subject matter of the case. For this reason, the legal assistant must understand what comprises public and private records, their sources, how they can be accessed, and limitations on accessing them.

PUBLIC RECORDS

Under federal legislation known as the Freedom of Information Act (FOIA), the Privacy Act and open records acts at the state level, federal, state and local governmental agencies (with limitations) must upon proper request make all of their records available to the public for inspection and copying.

Within this broad definition are two categories of records: public and private. Public records are those that a public agency is required by law to keep and make available, without any limitations other than those designed to maintain privacy and confidentiality. While examples vary from state to state, public records without any access limitations include records of a county recorder of deeds, court records, and records of state agencies pertaining to the professional licensing of individuals. Public records with a privacy or confidentiality limitation include birth and death records, since they can only be accessed by the person for whom the record was made or someone having a legal right to access them. Generally, such public records may have a direct bearing on a case.

Other public records concern the general activities of government. Although these records do not directly pertain to the case, a lawyer may want to access them because the information in these records

Secretary of State - Business names
County Recorder
 Skip Tracer - asset background check
214   *Discovery: Interviewing and Investigation*
 Contractors bond.

might have a substantial effect on the investigation and outcome of the case. They may even be admissible as evidence by judicial notice. An example is National Highway Traffic Safety Administration information concerning design and construction requirements for motor vehicles, utilized in the case of the automobile hitting the horse. This type of public record will be reviewed in more detail in Chapter 10.

Identification of Records

The first step in obtaining public records as evidence is to analyze the assembled case facts. Often the need for a public record will be obvious. For example, to pursue Social Security retirement benefits, a client will need an original birth certificate or a certified copy of it. But what if such did not exist or had been destroyed? Then evidence identification becomes more difficult and the legal assistant will have to utilize the identification techniques discussed in Chapter 8.

The legal assistant should keep in mind that most public records about people and entities emanate primarily from the local (county and city) level, then the state level, and finally at the federal level. Since people and entities do move, the legal assistant must identify all possible locations of records pertaining to the subject.

Identification of Record Sources

After the legal assistant has determined the possible location of a public record, the next step is to identify the specific governmental entity or agency that may have the record. The nature of the record sought indicates the source where it is kept or maintained.

Figure 9:1 illustrates some of an individual's public records and where they may be found.

FIGURE 9:1

Type of Record	Source		
	Local	State	Federal
Birth certificate	X	X	
Death certificate	X	X	
Marriage certificate	X	X	

Type of Record	Source		
	Local	**State**	**Federal**
Divorce records	X	X	
Tax returns	X	X	X
Driver's license		X	
Real property records	X	X	
Personal property records	X	X	
Earnings records			X
School records	X		
Voter records	X		
Court records	X	X	X
Military records	X		X

A legal assistant unfamiliar with specific sources of public records should obtain information about the governmental entity or agency believed to have the record, including materials on how to access its records. For federal records, two excellent sources are the official handbook of the Federal Government, *The United States Government Manual* and the *Washington Information Directory*, both of which provide comprehensive information, including World Wide Web sites, on the legislative, judicial, and executive government branches and its quasi-official agencies, boards, and commissions.

In the *Manual*, a typical agency description includes a list of principal officials, a summary statement of the agency's purpose and role, a brief history of the agency, including its legislative or executive authority, a description of its programs and activities, and a "Sources of Information" section. This last section provides information on the agency's consumer activities, contracts and grants, employment, publications, and similar materials.

Many states and local governmental entities and agencies publish similar official handbooks, and the legal assistant should obtain copies of such resource materials. Typically, these are agency-based and may contain statutory and regulatory references and case annotations.

Now with the Internet, at federal, state and local levels of government, there are accessible World Wide Web (Web) sites. These provide the legal assistant current information and forms, as compared to print

Credit Bureau - must have a very good reason to do so.

media which can be outdated. For example, the form in Figure 9:4 was downloaded and reproduced from the Internal Revenue Service's Web site.

The legal assistant should go to the proper governmental agency, consult with its personnel, and become familiar with its office functions and operational procedures. Particularly as to local records, the legal assistant should become competent in accessing records without assistance, especially computerized records. Usually agency supervisors and personnel support this approach and have prepared instructional materials on the use of their systems.

Figure 9:2 shows instructions provided by a local records department on finding ownership records.

FIGURE 9:2
INSTRUCTIONS ON FINDING OWNERSHIP RECORDS

RECORDS DEPARTMENT
FOLLOW THESE STEPS TO FIND OWNERSHIP RECORDS

1. Bring the legal description (name of subdivision) of the property to the records department.

2. If you do not have the legal description, go to the Taxpayer Assistance (S.E. Section) where the clerks will provide you with the legal description.

3. Proceed to the Index Section (Second Counter) and you will find the Subdivision Code Index. All subdivisions in Jackson County are listed alphabetically. On the right-hand column the correct Landlist Book and page of the property will be listed.

4. The Landlist Books (Third & Fourth Counters) list the current owner of the property, date of recording and microfilm book and page of the conveying document.

5. Please note, the Landlist Books, are used as reference only. Refer to the document on film. Also, if an error is found in the posting, the Grantor Index will have to be searched from the time the previous owner was posted to the present time.

---

6. Certified copies of documents are $2.00 per page and $1.00 for certification. If the copy desk clerks perform the search, the cost is $3.00. Fees are payable in cash only. If you need assistance, the copy desk clerks will be glad to help you.

Access Requirements and Limitations — State and Local Records

Many records must be made available within limitations by statutory requirement. For example, a local recorder or register of deeds office must make its records of all documents filed with it open for public inspection and copying, as required by recording and open records statutes. However, states have put many limitations on disclosure of an agency's records. In some states, the agency may require the requester to certify that he has a right to access the agency's records and the basis of that right. Other limitations include

- records that constitute the work product of an attorney

Rule of Evidence 34

- library patron and circulation records that pertain to identifiable individuals

- financial information submitted by contractors in qualification statements to any public agency

Production of Documents

- records that are privileged under the rules of evidence, unless the holder of the privilege consents to the disclosure.

The legal assistant should always review applicable open records statutes for access limitations when documentary evidence is needed from governmental entities or agencies. Even though access may be limited by statute, the statute is subject to interpretation. Typically, open records acts provide for civil remedies for a seeker of public records when an agency denies access. If the agency's denial was not in good faith and has no reasonable basis in fact or law, the seeker may request and be awarded attorneys' fees. However, if the agency made a correct denial, the reverse can be done. Thus, the lawyer should be certain of the case request before challenging an agency's decision.

Access Methods—State and Local Records

Because fifty states and innumerable local governmental entities and agencies all maintain records, it is impossible to identify specific methods of accessing state and local records. However, the following general access concepts or techniques have universal applicability.

1. Before accessing the records of the state or local governmental entity or agency, the legal assistant must review and thoroughly understand the statutes, regulations, rules, and access requirements and limitations applicable to the entity or agency.

2. Government or agency personnel may not understand or be aware of the requirements for accessing their records, and the legal assistant may have to "educate" them. While this task may be somewhat burdensome, occasionally it results in the release of a public record of questionable disclosure status.

3. Because accessing public records of a governmental entity or agency is a routine task, the legal assistant should create and maintain a public records filing system containing access information by type of record and by governmental entity or agency identification.

4. It is important to avoid stereotyping similar agencies, lest the legal assistant develop an unrealistic level of expectation. An experienced legal assistant knows that methods of accessing the records of one secretary of state can be far easier to obtain than those from another state. Small towns and rural counties may not have the record-keeping capacity or technology of urban cities and counties, although universal computerization of public records is making those records more accessible.

5. Whenever the public records of an entity or agency are accessible by internal computer terminals or externally through the use of a modem or through the Internet, the legal assistant must possess the computer competencies to use them. These electronic methods have become the dominant form of accessing public records.

Court records are generally accessible, absent statutory or court-imposed restrictions. Some records, such as adoption records and records of juvenile proceedings, are usually sealed. Sometimes, records or documents pertaining to a civil proceeding are sealed by order of the court by its own decision or upon request of the parties. (This is a customary practice and a requirement of settlement in many cases.)

Access Requirements and Limitations — Federal Records

While federal agencies generally must give the public access to their records (other than those falling under the FOIA exemptions), the Privacy Act controls information that an agency must make available, upon request, to the individual who is the subject of the requested record. The Privacy Act, which applies only to American citizens and aliens with permanent residence status, defines a system of records as a group of records from which information is retrieved by reference to a name or other personal identifier such as a Social Security number. Records include education, financial transactions, medical history, and criminal or employment history, such as:

- employment records of anyone who has worked for a federal agency

- military records of anyone who has served in the armed services

- Federal Bureau of Investigation (FBI) arrest records

- Veterans Administration (VA) records of anyone who has applied for or received benefits

- records of the Department of Health and Human Services of anyone who has received Medicare or Social Security benefits.

An agency may deny access to its system of records based upon any one of several exemptions set forth in the Privacy Act. These include:

- general exemptions applicable only to the Central Intelligence Agency and federal criminal law enforcement agencies

- classified documents concerning national defense and foreign policy

[handwritten margin notes: Safety Inspector / City / County / State } Always check all 3 sources]

- investigatory material compiled for law enforcement purposes

- Secret Service intelligence files

- files used solely for statistical purposes

- investigatory materials used in making decisions concerning federal employment, military service, federal contracts, and security clearances

- testing or examination material used solely for employment purposes

- evaluation material used in making decisions regarding promotions in the armed services.

Access Methods — Federal Records

The Privacy Act requires federal agencies to inform requesting persons whether the agency holds information about them. All agencies must also provide information about their systems of records and procedures for obtaining records from them, including the agency information official. The Superintendent of Documents publishes a compilation of all agencies and their records systems. It is available in law, reference, or university libraries, or it can be purchased for a nominal sum.

Often it is helpful to contact an agency by telephone, letter, or e-mail before a formal inquiry is made to ascertain its requirements for records access or requests for copies. A written request should be addressed to the head of the agency or to the specified agency information official. Along with the name and permanent address of the client, as much information as possible should be given about the record. Specificity shortens the response time. The letter must be signed by the individual whose records are requested or by the lawyer if an authorization is attached. Since agencies will require proof of identity before they release records, proof should be enclosed and/or the individual's signature should be notarized. "Privacy Act Request" should be written or typed on the bottom left-hand corner of the envelope. There is no charge for the search, but fees of 10 to 15 cents for standard size copies may be required. Electronic access is available through the Government Printing Office's website (www.access.gpo.gov).

FIGURE 9:3

SAMPLE REQUEST LETTER

Agency Head or Privacy Act Officer
Title
Agency
Address of Agency
City, State, Zip

      Re: Privacy Act Request

Dear _____:

Under the provisions of the Privacy Act of 1974, 5 U.S.C. 522a, I hereby request a copy of (or: access to) _____ (describe as accurately and specifically as possible the record or records you want, and provide all the relevant information you have concerning them).

If there are any fees for copying the records I am requesting, please inform me before you fill the request. (or:…please supply the records without informing me if the fees do not exceed $____.)

If all or any part of this request is denied, please cite the specific exemption(s) which you think justifies your refusal to release the information. Also, please inform me of your agency's appeal procedure.

In order to expedite consideration of my request, I am enclosing a copy of _____ (some document of identification).

Thank you for your prompt attention to this letter.

Sincerely,

Signature
Name
Address
City, State, Zip
Telephone Number

Since the records of some federal agencies such as the Internal Revenue Service (IRS) are frequently requested, they provide access request forms to help expedite the request.

Figure 9:4 contains IRS Form 4506, Request for Copy of Tax Form.

FIGURE 9:4

Form **4506**	**Request for Copy or Transcript of Tax Form**	
(Rev. May 1997)	► Read instructions before completing this form.	OMB No. 1545-0429
Department of the Treasury Internal Revenue Service	► Type or print clearly. Request may be rejected if the form is incomplete or illegible.	

Note: *Do not use this form to get **tax account information**. Instead, see instructions below.*

1a Name shown on tax form. If a joint return, enter the name shown first.	1b First social security number on tax form or employer identification number (see instructions)
2a If a joint return, spouse's name shown on tax form	2b Second social security number on tax form

3   Current name, address (including apt., room, or suite no.), city, state, and ZIP code

4   Address, (including apt., room, or suite no.), city, state, and ZIP code shown on the last return filed if different from line 3

5   If copy of form or a tax return transcript is to be mailed to someone else, enter the third party's name and address

6   If we cannot find a record of your tax form and you want the payment refunded to the third party, check here . . . . . . ► ☐
7   If name in third party's records differs from line 1a above, enter that name here (see instructions) ►

8   Check only one box to show what you want. There is **no charge** for items 8a, b, and c:
  a   ☐ Tax return transcript of Form 1040 series filed during the **current calendar year** and the **3 prior calendar years** (see instructions).
  b   ☐ Verification of nonfiling.
  c   ☐ Form(s) W-2 information (see instructions).
  d   ☐ Copy of tax form and all attachments (including Form(s) W-2, schedules, or other forms). **The charge is $23 for each period requested.**
     Note: *If these copies must be certified for court or administrative proceedings, see instructions and check here* . . . . . ► ☐

9   If this request is to meet a requirement of one of the following, check all boxes that apply.
     ☐ Small Business Administration   ☐ Department of Education   ☐ Department of Veterans Affairs   ☐ Financial Institution

10 **Tax form number** (Form 1040, 1040A, 941, etc.)	12 Complete only if **line 8d** is checked. Amount due;	
	a Cost for each period	$ 23.00
11 **Tax period(s)** (year or period ended date). If more than four, see instructions.	b Number of tax periods requested on line 11	
	c Total cost. Multiply line 12a by line 12b. .	$
	Full payment must accompany your request. Make check or money order payable to "Internal Revenue Service."	

Caution: *Before signing, make sure all items are complete and the form is dated.*

I declare that I am either the taxpayer whose name is shown on line 1a or 2a, or a person authorized to obtain the tax information requested. I am aware that based upon this form, the IRS will release the tax information requested to any party shown on line 5. The IRS has no control over what that party does with the information.

		Telephone number of requester ( )
Please Sign Here ► Signature. See instructions. If other than taxpayer, attach authorization document.	Date	Best time to call
► Title (if line 1a above is a corporation, partnership, estate, or trust)		**TRY A TAX RETURN TRANSCRIPT** (see line
Spouse's signature	Date	8a instructions)

SELECTED SOURCES OF PUBLIC RECORDS

It would be impossible to list and discuss all the various sources of public records available to legal assistants. The nature of the case will dictate what sources of public records need to be accessed. However, legal assistants will find that they access certain governmental entities and agencies more frequently than others.

FEDERAL AGENCIES

Federal agencies normally have some access limitations for their records. However, some agencies must provide records on the activities of others, for example, corporate documents filed with the Securities and Exchange Commission (SEC), the Federal Communications Commission (FCC), the Interstate Commerce Commission (ICC), and the Food and Drug Administration (FDA). Even the IRS can be accessed for the annual report of tax-exempt foundations and corporations. Legal assistants may find that they have frequent contact with the following federal agencies:

National Personnel Records Center (NPRC). Source of all permanent noncurrent military records; located in St. Louis, Missouri 63132.

Armed Services (Army, Navy, Air Force, Marine Corps, Coast Guard, Merchant Marine, and Merchant Seamen). Sources for personnel on active duty. Exact addresses contained in United States Government Manual.

Veterans Administration. Source for records of veterans pertaining to benefits.

Civil Service Commission. Source for records of all civil service employees employed by the federal government.

Department of Justice (Federal Bureau of Investigation (FBI) and Immigration and Naturalization Service (INS). Source for public records concerning the client. Access most likely through use of Privacy Act.

Social Security Administration.(SSA) Source for earnings and benefit estimate statement (Figure 9:5).

FIGURE 9:5

Form Approved
OMB No. 0960-0466

SP

Request for Earnings and Benefit Estimate Statement

☐ Please check this box if you want to get your statement in Spanish instead of English.

Please print or type your answers. When you have completed the form, fold it and mail it to us.

1. Name shown on your Social Security card:

First Name   Middle Initial

Last Name Only

2. Your Social Security number as shown on your card:

3. Your date of birth

Month   Day   Year

4. Other Social Security numbers you have used:

5. Your sex: ☐ Male ☐ Female

6. Other names you have used (*including a maiden name*):

For items 7 and 9 show only earnings covered by Social Security. Do NOT include wages from State, local or Federal Government employment that are NOT covered for Social Security or that are covered ONLY by Medicare.

7. Show your actual earnings (wages and/or net self-employment income) for last year and your estimated earnings for this year.

A. Last year's actual earnings: (*Dollars Only*)

$ ☐☐☐,☐☐☐.☐0☐0

B. This year's estimated earnings: (*Dollars Only*)

$ ☐☐☐,☐☐☐.☐0☐0

8. Show the age at which you plan to stop working.

☐☐ (*Show only one age*)

9. Below, show the average yearly amount (not your total future lifetime earnings) that you think you will earn between now and when you plan to stop working. Include cost-of-living, performance or scheduled pay increases or bonuses.

If you expect to earn significantly more or less in the future due to promotions, job changes, part-time work, or an absence from the work force, enter the amount that most closely reflects your future average yearly earnings.

If you don't expect any significant changes, show the same amount you are earning now (the amount in 7B).

Future average yearly earnings: (*Dollars Only*)

$ ☐☐☐,☐☐☐.☐0☐0

10. Address where you want us to send the statement.

Name

Street Address (Include Apt. No., P.O. Box, or Rural Route)

City   State   Zip Code

Notice:
I am asking for information about my own Social Security record or the record of a person I am authorized to represent. I understand that when requesting information on a deceased person, I must include proof of death and relationship or appointment. I further understand that if I deliberately request information under false pretenses, I may be guilty of a Federal crime and could be fined and/or imprisoned. I authorize you to use a contractor to send the statement of earnings and benefit estimates to the person named in item 10.

▲

Please sign your name (Do Not Print)

Date   (Area Code) Daytime Telephone No.

Form **SSA-7004-SM** (4-95) Destroy prior editions   ♺ Printed on recycled paper

National Archives and Records Administration. National Archives Building in Washington, DC, with 11 field branches. Source for records from regional governmental offices and inactive federal court records.

Internal Revenue Service (IRS). Source for tax returns and audit reports. Tax return information can be accessed through (800)-829-1040, but a power of attorney (Form 2848) must be on file before an IRS agent can communicate with a taxpayer's representative.

United States District Courts. Records are open unless specifically sealed by court order. Access is available electronically through Public Access to Court Electronic Records (PACER).

United States Bankruptcy Courts. Records are open unless sealed by court order. Many courts have set up a Voice Case Information System (VCIS) which allows case information to be accessed by use of a touchtone telephone.

Census Bureau. Source for personal information. Restricted to the individual concerned, but can be accessed by parent or guardian of a minor, and if deceased, then a blood relative, surviving spouse, beneficiary, and executor of decedent's estate.

STATE AGENCIES

Although each of the fifty states handles public records in its own way, most of them have the same agencies set up to handle common documents.

Vital Records Agencies

Every state now has a central office that has vital records pertaining to births, deaths, marriages, and divorces within its jurisdiction. There is no uniformity on how far back these records go, and many records are still on file with local agencies. Access to birth and death records is often sharply limited. Telephone contact can be difficult, and a written request may be more effective since it is eventually required anyway. The U.S. Department of Health and Human Services (DHHS) pamphlet, [DHHS Publication No. (PHS) 93-1142], is reproduced in Appendix 1.

The Secretary of State

This state agency is the primary source for information about corporate and other business entity filings, including documents pertaining to the creation and termination of these entities. Some states also require fictitious name registration. However, some states now limit access to financial data filed with the secretary of state if confidentiality is requested by the filer. This office handles all Uniform Commercial Code (UCC) financing statement filings (UCC-1) and UCC information requests and searches (UCC-3). Many accept fax, e-mail, and telephone requests where an account has been established with the secretary of state.

Figure 9:6 is an example of a UCC-3.

FIGURE 9:6
UCC-3 REQUEST FOR INFORMATION OR COPIES

Present in duplicate to filing officer, marked Attention: UCC Debtor(s)(last name first) and address(es):
Party requesting information or copies:
(name and address)

____information
Please furnish certificate showing whether there is request on file as of
_____,____ at __m., any presently effective financing statement naming the above debtor(s) and any statement of assignment thereof, and if there is giving the date and hour of filing of each such statement and the name(s) and address(es) of each secured party(ies) therein. Enclosed is the uniform fee of $____. The undersigned party further agrees to pay to the filing officer, upon receipt of this certificate, the sum of $____ for each financing statement and each statement of assignment reported on the certificate.

____copy
Filing officer please furnish exact copies of each request page of financing statements and statements of assignment listed below which are on file with your office. Enclosed is $____ fees for copies requested. In case any of said statements contain more than one page the undersigned agrees to pay for additional pages at the rate of $____.

Date _____
Signature of requesting party_____

File no._____
Date and hour of filing_____
Name(s) and address(es) of secured parties_____
_____

Certificate: the undersigned filing officer hereby certifies that:
_____the above listing is a record of all presently effective financing
statements and statements of assignment which name the above debtor(s) and
which are on file in my office as of _____,_____ at ____m.

_____the attached _____pages are true and exact copies of all available
financing statements or statements of assignments listed in the above request.

Additional fee requested $_____ date_____
Signature of filing officer_____

Licensing Agencies. Sources of records for all individuals and entities
licensed to perform professional services and business activities
requiring licensing or permits within the state.

Special Regulatory Agencies and Commissions. Regulate certain
industrial and business activities, and government regulated activities.
Commissions usually regulate banks, insurance companies, utilities, oil
and gas producers, alcoholic and beverage control, and state-authorized
gambling activities.

Workers' Compensation Agency. Administers state workers'
compensation laws. Records pertaining to previous claims and injuries
can be accessed

Department of Motor Vehicles. Accessible public records on motor
vehicle registrations and drivers licenses.

Department of Revenue. Tax records with access limitations.

Department of Health and Social Services. Regulates food and drug
industries and areas pertaining to employment, health care, family
support services, and child care.

State Highway Patrol/Investigative Agency. Access to files is limited but may be a source of criminal records check.

LOCAL ENTITIES AND AGENCIES

Dominant entities are cities, towns, counties, school boards, and local court systems. While local entities and agencies all have different forms and names from state to state, they all exist to support and regulate the personal and business activities of persons and entities within their jurisdictional limits. Because local entities and agencies are often the most utilized source of public records, access should be based upon the type of record sought and the agency that has it.

Occupational, Trade and Business Licensing. Records of licensing of certain occupations, tradespeople, and business establishments. In many instances, these will be connected to state licensing requirement, e.g., alcoholic beverages, child care, etc.

Zoning and Building Regulation. Accessible records of zoning applications, flood plain designations, building permits and inspections (structural and mechanical).

Health and Vital Records. Accessible records of health inspections and animal licensing. Many large urban areas keep birth, death, marriage licenses and certificates, and divorce records.

Assessment and Tax Records. The tax assessor's office maintains records concerning the ownership and valuation of real and personal property. Tax records are completely accessible.

county recorders office

Real Property Records. Public records for deeds, mortgages, subdivision plats, restrictions, easements, and miscellaneous filings such as oil and gas leases, land surveys, tax liens and judgments are found at the county level. UCC-1 financing statements may be required to be filed here and can be accessed with a UCC-3 request (Figure 9:6).

Voter Registration and Candidate Filings. Accessible records usually filed at the county level. Voter registration records indicate party

Corporation Commission
Annual Reports
Bylaws – license to do.
Articles of
Shares of Stock

affiliation, voting record, date of birth, and (possibly) social security number. Depending upon state statutes, candidates for political office must disclose occupational and business relationships.

Miscellaneous County Records. Powers of attorney, contracts, death certificates, military and school records can also be found at the county level.

College and School Records. The student and his or her parents or legal guardian, if the student is a minor, have a right to access the student's records.

Civil Court Records. Records pertaining to lawsuits, performance bonds, mechanic's liens, registered foreign judgments, garnishments and executions. Personal and financial information are often found in divorce or dissolution of marriage case files. Probate court records contain information on the administration of estates, guardianships, conservatorships, and regulation of private trusts.

PRIVATE RECORDS

Although public records will contain much of the case evidence, the legal assistant will find that certain private records are essential to the complete assembly of relevant documentary evidence and the outcome of the matter. While clients are the initial primary source of these documents and records, in many instances they may not have possession of them, or the document may have been lost, misplaced, or discarded.

Some clients may not understand the significance or the importance of keeping personal and business records for a period of time. The IRS says records must be kept as long as they may be needed in the administration of any Internal Revenue law. But telling a client this after the fact will not solve the problem created by the loss or destruction of essential records. However, businesses and institutions operate under stringent recordkeeping requirements, so some records may still be accessible during informal investigation or formal discovery.

Definition

Private records are any documents and records prepared, produced, maintained, or kept by or for any person or a nongovernmental entity or institution. There are no parameters as to what specific documents and records fall within this definition, nor is there a limitation as to the form they may take. The ultimate question is whether they can be considered case evidence. Most private records fall into four major categories: employment, business, health, and financial.

Employment Records

Federal and state reporting requirements require employers to maintain many records pertaining to their employees, including tax reporting, health and work-related injury information, and employment benefits. An employer will maintain a personnel file containing these and other records related to the employee's position. Many states statutorily require employers to give their employees complete access to their personnel files.

An employment file may have employment and noncompetition agreements, agreements assigning patents and copyrights, and other documents relating to the conditions of employment. Federal law requires employers who maintain employee benefit plans to provide a plan summary for each plan and access to the written plan documents.

Business Records

Business records include all documents and records pertaining to the operation of a business or activity, whether or not it is for profit. When a client operates the business, records are easily accessed, although they may not be complete. In such situations, the legal assistant may need to consult collateral sources such as banks, insurance companies, the client's agents, and governmental agencies.

Any contract of the client with a business becomes a business record. Sometimes the legal assistant will find that the client has an ownership interest in a business entity, but has been excluded from its management. If the entity is a corporation, state statutes give the client (if a stockholder or director) the right to inspect its bylaws, books of account, records of meetings, and other books and records and to make copies thereof.

Health Records

Normally, the legal assistant has very limited access to medical records. There must be a legal reason for obtaining them. Interestingly, if a person gives another a power of attorney for healthcare decisions, the latter has the right to access the medical records so that he or she can carry out the responsibilities of the relationship.

Medical records should include any diagnosis, testing, and medical-related information pertaining to an individual. They are not limited solely to the records kept by physicians, hospitals and associated medical providers; the legal assistant should search for records of healthcare insurers and medical laboratories that do medical testing for insurance companies.

Financial Records

Clients routinely generate many records containing information about their financial holdings, assets and liabilities, and their business and personal transactions: financial statements, loan applications and documents, negotiable instruments, canceled checks, and records maintained by credit agencies. Normally, the client will have the right to access and copy such documents, but copying can be expensive (as in the case of canceled checks that are microfilmed by banks). If the client's credit status is important to the case, under consumer credit laws, credit bureau records pertaining to the client can be reviewed.

Denial of Access

If access to private records about the client is denied during informal discovery, the individual or entity having possession of the records should be informed that they will be formally involved if a lawsuit is filed through the use of a records deposition, subpoena of business records, or even as a party to the proceedings. The legal assistant should not threaten, but should educate the recalcitrant record holder

gently that the subpoena possibilities exist by showing a sample of the
business records subpoena, as set out in Figure 9:7.

FIGURE 9:7

SUBPOENA OF BUSINESS RECORDS

DISTRICT COURT OF_____

_____
Plaintiff/Petitioner
vs.   CASE NO._____
                                   COURT_____

_____
Defendant/Respondent

SUBPOENA OF BUSINESS RECORDS

TO:_____

_____

_____

You are commanded to produce the records listed below before the Clerk of
District Court on the _____ day of _____, _____ at
_____ a.m./p.m. and to testify on behalf of the above named parties. Failure
to comply with this subpoena may be deemed a contempt of the court.

Records to be produced: _____You may
make written objection to the production of any or all of the records listed
above by serving such written objection upon _____ attorney,
at_____ within 10 days after service of this
subpoena – OR – on or before _____, _____. If such
objection is made, the records need not be produced except upon order of the
court.

Instead of appearing at the time and place listed above, it is sufficient
compliance with this subpoena if a custodian of the business records delivers to
the Clerk of the Court by mail or otherwise a true and correct copy of all the
records described above and mails a copy of the attached affidavit to
_____ at _____ within 10 days after receipt
of this subpoena.

The copy of the records shall be separately enclosed in a sealed envelope or wrapper on which the title and number of the words "return requested" must be inscribed clearly on the sealed envelope or wrapper. The sealed envelope or wrapper shall be delivered to the Clerk of the Court.

The records described in this subpoena shall be accompanied by the affidavit of a custodian of the records, a form for which is attached to this subpoena.

If the business has none of the records described in this subpoena, or only part thereof, the affidavit shall so state, and the custodian shall send only those records of which the custodian has custody. When more than one person has knowledge of the facts required to be stated in the affidavit, more than one affidavit may be made.

The reasonable costs of copying the records may be demanded of the party causing this subpoena to be issued. If the costs are demanded, the records need not be produced until the costs of copying are advanced.

The copy of the records will not be returned unless requested by the witness.

Clerk of District Court

DATED:_____   by:_____

DISTRICT COURT OF _____

_____
Plaintiff/Petitioner
vs.   CASE NO._____
                            COURT_____

_____
Defendant/Respondent

AFFIDAVIT OF CUSTODIAN OF BUSINESS RECORDS

I,_____, being first duly sworn, on oath, depose and say that: I am a duly authorized custodian of the business records of and have the authority to certify those records.

The copy of the records attached to this affidavit is a true copy of the records described in the subpoena.

The records were prepared by the personnel or staff of the business, or persons acting under their control, in the regular course of the business at or about the time of the act, condition or event recorded.

_____
(Signature of Custodian)

Subscribed and sworn to before the undersigned on

_____, _____.

My Appointment Expires:_____

_____
(Notary Public)

CERTIFICATE OF MAILING

I hereby certify that on _____, _____, I mailed a copy of the above affidavit to _____ at
_____ _____ by depositing it with the United States Postal Service for delivery with postage prepaid.

_____
(Signature of Custodian)

Subscribed and sworn to before the undersigned on _____,

_____.

My Appointment Expires:_____

_____
(Notary Public)

Chapter Ten

SOURCES OF INFORMATION

GENERAL CONCEPTS

One of the investigative legal assistant's most important duties is to locate, access, and utilize information pertaining to the case. Legal assistants who become proficient in these skills should make special note of them on their resumes. Many clients no longer seek representation for simple matters, but bring to the lawyer unusual case situations that will require extensive nonlegal research and information development. The following is an actual example:

The client comes to the lawyer because the bank has just foreclosed on the client's small apple farm due to nonpayment of the mortgage. The client couldn't make the payments because the price of apples fell dramatically after negative health publicity concerning the use of Alar, a chemical used by some apple growers to keep their fruit firm after harvest and to enhance its shelf life. The client didn't use this chemical and wants "somebody" to pay for the loss of the farm.

While the lawyer determines what legal remedies, if any, are available to the client, the legal assistant will be required to collect information relevant to the case. Two obvious pieces of starting information will be the chemical Alar and the nature of the publicity given to its use on apples. The information gathered by the legal assistant will have a dramatic and crucial effect on the development and outcome of the case.

FACTORS

Several factors affect the legal assistant's ability to gather information. First of all, as a result of the information explosion, a tide of knowledge has inundated government, institutions, and the private sector. Knowledge has become a product, and its management and access have resulted in a viable service industry. Thus, it is impossible for legal assistants to be universally knowledgeable, but they should know the techniques for accessing sources of information. Knowing how to find information is as important as knowing the information itself.

Information Exists

The legal assistant seeking information should assume that it exists and that it may be located in more than one source. While the information may not exist, the legal assistant must work under the assumption that it exists somewhere until research verifies that it does not. When every conceivable topic has been studied and described without success, a good question to ask when gathering information is, "Who else would have wanted to know this, even if it was for some other reason?"[1]

Access Limitations

Even though information exists, access to it may be limited. Some limitations will be legal in nature, like the exemptions to the Freedom of Information Act (FOIA); others are financial, such as the costs of purchasing database information. One of the most serious limitations occurs when the necessary knowledge for understanding the information is beyond the understanding of the lawyer and the legal assistant (very technical chemical analyses, for example). In such a case, the lawyer and legal assistant should recognize that the nature of the information is beyond their comprehension and take steps to retain the services of an expert.

Focus

To seek information on unfamiliar topics, the legal assistant should start with general concepts and work towards specificity. For example, in the case of the farmer allegedly victimized by Alar, the legal assistant should start by reviewing materials about Alar in general and chemical encyclopedias. Then the research can be expanded to scientific or technical articles concerning Alar's use and the risks involved.

Case Parameters

The nature of the case will determine the information sources to be located, accessed, and used. In the apple farm case, the lawyer will want information about the negative health publicity to help in deciding if it caused the client's deteriorated financial situation. The information obtained will have to demonstrate a causal link between the publicity and the client's plight.

Duplication and Overlap

Accompanying the information explosion is the availability of a tremendous duplication of sources for legal assistants. If the legal assistant fails to identify the primary source in the initial investigation and falls back on a secondary source having similar but incomplete information, efforts also will be duplicated. Sources can overlap. For example, a regional office of the Environmental Protection Agency (EPA) may have information about hazardous materials within its jurisdiction, but a state agency might have similar information about the state within the EPA region.

Erroneous, Incomplete, or Obsolete Information

When computers helped open up access to information, information specialists recognized that not all information accessed was factually true or correct. In other words, "garbage in, garbage out." This, of course, does not apply only to information accessed via computer! Information may be incomplete, or it may lack some important fact. In the same vein, the legal assistant should be alert for obsolete information. In the technological age, the rapidity at which new information becomes available can be overwhelming, and the legal assistant must always verify the freshness of any information obtained. With all forms of information, print or electronic, an evaluation should be made about the credentials of the author and publisher, perspective of the information, reference to other resources, accuracy, and currency.

Language and Terminology

In seeking information related to the case, the legal assistant will access and deal with a wide variety of sources, including government entities and agencies, business and institutional sources, and libraries. Although English is the common language of the foregoing, each speaks and operates with its own version of our language. The legal assistant must be able to communicate with a source and its personnel in their language, using their terminology.

USES OF INFORMATION

Information located and accessed can be used during many stages of a case. At the beginning of client representation, case-related information can be used to develop an investigation plan, or it can be used to prepare for the initial client interview by the lawyer and any substantive interviews conducted by the legal assistant.

Informal Discovery

During this stage, information can give the legal assistant factual background on the subject matter of the case in order to fully prepare for witness interviews. This becomes particularly important when the legal assistant has to locate and interview expert witnesses, or determine what documentary and physical evidence is necessary for the case.

Formal Discovery

If a lawsuit must be filed, case-related information gains importance during formal discovery. First, it will implement the drafting of interrogatories using language and terminology appropriate for the case. Second, with complete information development, the legal assistant will be able to prepare requests for the production of documents and things in specific terms so that there is no question of what items are being sought. Third, the lawyer needs complete factual information to prepare for and take depositions.

Judicial Notice

To expedite lawsuits, the courts often take judicial notice of certain laws, facts, and principles, accepting the truth of a proposition without requiring evidence. Upon proper application and at the court's discretion, judicial notice can be made before trial. Often a court will encourage the parties to stipulate to factual information in the place of the court taking judicial notice. To successfully persuade a court to take judicial notice, the lawyer must satisfy the court as to the certainty of the source of information. Many courts in automobile cases take judicial notice as a matter of course for the following:[2]

- Speed – a car travels 1.5 times its speed in feet per second.

- Vehicle's width – based upon the manufacturer's specifications.

- Maneuverability – present day automobiles respond quickly and accurately when the steering wheel is turned.

- Headlights – illuminate not only the road ahead, but to its sides for a considerable distance.

- Time of sunrise/sunset – this information is considered common knowledge.

Each item of judicial notice was based upon a source of factual information that existed outside the case or direct facts of the automobile accident to which it was applied.

Certified/Authenticated Copies

Whenever the legal assistant believes that the information will be used as evidence, it should be obtained in certified or authenticated form. At the federal level, according to 28 U.S.C. Section 1733, books, records, papers, or documents of any department or agency of the United States are admissible to prove the act, transaction, or occurrence as a memorandum of which the same were made or kept. Properly authenticated copies of such can be admitted into evidence in place of the originals. For state proceedings, the legal assistant should review the applicable state statutes before contacting sources of information to save time and duplication of effort.

GOVERNMENT SOURCES

Innumerable sources of information within the public sector exist. For the sake of time, the legal assistant cannot afford to be caught in a bureaucratic maze when trying to locate information. With rare exceptions, governmental agencies move slowly.

In one case, the author obtained information about a pertinent document from an agency by telephone because the information existed in its database, but received a copy of the document four months later. When the legal assistant has frequent dealings with a particular agency, he or she should develop contacts within the agency who can facilitate an information request.

When dealing with government personnel by telephone or e-mail, the legal assistant should always obtain the name of the individual who is handling the information request. Because many agencies are conscious of their image with the public, the agency employee may give better service if the employee fears being reported to a superior.

FEDERAL SOURCES

There are certain advantages in dealing with federal information sources as compared to those at the state and local levels. First, federal agencies have nationwide resources and contacts; they have no state jurisdictional limits. Their personnel tend to be better qualified. Many agencies are regionalized and operate fairly independently of the home office (Washington, DC). While the staff may be qualified, the administrator may be a political appointee who is unknowledgeable about the workings of the agency. Unfortunately, some agencies work at a snail's pace, no matter what the immediate needs of the legal assistant.

Source Identification

In accessing information of the federal government, a major obstacle is proper identification of the source. The government provides assistance in this task in several ways. The *United States Government Manual* is available from the Superintendent of Documents and its bookstores and can be found in public libraries. Federal information centers throughout the country can be contacted by a toll-free telephone call or in writing. Hundreds of depository libraries in local public libraries have selected government publications, and fifty regional depositories receive every unclassified government publication of interest to the public. Legal assistants can locate the depository libraries in their areas by contacting local libraries or writing the Superintendent of Documents, Washington, DC 20402. Available private publications, such as Information, U.S.A., list governmental sources of information by topic. The "blue pages" of a local telephone book list federal, state, and local agencies in its community.

All federal information resources are on the Internet. Many federal agencies are interactive and allow an Internet user to provide and access information. Because of Internet availability and use, the legal assistant should identify and have Web addresses for key agencies.

National Archives

Legal assistants can utilize the facilities of the National Archives and Records Administration at the National Archives Building in Washington, D.C., or any of the eleven regional National Archives Branches set out in Figure 10:1. Records of federal agencies are available for research, but may vary from region to region.

FIGURE 10:1

NATIONAL ARCHIVES BRANCHES

ATLANTA
1557 St. Joseph Avenue
East Point, GA 30344
(404) 246-7477

CHICAGO
7358 South Pulaski Road
Chicago, IL 60629
(312) 581-7816

FORT WORTH
P.O. Box 6216
Fort Worth, TX 76115
(817) 334-5525

LOS ANGELES
2400 Avila Rd., 1st Floor
Laguna Niguel, CA 92677
(714) 643-4241

BOSTON
380 Trapelo Road
Waltham, MA 02154
(617) 647-8100

DENVER
P.O. Box 25307
Denver, CO 80225
(303) 236-0817

KANSAS CITY
2312 East Bannister Rd.
Kansas City, MO 64131
(816) 926-6934

NEW YORK
Bldg. 22, Mil. Ocean Ter.
Bayonne, NJ 07002
(201) 823-7252

PHILADELPHIA
9th & Market Sts., Rm. 1350
Philadelphia, PA 19107
(215) 597-3000

SAN FRANCISCO
1000 Commodore Drive
San Bruno, CA 94066
(415) 876-9009

SEATTLE
6125 Sand Point Way, NE
Seattle, WA 98115
(206) 526-6507

Accessing Specific Federal Sources of Information

Once the legal assistant has identified a specific federal agency with information of value, steps must be taken to access it. If the information is located in a depository library or the National Archives, or it is published by the Superintendent of Documents, it is not necessary to contact the agency directly.

The Freedom of Information Act (FOIA)

Sometimes the legal assistant has to obtain information or access records of a specific agency in person, by correspondence, or by telephone. This task will be governed by the provisions of the Freedom of Information Act (FOIA), which requires all federal administrative agencies to make available to the public all records that do not fall within one of the nine specific exceptions. The FOIA does not apply to information maintained by the legislative and judicial branches, nor are presidential papers subject to it.

Many government documents may be useful to the legal assistant involved in the investigation of the case. For example:

- reports compiled by the Department of Health and Human Services concerning conditions in federally supported nursing homes

- data collected by the Agriculture Department regarding the purity and quality of meat and poultry products and the harmful effects of pesticides

- records of regulatory agencies concerning such matters as air-pollution-control programs, the adverse effects of television violence, and the safety records of airlines

- test results maintained by departments and agencies concerning the nutritional content of processed foods, the efficacy of drugs, and the safety and efficiency of all makes of automobiles

- consumer complaints registered with the Federal Trade Commission regarding interstate moving companies, corporate marketing practices, and faulty products.

The FOIA does not obligate federal agencies to do research, analyze documents, or collect information it does not have.

The FOIA Request

Once it is determined that an agency has the needed information, the legal assistant can write a letter to the agency's FOIA officer or the agency's official directly responsible for the record containing the information. "Freedom of Information Request" should be written on the bottom left corner of the envelope of the letter.

Unlike the Privacy Act, a FOIA request does not require the signature or authorization of the client. In the letter, the legal assistant should identify the records wanted as accurately as possible, although specifying a document by name or title is not required. Requests must reasonably describe the information sought; the more specific and limited the request, the greater the likelihood that it will be processed expeditiously. The agency should be contacted for fee information before the letter is sent. Figure 10:2 is a sample request letter under the FOIA.

FIGURE 10:2
SAMPLE REQUEST LETTER UNDER THE FOIA.

Agency Head or FOIA Officer
Title
Name of Agency
Address of Agency

City, State, Zip

Re: Freedom of Information Act Request

Dear _____ :

Under the provisions of the Freedom of Information Act, 5 U.S.C. 552, I am requesting access to [identify the records as clearly and specifically as possible].

If there are any fees for searching for or copying the records I have requested, please inform me before you fill the request. [Or.... please supply the records without informing me if the fees do not exceed $____ .

[Optional] I am requesting this information [state the reason for the request if it will assist in obtaining the information].

[Optional] As you know, the act permits you to reduce or waive fees when the release of the information is considered as "primarily benefiting the public." I believe that this request fits that category, and I therefore ask that you waive any fees.

If all or any part of this request is denied, please cite the specific exemption(s) which you think justifies your refusal to release the information, and inform me of the appeal procedures available to me under the law.

I would appreciate your handling this request as quickly as possible, and I look forward to hearing from you within 10 days, as the law stipulates.

Sincerely,

[Signature]
Name
Address
City, State, Zip
Telephone Number

Federal agencies must respond to all requests for information within 10 working days (excluding Saturdays, Sundays, and national holidays) after receipt of the request. If the material is needed right away, the request letter should be sent by certified mail, return receipt requested, so that the legal assistant will know exactly when the 10 days run out. If a reply has not been received by the end of that time (allowing for the return mail), the legal assistant should follow up by letter or telephone inquiry. If an agency refuses to disclose information requested under the FOIA, then it must give a reason falling within one or more of the following exemptions to the act:

1. Documents concerning National Defense and Foreign Policy properly classified as "Confidential," "Secret," and "Top Secret" under the terms and procedures of the presidential order establishing the classification system.

2. Internal agency matters relating to personnel rules and practices.

3. Information specifically exempted from disclosure by statute.

4. Trade secrets and commercial or financial information obtained from a person which are privileged or confidential.

5. Inter and intra-agency memoranda or letters otherwise not available by law to a party other than an agency in litigation with the agency.

6. Personnel and medical files and similar files, disclosure of which would constitute an invasion of privacy.

7. Investigatory records compiled for law enforcement purposes to the extent disclosure would interfere with enforcement proceedings, deprive a person of a right to a fair trial or an adjudication, constitute an invasion of personal privacy, disclose a confidential source, disclose investigative techniques and procedures, or endanger the life or physical safety of law enforcement personnel.

8. Information and materials contained in or related to examination, operating, or condition reports prepared by, on behalf of, or for the use of an agency responsible for the regulation or supervision of financial institutions.

9. Geological and geophysical information and data, including maps concerning wells.

Even though a requested document may fall within an exemption, an agency may choose to voluntarily disclose the information. Sometimes the legal assistant will receive a response where exempted information has been extracted or deleted from the materials provided. In either case, the legal assistant should consult with the lawyer to determine whether the denial warrants an agency appeal, and, if that is denied, a lawsuit in federal district court. In such situations, the legal assistant may want to contact the Freedom of Information Clearinghouse, Suite 700, 2000 P Street NW, P. O. Box 19367, Washington, DC. 20402, (202) 783-3238.

Publications/Internet Resources

Since federal government publications number in the thousands, the legal assistant seeking one of its publications should identify the informational area that may be covered by publications. Federal government publications fall into the following categories:

- *Legislative*. Congressional publications.
- *Administrative*. Agency rules and regulations.
- *Reportorial*. Annual reports of government agencies.
- *Service*. Data and statistical information.
- *Research*. Conducted or supported.
- *Informational*. Pamphlets for consumers, on health care, etc.

Most federal government publications are broken into more than 220 "Subject Bibliographies" (SBs), and they (and an index to them) can be obtained without charge from the Superintendent of Documents, U.S. Government Printing Office (GPO), Washington, DC. 20402. Each SB lists titles of publications falling within its subject designation, costs, and order information, including telephone orders, (202) 783-3238. Subjects covered by the SBs include Child Abuse and Neglect, Directories and Lists of Persons and Organizations, Motor Vehicles, Environmental Education and Protection, and Federal Trade Commission Decisions and Publications.

The GPO publishes a quarterly catalog entitled "U.S. Government Books" which features listings of popular government books. This can be obtained from the GPO or from any one of the U.S. Government Bookstores around the country. (The legal assistant should check local "blue pages" for the nearest one.)

Titles of interest to the legal assistant involved in interviewing and investigation include:

1. *Crime Scene Search & Physical Evidence Handbook* (S/N 027-000-01195-1)

2. *Fire Investigation Handbook* (S/N 003-003-02223-3)

3. *Forensic Evidence and the Police: The Effects of Scientific Evidence on Criminal Investigations* (S/N 027-000-0206-0)

4. *Forensics: When Science Bears Witness* (S/N 027-000-01202-7)

5. *A Citizen's Guide on How to Use the Freedom of Information Act and the Privacy Act in Requesting Government Documents* (S/N 052-071-00540-4)

6. *Finding the Law: A Workbook on Legal Research for Laypersons* (S/N 024-011-00248-4)

7. *The United States Government Manual* (S/N 022-003-01118-8)

8. *Where to Write for Vital Records: Births, Deaths, Marriages & Divorces* (S/N 017-022-00847-5)

9. *Managing Correspondence, Form and Guide Letters* (S/N 022-003-00903-5)

10. *United States Government Printing Office Style Manual* (S/N 021-000-00120-1)

Sometimes information and publications are assembled into catalogs or handbooks for certain subjects such as the *Consumer's Resource Handbook*, available from the Consumer Information Center, Pueblo, CO 81009. Many agencies publish extensive guides to their publications, such as the pamphlet published by the Federal Aviation Administration (FAA), entitled "Guide to Federal Aviation Administration Publications," FAA-APA-PG-12.

For the legal assistant trying to find the "right" government employee for assistance in locating agency information sources, the Superintendent of Documents makes available Internal Telephone Directories for federal agencies with names, titles, and telephone numbers of the individuals in specific divisions.

The websites of the federal government are too innumerable to list here. Some are provided in Appendix 2. As in the private sector, they vary in quality. An example of a site that provides excellent materials is the Social Security Administration (www.ssa.gov).

Selected Departments, Agencies, and Commissions

While it would be impossible to list every department, agency, and commission of the federal government that the legal assistant may access for information, the following are suggested for contact files:

- Bureau of Alcohol, Tobacco and Firearms
- Bureau of the Census
- Consumer Product Safety Commission
- Department of Agriculture
- Department of Commerce
- Department of Education
- Department of Energy
- Department of Health and Human Services
- Department of Justice
- Department of Labor
- Department of the Treasury
- Department of Transportation
- Drug Enforcement Administration
- Environmental Protection Agency
- Equal Employment Opportunity Commission
- Federal Aviation Administration
- Federal Bureau of Investigation
- Federal Communications Commission
- Federal Emergency Management Agency
- Federal Energy Regulatory Commission
- Federal Highway Administration
- Federal Railroad Administration

- Federal Trade Commission
- Food and Drug Administration
- Immigration and Naturalization Service
- Internal Revenue Service
- National Archives and Records Administration
- National Bureau of Standards
- National Highway Traffic Safety Administration
- National Institute of Health
- National Labor Relations Board
- National Technical Information Service
- National Transportation Safety Board
- Occupational Safety and Health Administration
- Occupational Safety and Health Review Commission
- Patent and Trademark Office
- Railroad Retirement Board
- Securities and Exchange Commission
- Small Business Administration
- Social Security Administration
- Veterans Administration

STATE GOVERNMENT SOURCES

The legal assistant seeking information from public sources at the state
level obviously will focus on the agencies and resources of the state
having jurisdiction over the aspect of the case for which information is
sought. Information available at state government sources (and
necessarily at local sources, since they are political subdivisions of a
state) is similar in form to that available under the FOIA and includes:
documents, correspondence, original papers, maps, drawings, charts,
indexes, plans, memoranda, sound recordings, microfilm, motion-
picture or other photographic records, computer disks and tapes, or
other materials of the department or agency.

Source Identification

Methods of identifying state government sources are similar to those
used for federal sources, but the extent of identification will vary from
state to state. The more people living in a state, the greater the size of
its government. Department labels change from state to state: a

Division of Social and Rehabilitation Services in one state may be the Welfare Department in another.

Many states publish "bluebooks" or directories similar in content to the *United States Government Manual*, listing their agencies and their functions. The legal assistant should obtain the telephone book of the state capitol, since it will have "blue pages" for all state departments and agencies. If it is available at the local library, the legal assistant should utilize Braddock's *Federal-State-Local Government Directory*, particularly Volume II, for names, addresses, and telephone numbers of major state officials, or the *State Executive Directory*.

The digest volume of *Martindale-Hubbell Law Directory* identifies state departments and agencies associated with substantive state statutes. Other directories include the *Book of the States* and the *National Directory of State Agencies*. Perhaps the best and most current directory of a state's departments and agencies is the index to its statutes and its departments, commissions, and agencies' rules and regulations.

With states providing extensive Internet access to their agencies, print media in this area is fast becoming obsolete or has been relegated to "second choice" status. Therefore, it is essential that the legal assistant develop his or her own directory of key state-related websites. For example, a legal assistant working in the business area of law would want to identify state-specific websites in that area, e.g., the secretary of state, real estate commission, utility regulatory agency, banking commission, etc.

Accessing

The state open records acts and statutes apply when the legal assistant seeks to access public records of a state department or agency. Allowing for individual state requirements, the legal assistant should direct requests for inspection and/or copying to the public records custodian of the appropriate department or agency. The department or agency usually must furnish the records custodian's name and address as well as information on access or copy fees and the procedure for requesting information or documents.

The request should contain the name and address of the requesting party and a reasonably specific description of the information or documents requested. The response time of the department or agency may not be specified in days as provided in the FOIA, but generally it should be timely. If the response is a complete or partial denial under a claimed statutory exemption, a court action similar to that under the FOIA may be necessary.

Publications

States have printing offices similar to the Government Printing Office (GPO) to handle the printing and publication of all materials of the state governmental institutions. Some agencies may use commercial printing of publications. In any event, the legal assistant should first contact the agency directly and ascertain what publications it makes available to the public. If possible, the legal assistant should obtain the agency's publication manual, a summary of its books, pamphlets and forms. Certain professional groups involved with the activities of a state department or agency publish manuals and professional education materials with information about the department or agency. The Library of Congress publishes the *Monthly Checklist of State Publications*, listing all state publications sent to the Library for deposit. The Council of State Governments can be contacted for information on state government.

Selected Departments and Agencies

The importance or even the existence of a department or agency may vary from state to state. For example, Texas, California, and Oklahoma have agencies dealing with oil and gas production and regulation, but most other states do not. Landlocked states will not have any agency dealing with coastal waters.

All states, however, must deal with the recording, management, and preservation of their records, and all have established an agency, department, historical society, or commission to oversee these records, including local records. The following list of state departments and agencies represents those agencies the legal assistant may have more frequent contact with:

1. ***Secretary of State***
   - Business Entities
   - Securities Regulation

2. ***Department of Agriculture***
   - Food and Drug

3. ***Attorney General***

4. ***Health and Welfare***
   - Workers' Compensation
   - Employment
   - Occupational Safety

5. ***Business and Commerce***
   - Banking
   - Regulatory Agencies and Commissions
   - Highways and Vehicles

6. ***Natural Resources***
   - Environmental and Energy
   - Oil and Gas Regulation
   - Mines and Minerals
   - Land

7. ***Taxation***
   - Revenue
   - Sales

8. ***Civil Rights***
   - Discriminatory Practices
   - Handicapped Persons.

LOCAL GOVERNMENT SOURCES

Source Materials

Local governments number in the thousands: cities, towns, villages, townships, counties, and other governmental subdivisions such as water boards, school boards, waste water boards, public safety commissions, granted governing authority by state statutes. All are subject to the open records act or statute of their state. Because of the diversity in size and type of local entities, legal assistants seeking information from local government sources should concentrate on those in their locale and develop good information contacts with their personnel.

Many larger municipalities and counties publish pamphlets and information guides about their functions, departments, and services available. Lacking such a guide, the legal assistant should start with the clerk's office for the municipality and county or the clerk or secretary's office for other local sources.

Accessing

While open records acts and statutes have diminished the legal problem of accessing local records, in many localities the legal assistant will still encounter resistance when attempting to obtain information and records. Local government personnel are often more sensitive because they are closer to the governed, especially in smaller communities. In such cases the legal assistant will need excellent communication and persuasion skills and should come armed with cases where the local government was required to disclose the information or records requested, such as any of the following:[3]

1. *Cooper v. Bales*, 233 S.E.2d 770 (1977) Transcripts of portions of an agency meeting that were required to be open to the public

2. *Cohen v. Everett City Council*, 535 P.2d 801 (1975) Transcripts of council meetings that did not otherwise have to be available for public inspection

3. *Gold v. McDermott*, 347 A.2d 643 (1975) Information concerning assessments compiled pursuant to a reevaluation of the taxable properties within a municipality

4. *Cunningham v. Health Officer*, 385 N.E.2d 1011 (1979) Complaints filed with a government agency

OTHER SOURCES

Beyond government sources of information, legal assistants have at their disposal many other sources: businesses, institutions, organizations, individuals, libraries, and databases. These information sources are generally accessed for information about themselves or their possessions. Numerous books and electronic resources address these information sources, and the legal assistant should not limit a search for information to any of the materials mentioned in the following discussion.

Business Sources

Information about businesses may be needed for a variety of reasons. Occasionally, legal assistants need information about the nature of a business; at other times, they need to know about a particular business.

Unlike government sources, businesses usually seek publicity and voluntarily give out information about themselves beyond required governmental reporting requirements. As President Coolidge remarked, "The business of America is business."

Thus, the information about businesses is there; the difficulty lies in finding it. Fortunately, a number of books, materials, and electronic resources can help legal assistants in their search.

Books and Publications

Before seeking sources of business information or utilizing the materials listed below, the legal assistant inexperienced in this kind of nonlegal research should first review *How to Find Information about Companies*. This comprehensive guide to sources of information at the federal, state, and local levels explains the types of information one is likely to find.

The following materials and guides are usually found in the business and technical or reference department of a library, often on CD-ROMs.

1. *Moody's Manuals*. Information on publicly traded companies.

2. *Standard & Poor's Register of Corporations.* Format similar to Moody's.

3. *Standard & Poor's Register of Directors and Executives.* Information on officers and directors of businesses.

4. *Standard & Poor's Stock Reports.* Company profiles.

5. *Standard & Poor's Stock Price Record.* Traded stock price information.

6. *Dun & Bradstreet Million Dollar Directory.* Information about both publicly and privately held companies.

7. *Directory of Corporate Affiliations.* Information on parent companies, subsidiaries, and affiliates.

8. *Thomas' Register of American Manufacturers.* Information on specific products.

9. *Moody's Industry Review* (Monthly). Statistical financial information and operating data for thousands of companies.

10. *Business Periodical Index.* Index to about 150 periodicals in business, finance, labor, taxation, economics, management and related subjects.

Local Sources

Local business information is available from the chamber of commerce, local business and trade publications, and sometimes very effectively from the yellow pages and through similar Internet resources. For example, your author found a nationwide listing for himself and others with the same last name on the Internet.

The legal assistant should not overlook the resources of the business and technical departments of the public library. In many large urban areas, these departments maintain files on major companies in their area, including annual reports, newspaper articles, and other materials.

Institutions and Organizations

The legal assistant may need to seek information about these entities in addition to information already available on research, development, or the operations of a nonbusiness entity. The nature of the information sought will substantially influence the sources utilized, but finding these sources can be an arduous task.

Our complex society is institutionalized and organized, even more so in the private sector than in our government. Legal assistants can assume that an existing institution or organization has the needed information or resources. Although the following books and publications available on CD-ROM will help in identifying and locating these sources, the legal assistant should remember to contact local sources.

- *Research Centers Directory*. A directory by topic of institutions and organizations doing research.

- *Encyclopedia of Associations*. Comprehensive subject listing of organizations and associations.

- *Directories in Print*. Very complete listing of directories.

- *Lawyer's Desk Reference*. Lists institutions and organizations by legal subject areas.

- *National Trade & Professional Associations of the United States*. Alphabetical and subject listings.

- *Social Science Organizations and Agencies Directory*. Arranged in subject categories.

Individuals

When seeking information about well-known or prominent individuals, the legal assistant should use *Who's Who in America* or similar biographical books. There are now "who's who" books for persons not based on prominence, but on their association with a subject area (for example, *Who's Who in Barbed Wire*). *The Biography Index* (H.W.

Wilson Co.) or *Gale's Biographical Index* Series provides access to biographical directories. For private individuals, local sources such as newspaper files, libraries, and local publications and directories are useful. And, several Internet search engines offer access to detailed information about individuals.

Information Specialist

Occasionally, the employment of an information specialist will be necessary. Information specialists are frequently used to conduct extensive databases searches or to find and interpret scientific and technical information. Factors to consider in selecting an information specialist include:

1. The credentials, qualifications, experience, and references of the information specialist should be thoroughly reviewed and verified.

2. If the search will be conducted with computer databases, the legal assistant should verify the information specialist's database experience.

3. Time and costs are very important, since information searches are uniformly expensive and time-consuming. Parameters of time and cost should be specified by contract once the information specialist is selected.

LIBRARIES

The search for sources of information will invariably lead to a library. Libraries have changed. No longer are they just places for finding books and periodicals; they are now "virtual" media and research centers and access points to other information sources — "windows to the world." Libraries have become complex information sources that require technical skills for their proper utilization.

Identification

Before identifying a particular library as a source of information, the legal assistant should ascertain exactly what is needed. Sometimes the needed information will be obvious — for example, a product liability case against a drug manufacturer where information is needed on the material adverse effects of the drug. The initial information will be found in the public library's medical reference section, but as the case progresses more specific information will be required from a medical library.

A legal assistant should routinely be familiar with the identities of all available libraries.

Public Libraries

Perhaps the most familiar library will be the public library. Most large public library systems will have a main library and several branches. While branches serve limited information needs, for the most part only the main library will have copies of all available reference materials. However, if a branch library is connected to the main library through a system-wide computer, microfilm catalog, or the Internet, materials from the main library or external libraries can be ordered.

No matter the situation, the legal assistant must become familiar with local public library resources and how they can be used. These include the catalog of materials, the reference materials, interlibrary loans, depository library designation, and the librarian. The librarian is indispensable to effective nonlegal research, and legal assistants should not be shy about asking for the librarian for assistance, provided they are prepared to explain their information problem thoroughly.

Academic Libraries

Depending on their size and location, academic libraries may better fulfill the legal assistant's nonlegal research needs. Most university libraries have extensive research materials to support their faculty and students needs, and most use the latest in research technologies. The legal assistant should have complete resident access to an academic library located at a publicly funded state university or college, and even a private institution will probably allow access to its library for a nominal user's fee.

State Libraries

To meet the needs of their citizens and government, states have established libraries at their capitols. Many have extensive legal materials, including the statutes of all fifty states, which can be most helpful to the legal assistant. Many state libraries have created state-wide Internet systems to facilitate access to books and materials of all libraries within their state.

Historical and Museum Libraries

A state historical library is located at the state capitol, and most public libraries will have a "historical library" section for their patrons, focusing on maps, archives, and genealogical information. Museum libraries usually focus on the subject of the museum itself, but may limit access.

Law Libraries

While the focus of law libraries, particularly at the university level, is on legal materials, many supplement their collections with nonlegal materials.

Medical Libraries

These will usually be located at medical schools and, as academic libraries, will have materials to support the research needs of the faculty and medical students. However, they commonly will allow access by outsiders with or without a user's fee. In addition to medical journals, books, and research materials, they usually have "state of the art" audio and video materials on medical procedures.

Scientific and Technical Libraries

The legal assistant may be fortunate to have one of these libraries in the community. They have extensive holdings on scientific and technical journals and publications.

Special Libraries (Special Collections)

These libraries or collections, sometimes found in public libraries, focus on a particular subject area. For example, the Centers for Disease Control in Atlanta, Georgia, has a collection of over 15,000 items on mosquitoes.[4]

Company Libraries

Similar in purpose to special libraries, many companies maintain libraries related to their corporate purpose. Since they are in essence private libraries, they may be difficult to access.

Locating Libraries

When legal assistants must use a library or library materials beyond their immediate locale, they have available at their local public library several publications and Internet resources to help locate information at these sources:

American Library Directory

An annual directory of libraries with type, location and holdings data for each listing.

Directory of Special Libraries and Information Centers

A comprehensive guide to information centers, archives, and special and research libraries maintained by businesses, educational institutions, nonprofit organizations, and government agencies.

Subject Collections

A geographical arrangement of libraries and special collections in libraries by subject area.

Virtual Libraries

Through Internet access the legal assistant can research library resources and collections, throughout the world. In addition, with more and more "publishing" on the Internet, current information about a subject area is instantly available.

REFERENCE MATERIALS

While it would be impossible to identify every reference book or material that one may ever need to consult, a number of standard works should be on everyone's reference list. If a library does not have a reference book or material for consultation or checkout, it can be requested through interlibrary loan. Besides the books and materials identified earlier in this chapter and previously in this book, the following are suggested for the legal assistant's reference list:

Reference Books

Guide to Reference Books, Comprehensive guide to reference books and materials; *Where to Find What: A Handbook to Reference Service*; *Where to Find More: A Handbook to Reference Service*.

General Encyclopedias

Encyclopedia Americana, Encyclopedia Britannica, World Book Encyclopedia. Useful as introductions to unfamiliar subjects and as sources of specific information on well-settled topics.

Almanacs

The World Almanac and Book of Facts, Information Please Almanac, Reader's Digest Almanac, The Hammond Almanac. Facts, figures, and data on a wide range of subjects.

Factual Sourcebooks

Facts on File, The Information Age Source Book, First Facts. Compilations of factual information. Some may be professional in scope.

Atlases

The Times Atlas of the World, Rand McNally Commercial Atlas and Marketing Guide, Rand McNally Road Atlas. Sources for geographical information.

Books

Subject, Author, and Title Guide to Books in Print. Lists all books currently in print in separate volumes by subject, author, and title.

Medical Sourcebooks

Physicians' Desk Reference (PDR), a comprehensive listing of prescription and nonprescription drugs and their manufacturers, and *Gray's Human Anatomy*.

Library Research

Concise Guide to Library Research, Knowing Where to Look, Find It Fast, Indexes, Abstracts and Digests. Sourcebooks for how to conduct library research and searching the contents of materials.

Periodicals and Newspapers

Sources of information in these publications are accessed through the use of indexes, available in books (such as the *Standard Periodical Directory*), microfilm, and in-library computer database form (for example, InfoTrac II). The most familiar index in book form, the *Readers' Guide to Periodical Literature*, is published by H.W. Wilson Company, which also publishes indexes for the following areas of interest:[5]

Area of Interest	Wilson Guide
Fire, mineralogy, oceanology, plastics, transportation, and similar applied scientific subjects	*Applied Science and Technology Index*

Area of Interest	**Wilson Guide**
Architecture, art history, film, industrial design, landscape design, painting, photography	*Art Index*
Animal breeding, food science, nutrition, pesticides	*Biological and Agriculture Index*
Accounting, advertising, banking, economics, finance, investment, labor, management, marketing, public relations, specialized industries	*Business Periodicals Index*
Curriculums, school supervision and teaching methods	*Education Index*
Astronomy, physics, and scientific areas	*General Science Index*
Archaeology, classical studies, folklore, history, language and literature, literary and political criticism, performing arts, philosophy, religion, theology	*Humanities Index*
Anthropology, environmental science, psychology, sociology	*Social Sciences Index*

A microfilm magazine index is the *Magazine Index*; this automated system displays the index on a microfilm reader. However, Infocat in CD-ROM form is becoming very popular. For newspapers, the *New York Times Index* and the *Wall Street Journal Index* provide an index for those two publications, and the *National Newspaper Index* and the *Newspaper Index* provide access to several major newspapers. Many newspapers, including the above, are accessible through the Internet.

DATABASES

Many legal assistants are familiar with and use legal databases. The two most prominent are LEXIS and WESTLAW. With either of these systems, the legal assistant can perform computerized legal research without leaving the law office. However, they are expensive and many lawyers use lawbooks for their legal research.

Nonlegal databases, on the other hand, are more numerous and may be more accessible because libraries provide access to these databases through commercial systems. Legal assistants can use them on an as-needed basis, without the law firm paying ongoing subscription costs. Because of the Internet, many are available without charge.

Advantages and Disadvantages

In deciding to subscribe or use a nonlegal database, advantages and disadvantages must be considered.

Advantages

Using a computerized database, one can access, at great speed, enormous amounts of information not even accessible at libraries. Computerized research in databases allows the researcher to specify exactly what is wanted from the database. An active database can provide the most current information available, while regular library books and materials may be out-of-date or obsolete.[6]

Disadvantages

Costs may be prohibitive. While it may be possible to pass on to clients the cost of a database search, they may be concerned if it costs hundreds of dollars. While information obtained from a database may bear on the case, it may lack the substantive weight necessary for relevancy. As with all databases, the frequency of use may not be enough to justify maintaining a subscription, when access is available at the public library.

Identification

If the decision is made to conduct a database search, identify the area or areas of the search. One technique to save costs is to do a library search of the subject to provide a good understanding of its content. A number of nonlegal databases are recognized as substantive sources of information useful in client cases, including:

Business

   Dun & Bradstreet Million Dollar Directory
   Claims/U.S. Patent Abstracts
   PTS F & S/Funk and Scott Index
   Dow Jones News/Retrieval
   Disclosure II
   PTS Prompt

Medical and Technical

   Pharmaceutical News Index
   Medline
   Toxline
   NTIS
   Chemical Exposure
   Scisearch
   International Pharmaceutical Abstract

News

   Newsearch
   NEXIS
   National Newspaper Index
   VU/TEXT

Database Vendors

Because so many databases are available for every conceivable subject, there are companies that act as vendors or information brokers for multiple databases. The user of their services can reduce costs and channel the search through the vendor's computer. The two largest vendors are DIALOG and BRS.

DIALOG

This largest of information brokers has hundreds of databases covering science, technology, engineering, social sciences, business and economics. Fees for access vary with the database. DIALOG provides its subscribers with a listing of the various databases within the system and their various search fields.

DIALOG does not provide full text in the searches, but only summary statements or abstracts of their contents. A user who chooses not to locate the cited material from a library can make use of the online ordering service to order full text.[7]

BRS

Smaller than DIALOG, BRS offers databases in the areas of medical and scientific topics: sciences, medicine, business, reference, education, social science, and humanities. It costs less than DIALOG.

Search Techniques

Since most database searches are conducted by professional inter-mediaries such as librarians, utilize the following search techniques when another person conducts the search.

- A search plan or strategy should be set out beforehand.

- The search topic should be described with different words and synonyms that can be used if key words don't work.

- The search should start with narrow parameters first and then expanded as information is produced.

When using another person to conduct the search, the legal assistant should always guard against making any disclosures that breach client confidentiality.

THE INTERNET

With the arrival of the Internet in the mid-1990s, the primary functions of the legal assistant as a fact gatherer and communicator have taken on new significance. Research, both legal and nonlegal, now includes substantial use of the Internet. For example, for the horse-car accident situation discussed in Chapter 8, nonlegal research on the Internet would include accessing the websites of the following: National Highway Traffic Safety Administration, Consumer Product Safety Commission, Federal Highway Administration, accident reconstructionists, medical and product experts, traffic experts, private investigators, horse breeding associations, state highway agency, and the automobile manufacturer. And, this is a relatively simple situation. In complex cases, such as tobacco litigation, extensive websites have been established.

As discussed previously, the legal assistant must develop a personal Internet directory that will expand with experience. For starters, there are Internet directories available in print form, including *The Internet Compendium* and *Law on the Net*. An Internet resources directory relating to the materials presented in this book can be found in Appendix 2.

NOTES

---

[1] G. Finnigan & M. Kennedy, *Effective Factual Research for Paralegals*, 5 (1983).
[2] W. Corrigan, Jr., "Using Judicial Notice in a Personal Injury Case," 47 *Journal of the Missouri Bar* 179 (1991).
[3] C. Rhyne, *The Law of Local Government Operations*, 149-150 (1980).
[4] L. Horowitz, *Knowing Where To Look*, 19 (1984).
[5] R. Berkman, *Find It Fast*, 22 (1987).
[6] Id., 141.
[7] M. Mason, *Using Computers in the Law*, 110-112 (2nd Ed. 1988).

Chapter Eleven

SERVICE OF SUMMONS AND COMPLAINT: SERVING SUBPOENAS

In this last chapter, we will discuss the legal assistant's role during discovery when filing and maintaining the lawsuit, particularly the task of serving the summons and complaint on the defendant (process), and serving subpoenas.

SERVICE OF SUMMONS AND COMPLAINT: FEDERAL DISTRICT COURTS

When a lawyer is unable to settle or resolve a client's claim or dispute, it may be necessary for a lawsuit to be filed. Most lawsuits are adversarial in nature, with at least one plaintiff and one defendant, but occasionally, there will be no defendant. For example, the client wants to change his or her name.

In some divorce or marriage dissolution or adoption cases, defendants voluntarily submit to the jurisdiction of the court and enter their appearance without the formal service of summons. A legal assistant involved in these types of legal matters should review and follow the procedures outlined in the statutes and court rules, both state and local, applicable to such matters in their state. The following will be applicable in adversarial situations.

Filing of the Lawsuit

The adversarial process begins when the plaintiff's lawyer files a lawsuit with the clerk of the court having jurisdiction. The documents required for such vary from state to state and in the federal courts, but a complaint or petition is required everywhere. The complaint must conform to the requirements of the courts as to style, form, attachments, execution by the plaintiff and/or the lawyer, or it will not be accepted. For this reason, the legal assistant with the responsibility to effect service should obtain state and local court rules pertaining to service and contact the local clerk's office for information and applicable forms.

Because of the diversity among state trial courts as compared to the requirements under the Federal Rules of Civil Procedure (FRCP) applicable to federal district courts, our discussion of other documents associated with the filing of the lawsuit will be broken into those two categories.

The original of the complaint is filed with the clerk along with a copy for each named defendant and a file copy, all of which will be "filed-stamped" by the clerk to indicate the date and time the complaint was filed. In the federal district courts, a Civil Cover Sheet Form (Figure 11:1) must be completed, signed by the lawyer, and filed with the complaint and required filing fee, under 28 U.S.C. Section 1914. Some may also require a completed Designation Form indicating the category of the case for calendar assignment, designation of place of trial, and jury demand, if any.

FIGURE 11:1A

JS 44
(Rev. 12/96)

CIVIL COVER SHEET

The JS–44 civil cover sheet and the information contained herein neither replace nor supplement the filing and service of pleadings or other papers as required by law, except as provided by local rules of court. This form, approved by the Judicial Conference of the United States in September 1974, is required for the use of the Clerk of Court for the purpose of initiating the civil docket sheet. (SEE INSTRUCTIONS ON THE REVERSE OF THE FORM.)

I. (a) PLAINTIFFS

DEFENDANTS

(b) COUNTY OF RESIDENCE OF FIRST LISTED PLAINTIFF
(EXCEPT IN U.S. PLAINTIFF CASES)

COUNTY OF RESIDENCE OF FIRST LISTED DEFENDANT
(IN U.S. PLAINTIFF CASES ONLY)
NOTE: IN LAND CONDEMNATION CASES, USE THE LOCATION OF THE TRACT OF LAND INVOLVED.

(c) ATTORNEYS (FIRM NAME, ADDRESS, AND TELEPHONE NUMBER)

ATTORNEYS (IF KNOWN)

II. BASIS OF JURISDICTION (PLACE AN "X" IN ONE BOX ONLY)

☐ 1 U.S. Government Plaintiff
☐ 2 U.S. Government Defendant
☐ 3 Federal Question (U.S. Government Not a Party)
☐ 4 Diversity (Indicate Citizenship of Parties in Item III)

III. CITIZENSHIP OF PRINCIPAL PARTIES (PLACE AN "X" IN ONE BOX FOR PLAINTIFF
(For Diversity Cases Only) AND ONE BOX FOR DEFENDANT)

	PTF	DEF		PTF	DEF
Citizen of This State	☐ 1	☐ 1	Incorporated or Principal Place of Business In This State	☐ 4	☐ 4
Citizen of Another State	☐ 2	☐ 2	Incorporated and Principal Place of Business In Another State	☐ 5	☐ 5
Citizen or Subject of a Foreign Country	☐ 3	☐ 3	Foreign Nation	☐ 6	☐ 6

IV. ORIGIN (PLACE AN "X" IN ONE BOX ONLY)

☐ 1 Original Proceeding
☐ 2 Removed from State Court
☐ 3 Remanded from Appellate Court
☐ 4 Reinstated or Reopened
☐ 5 Transferred from another district (specify)
☐ 6 Multidistrict Litigation
☐ 7 Appeal to District Judge from Magistrate Judgment

V. NATURE OF SUIT (PLACE AN "X" IN ONE BOX ONLY)

CONTRACT	TORTS		FORFEITURE/PENALTY	BANKRUPTCY	OTHER STATUTES
☐ 110 Insurance	**PERSONAL INJURY**	**PERSONAL INJURY**	☐ 610 Agriculture	☐ 422 Appeal 28 USC 158	☐ 400 State Reapportionment
☐ 120 Marine	☐ 310 Airplane	☐ 362 Personal Injury – Med. Malpractice	☐ 620 Other Food & Drug		☐ 410 Antitrust
☐ 130 Miller Act	☐ 315 Airplane Product Liability		☐ 625 Drug Related Seizure of Property 21 USC 881	☐ 423 Withdrawal 28 USC 157	☐ 430 Banks and Banking
☐ 140 Negotiable Instrument	☐ 320 Assault, Libel & Slander	☐ 365 Personal Injury – Product Liability	☐ 630 Liquor Laws		☐ 450 Commerce/ICC Rates/etc.
☐ 150 Recovery of Overpayment & Enforcement of Judgment	☐ 330 Federal Employers Liability	☐ 368 Asbestos Personal Injury Product Liability	☐ 640 R.R. & Truck	**PROPERTY RIGHTS**	☐ 460 Deportation
☐ 151 Medicare Act	☐ 340 Marine		☐ 650 Airline Regs.	☐ 820 Copyrights	☐ 470 Racketeer Influenced and Corrupt Organizations
☐ 152 Recovery of Defaulted Student Loans (Excl. Veterans)	☐ 345 Marine Product Liability	**PERSONAL PROPERTY**	☐ 660 Occupational Safety/Health	☐ 830 Patent	☐ 810 Selective Service
☐ 153 Recovery of Overpayment of Veteran's Benefits	☐ 350 Motor Vehicle	☐ 370 Other Fraud	☐ 690 Other	☐ 840 Trademark	☐ 850 Securities/Commodities/ Exchange
☐ 160 Stockholders' Suits	☐ 355 Motor Vehicle Product Liability	☐ 371 Truth in Lending	**LABOR**	**SOCIAL SECURITY**	☐ 875 Customer Challenge 12 USC 3410
☐ 190 Other Contract	☐ 360 Other Personal Injury	☐ 380 Other Personal Property Damage	☐ 710 Fair Labor Standards Act	☐ 861 HIA (1395ff)	☐ 891 Agricultural Acts
☐ 195 Contract Product Liability		☐ 385 Property Damage Product Liability	☐ 720 Labor/Mgmt. Relations	☐ 862 Black Lung (923)	☐ 892 Economic Stabilization Act
REAL PROPERTY	**CIVIL RIGHTS**	**PRISONER PETITIONS**		☐ 863 DWC/DIWW (405(g))	☐ 893 Environmental Matters
			☐ 730 Labor/Mgmt. Reporting & Disclosure Act	☐ 864 SSID Title XVI	☐ 894 Energy Allocation Act
☐ 210 Land Condemnation	☐ 441 Voting	☐ 510 Motions to Vacate Sentence	☐ 740 Railway Labor Act	☐ 865 RSI (405(g))	☐ 895 Freedom of Information Act
☐ 220 Foreclosure	☐ 442 Employment	**HABEAS CORPUS:**		**FEDERAL TAX SUITS**	☐ 900 Appeal of Fee Determination Under Equal Access to Justice
☐ 230 Rent Lease & Ejectment	☐ 443 Housing/ Accommodations	☐ 530 General	☐ 790 Other Labor Litigation		☐ 950 Constitutionality of State Statutes
☐ 240 Torts to Land		☐ 535 Death Penalty		☐ 870 Taxes (U.S. Plaintiff or Defendant)	☐ 890 Other Statutory Actions
☐ 245 Tort Product Liability	☐ 444 Welfare	☐ 540 Mandamus & Other	☐ 791 Empl. Ret. Inc. Security Act	☐ 871 IRS – Third Party 26 USC 7609	
☐ 290 All Other Real Property	☐ 440 Other Civil Rights	☐ 550 Civil Rights			
		☐ 555 Prison Condition			

VI. CAUSE OF ACTION (CITE THE U.S. CIVIL STATUTE UNDER WHICH YOU ARE FILING AND WRITE BRIEF STATEMENT OF CAUSE
DO NOT CITE JURISDICTIONAL STATUTES UNLESS DIVERSITY)

VII. REQUESTED IN COMPLAINT: CHECK IF THIS IS A **CLASS ACTION** ☐ UNDER F.R.C.P. 23
DEMAND $
CHECK YES only if demanded in complaint:
JURY DEMAND: ☐ YES ☐ NO

VIII. RELATED CASE(S) IF ANY (See instructions): JUDGE _____ DOCKET NUMBER _____

DATE
SIGNATURE OF ATTORNEY OF RECORD

FOR OFFICE USE ONLY

RECEIPT # _____ AMOUNT _____ APPLYING IFP _____ JUDGE _____ MAG. JUDGE _____

FIGURE 11:1B

JS 44 Reverse
(Rev. 12/96)

INSTRUCTIONS FOR ATTORNEYS COMPLETING CIVIL COVER SHEET FORM JS-44
Authority For Civil Cover Sheet

The JS-44 civil cover sheet and the information contained herein neither replaces nor supplements the filings and service of pleading or other papers as required by law, except as provided by local rules of court. This form, approved by the Judicial Conference of the United States in September 1974, is required for the use of the Clerk of Court for the purpose of initiating the civil docket sheet. Consequently a civil cover sheet is submitted to the Clerk of Court for each civil complaint filed. The attorney filing a case should complete the form as follows:

I.   (a) Plaintiffs – Defendants. Enter names (last, first, middle initial) of plaintiff and defendant. If the plaintiff or defendant is a government agency, use only the full name or standard abbreviations. If the plaintiff or defendant is an official within a government agency, identify first the agency and then the official, giving both name and title.

(b) County of Residence. For each civil case filed, except U.S. plaintiff cases, enter the name of the county where the first listed plaintiff resides at the time of filing. In U.S. plaintiff cases, enter the name of the county in which the first listed defendant resides at the time of filing. (NOTE: In land condemnation cases, the county of residence of the "defendant" is the location of the tract of land involved.)

(c) Attorneys. Enter the firm name, address, telephone number, and attorney of record. If there are several attorneys, list them on an attachment, noting in this section "(see attachment)".

II.   Jurisdiction. The basis of jurisdiction is set forth under Rule 8(a), F.R.C.P., which requires that jurisdictions be shown in pleadings. Place an "X" in one of the boxes. If there is more than one basis of jurisdiction, precedence is given in the order shown below.

United States plaintiff. (1) Jurisdiction based on 28 U.S.C. 1345 and 1348. Suits by agencies and officers of the United States are included here.

United States defendant. (2) When the plaintiff is suing the United States, its officers or agencies, place an "X" in this box.

Federal question. (3) This refers to suits under 28 U.S.C. 1331, where jurisdiction arises under the Constitution of the United States, an amendment to the Constitution, an act of Congress or a treaty of the United States. In cases where the U.S. is a party, the U.S. plaintiff or defendant code takes precedence, and box 1 or 2 should be marked.

Diversity of citizenship. (4) This refers to suits under 28 U.S.C. 1332, where parties are citizens of different states. When Box 4 is checked, the citizenship of the different parties must be checked. (See Section III below; federal question actions take precedence over diversity cases.)

III.   Residence (citizenship) of Principal Parties. This section of the JS-44 is to be completed if diversity of citizenship was indicated above. Mark this section for each principal party.

IV.   Origin. Place an "X" in one of the seven boxes.

Original Proceedings. (1) Cases which originate in the United States district courts.

Removed from State Court. (2) Proceedings initiated in state courts may be removed to the district courts under Title 28 U.S.C., Section 1441. When the petition for removal is granted, check this box.

Remanded from Appellate Court. (3) Check this box for cases remanded to the district court for further action. Use the date of remand as the filing date.

Reinstated or Reopened. (4) Check this box for cases reinstated or reopened in the district court. Use the reopening date as the filing date.

Transferred from Another District. (5) For cases transferred under Title 28 U.S.C. Section 1404(a). Do not use this for within district transfers or multidistrict litigation transfers.

Multidistrict Litigation. (6) Check this box when a multidistrict case is transferred into the district under authority of Title 28 U.S.C. Section 1407. When this box is checked, do not check (5) above.

Appeal to District Judge from Magistrate Judgment. (7) Check this box for an appeal from a magistrate judge's decision.

V.   Nature of Suit. Place an "X" in the appropriate box. If the nature of suit cannot be determined, be sure the cause of action, in Section IV above, is sufficient to enable the deputy clerk or the statistical clerks in the Administrative Office to determine the nature of suit. If the cause fits more than one nature of suit, select the most definitive.

VI.   Cause of Action. Report the civil statute directly related to the cause of action and give a brief description of the cause.

VII. Requested in Complaint. Class Action. Place an "X" in this box if you are filing a class action under Rule 23, F.R.Cv.P.

Demand. In this space enter the dollar amount (in thousands of dollars) being demanded or indicate other demand such as a preliminary injunction.

Jury Demand. Check the appropriate box to indicate whether or not a jury is being demanded.

VIII. Related Cases. This section of the JS-44 is used to reference related pending cases if any. If there are related pending cases, insert the docket numbers and the corresponding judge names for such cases.

Date and Attorney Signature. Date and sign the civil cover sheet.

Issuance of Summons

With the filing of the complaint, the plaintiff's lawyer presents a summons prepared for the clerk's signature under the seal of the court. The purpose of the summons is to notify the defendant that he or she must appear in the court and advise him or her of the consequences of failing to do this. The summons, directed to the defendant, must contain the name of the court, names of the parties, the name and address of the plaintiff's lawyer, and the time within which the defendant must appear and defend. The summons must also notify the defendant that, if he or she fails to appear and answer, a default judgment will be rendered against him or her for the relief demanded in the complaint. If the summons is in proper form, the clerk issues it to the plaintiff for service on the defendant (Rule 4(a) FRCP) with a copy of the complaint. Figure 11:2 is the summons form used in the federal district courts.

FIGURE 11:2A

United States District Court

_____ DISTRICT OF _____

SUMMONS IN A CIVIL ACTION

V.   CASE NUMBER:

TO: (Name and Address of Defendant)

YOU ARE HEREBY SUMMONED and required to file with the Clerk of this Court and serve upon

PLAINTIFF'S ATTORNEY (name and address)

an answer to the complaint which is herewith served upon you, within _____ days after service of this summons upon you, exclusive of the day of service. If you fail to do so, judgment by default will be taken against you for the relief demanded in the complaint.

CLERK _____   DATE _____

BY DEPUTY CLERK _____

FIGURE 11:2B

AO 440 (Rev. 1/90) Summons in a Civil Action

RETURN OF SERVICE

Service of the Summons and Complaint was made by me[1]	DATE
NAME OF SERVER (PRINT)	TITLE

Check one box below to indicate appropriate method of service

☐ Served personally upon the defendant. Place where served : _____

☐ Left copies thereof at the defendant's dwelling house or usual place of abode with a person of suitable age and discretion then residing therein.
Name of person with whom the summons and complaint were left: _____

☐ Returned unexecuted: _____

☐ Other (specify): _____

STATEMENT OF SERVICE FEES

TRAVEL	SERVICES	TOTAL

DECLARATION OF SERVER

I declare under penalty of perjury under the laws of the United States of America that the foregoing information contained in the Return of Service and Statement of Service Fees is true and correct.

Executed on _____   _____
              Date   *Signature of Server*

                            _____
                            Address of Server

1) As to who may serve a summons see Rule 4 of the Federal Rules of Civil Procedure.

Service of the Summons and Complaint (Process)

Normally, the plaintiff must serve the summons and a copy of the complaint on the defendant within 120 days after the filing of the complaint, or the court will take the initiative and, after notifying the plaintiff, dismiss the action without prejudice as to that defendant.

However, if the plaintiff shows good cause for failure to serve, the court shall extend the time for service appropriately (Rule 4(j) FRCP).

Service may be effected by any person who is not a party and is not less than 18 years of age. Upon the request of the plaintiff, the court may direct that service be effected by a person or officer, including a U.S. marshal or deputy, specifically appointed by the court for that purpose. Special appointments by the court shall be made in cases involving paupers under 28 U.S.C. Section 1915 and in seaman's suits under 28 U.S.C. Section 1916 (Rule 4(c) FRCP. Figure 11:3 illustrates a motion and Order for Special Appointment to Serve the Summons and Complaint. If a special appointment is made of a process server, then following service, he or she must comply with Rule 4(g), FRCP, and file Proof of Service as set forth in Figure 11:4. Some district courts do not require a motion and order for special appointment, but this should be verified with the clerk.

FIGURE 11:3

MOTION AND ORDER FOR SPECIAL APPOINTMENT TO SERVE SUMMONS AND COMPLAINT

IN THE UNITED STATES DISTRICT COURT
FOR THE STATE OF _____

Plaintiff,

CIVIL ACTION
V.   NO._____

Defendant.

MOTION FOR SPECIAL APPOINTMENT TO SERVE
SUMMONS AND COMPLAINT

Pursuant to Rule 4(c) of the Federal Rules of Civil Procedure, _____
in the above captioned action moves this Court to specifically appoint
_____ to serve summons and complaint upon _____ in this
action. Said person to be appointed is not less than eighteen years of age and is
not a party to this action. This appointment will bring a savings in costs of
service.

_____
Attorney for Plaintiff

ORDER

On this ____ day of _____, ____ it is ORDERED that _____ be and
is hereby appointed to serve the summons and complaint upon _____
in this action. Proof of service shall be made by affidavit in accordance with
Rule 4(g) of the Federal Rules of Civil Procedure.

BY THE COURT

_____
United States District Court Judge

FIGURE 11:4

PROOF OF SERVICE

IN THE UNITED STATES DISTRICT COURT
FOR THE STATE OF _____

_____
Plaintiff,

                     CIVIL ACTION

V.   NO._____

_____
Defendant.

PROOF OF SERVICE

I certify that I personally served the summons and complaint in the above
captioned action at _____.m. on the ____ day of _____, ____ on the
below named individual, company, corporation, etc. and at the address
following (his, her, its) name:

Under penalty of perjury, I declare that the foregoing is true and correct.

> (Signature)
>
> _____
> (Typed Name)
> Date: _____

Service by Mail (Notice and Acknowledgment)

When the defendant is an individual, other than an infant or an incompetent person, a domestic or foreign corporation, or a partnership or other incorporated association, to encourage the saving of costs of service, Rule 4(c)(2)(C)(ii) FRCP allows the plaintiff to mail a copy of the complaint with a waiver of service of summons by first-class mail, postage prepaid, to the defendant along with a postage-prepaid return envelope addressed to the sender. The notice and acknowledgment form must be "filed-stamped" by the clerk before mailing. If the sender does not receive a completed waiver form within twenty days, then service should be by process server or U.S. Marshal, if available.

Rule 4 (c)(2)(D) FRCP provides that if the defendant fails to comply, the court shall order the costs of subsequent personal service be paid by the defendant. Figure 11:5 is an example of the notice of lawsuit and request for waiver of service of summons form. While first-class mailing is sufficient in difficult service of process situations, it is best that the notice and acknowledgment and other documents be sent to the defendant by certified mail, "Restricted Delivery Only." In this way the plaintiff will have proof of mailing if the defendant does not respond.

FIGURE 11:5

UNITED STATES DISTRICT COURT
FOR THE DISTRICT OF

NOTICE OF LAWSUIT AND REQUEST FOR
WAIVER OF SERVER FOR SUMMONS

To: (A) _____

As (B) _____ OF (C) _____

A lawsuit has been commenced against you (or the entity on whose behalf you are addressed). A copy of the complaint is attached to this notice. It has been filed in the United States District Court for the (D) District of _____ and has been assigned docket number (E) _____.

This is not a formal summons or notification from the court, but rather my request that you sign and return the enclosed waiver of service in order to save the cost of serving you with a judicial summons and an additional copy of the complaint. The costs of service will be avoided if I receive a signed copy of the waiver within (F) _____ days after the date designated below as the date on which this Notice and Request is sent. I enclose a stamped and addressed envelope (or other means of cost-free return) for your use. An extra copy of the waiver is also attached for your records.

If you comply with this request and return the signed waiver, it will be filed with the court and no summons will be served on you. The auction will then proceed as if you had been served on the date the waiver is filed, except that you will not be obligated to answer the complaint before 60 days from the date designated below as the date on which this notice is sent (or before 90 days from that date if your address is not in any judicial district of the United States).

If you do not return the signed waiver within the time indicated, I will take appropriate steps to effect formal service in a manner authorized by the Federal Rules of Civil Procedure and will then, to the extent authorized by those Rules, ask the court to require you (or the party on whose behalf you are addressed) to pay the full costs of such service. In that connection, please read the statement concerning the duty of parties to waive the service of the summons, which is set forth on the reverse side of the waiver form.

I affirm that this request is being sent to you on behalf of the plaintiff this _____ day of _____, _____.

_____
Signature of Plaintiff's Attorney or
Unrepresented Plaintiff

A: Name of individual defendant (or name of agent of corporate defendant)
B: Title or other relationship of individual to corporate defendant
C: Name of corporate defendant, if any
D: District
E: Docket number of action (case number)
F: Addressee must be given at least 30 days (60 days if located in foreign country) in which to return waiver

Personal Service Requirements

Rule 4(d) FRCP sets out the service requirements necessary to effect personal service over an individual, infants and incompetents, corporations and associations, the United States and its agencies, and foreign, state or local governments. These requirements are summarized below.

Individual. Service upon an individual is made by delivering a copy of the summons and the complaint to him or her personally. The copies can be left at the person's dwelling house or usual residence with some person of suitable age and discretion residing therein. A person of "suitable age and discretion" is not less than 14 years of age, but this may vary in some states; discretion means that he or she has the presence of mind to realize that it is important to get the papers to the defendant. A copy of the summons and complaint can be delivered to an agent authorized by appointment or by law to receive service of process. However, some states require service by mail or personal service on the defendant, and leaving the summons and complaint at their residence would be insufficient.[1]

Infant or an Incompetent Person. Service on an infant or an incompetent person is made in the manner prescribed by the law of the state in which service is made for the service of summons in an action brought in the courts of that state.

Domestic or Foreign Corporation, Partnership, Unincorporated Association Subject to Suit under a Common Name. Service is made on these entities by delivering a copy of the summons and of the complaint to an officer, a managing or general agent, or to any other agent authorized by appointment or by law to receive service of process. If the agent is one authorized by statute to receive service and the statute so requires, then service is also made by mailing a copy to the defendant. In most states, the secretary of state serves as the process agent for foreign corporations, and thus the secretary of state would be served and a copy of the summons and complaint would be mailed to the out-of-state corporation.[2]

The United States. Service upon the United States is made by delivering a copy of the summons and complaint to the United States attorney for the district in which the action is brought, or an assistant United States attorney or clerical employee designated by the United States attorney in a writing filed with the clerk of the court. It can also be performed by sending a copy of the summons and complaint by registered or certified mail to the Attorney General of the United States at Washington, DC. Where the action attacks the validity of an order of an officer or agency of the United States not made a party, then a copy of the summons and the complaint is to be sent by registered or certified mail to the officer or agency.

An Officer or Agency of the United States. Service is made by serving the United States and by sending a copy of the summons and complaint by registered or certified mail to the officer or agency. If the agency is a corporation, the copy shall be delivered as set out in paragraph 3 above. The enabling statutes of most agencies set out specific service requirements.

A State or Municipal Corporation or Other Governmental Organization. Service is achieved by delivering a copy of the summons and complaint to the chief executive officer of the entity or in the manner prescribed by the law of that state for the service of summons upon any such defendant.

SERVICE OF SUMMONS AND COMPLAINT
STATE COURTS

Because we are dealing with fifty separate and distinct court systems, each with its own statutes and court rules, it is impossible to cover all the variations that exist for the service of the summons and petition once a lawsuit is filed in a particular state court system. When a legal assistant is assigned the task of carrying out service of process on a defendant in a state court matter, the following should be accomplished:

1. Review the petition and case file documents to identify the defendants to be served, including address and location.

2. Determine from the lawyer the type of service of process to be obtained, e.g., sheriff, in or out of state, certified mail, or special process server.

3. Gather and review current state statutes and court rules, including local court rules, applicable to service of process.

4. Obtain applicable forms and instructions, if any, from clerk of the court where the complaint will or has been filed.

Following the lead of the federal district courts, many state courts place complete responsibility for the service of process on plaintiffs and their lawyers; however, many, particularly at the local level, willingly provide sample forms and assistance. In some jurisdictions, the legal assistant can obtain computer disks containing formats for summons, subpoenas, garnishments, executions, etc. In others, the courts supply pre-printed forms with fill-in blanks for pertinent data.

Figure 11:6 is an example of a summons with return of service form found in the Kansas statutes.

FIGURE 11:6

EXAMPLE OF SUMMONS WITH RETURN OF SERVICE FORM
[To be used for personal or certified mail service]

IN THE DISTRICT COURT
OF _____ COUNTY, KANSAS

_____
                           Plaintiff,

vs.   No. _____

_____
                           Defendant.

SUMMONS

TO THE ABOVE NAMED DEFENDANT:

You are hereby summoned and required to serve upon _____,
plaintiff's attorney, whose address is _____, a pleading to
the petition which is herewith served upon you, within 20 days after service of
this summons upon you, exclusive of the day of service. If you fail to do so,
judgment by default will be taken against you for the relief demanded in the
petition. Your pleading must also be filed with the court. As provided in
subsection (a) of K.S.A. 60-213, and amendments thereto, your answer must
state as a counterclaim any related claim which you may have against the
plaintiff, or you will thereafter be barred from making such claim in any other
action.

                                        _____
                                        Clerk of the District Court

RETURN OF SERVICE OF SUMMONS

____ Personal Service

I hereby certify that I have served the within summons:

(1) By delivering on the ____ day of _____, ___, a copy of the summons
and a copy of the petition to each of the within-named defendants
_____.

(2) By leaving on the ____ day of _____, ____ for each of the within-named
defendants _____a copy of the summons
and a copy of the petition at the respective dwelling place or usual place of
abode of such defendants with some person of suitable age and discretion
residing therein.

(3) By delivering on the ____ day of _____, ____, a copy of the summons
and a copy of the petition to each of the following agents authorized by
appointment or by law to receive service of process
_____.

(4) By leaving a copy of the summons and a copy of the petition at the
dwelling house or usual place of abode and mailing by first- class mail to each
of the following defendants a notice that such copy has been so left _____
on the ____ day of _____, ____. All done in _____ County,
Kansas.

Sheriff of _____ County, Kansas

By _____

___ Service by Certified Mail

I hereby certify that I have served the within summons:

(1) By mailing on the ____ day of _____, ____, a copy of the summons and a copy of the petition in the above action as certified mail return receipt requested to each of the within-named defendants;

(2) the name and address on the envelope containing the process mailed as certified mail return receipt requested were as follows:

_____

_____

Sheriff of _____ County, Kansas, (or the party or the party's attorney) By _____ Certified mail, return receipt requested was refused. I hereby certify that on the ____ day of _____, ____, I mailed a copy of the summons and petition in the above action by first-class mail, postage prepaid, addressed to _____ at

_____.

Sheriff of _____ County, Kansas

(or the party or the party's attorney)

By _____

Seal of the court

Dated _____

Methods of Service of Process

In Kansas, as with most states, upon the filing of a request (praecipe) for the issuance of the summons by the clerk of the court, service of process may be effected by any one of the following methods:

1.   *Personal and residence service through the office of the sheriff of the county where the court is located and the defendant resides; or through a sheriff of the county where the defendant resides if other than where the court is located, particularly if a different state.* Typically,

the sheriff should be given instructions on the defendant's exact location. If service is at the residence, then directions to its location should be furnished. If residence service is effected by leaving a copy, then statutes or court rules may require that notice of such service be sent to the defendant by first-class mail.

2.   *Personal and residence service by an appointed process server. Depending upon the state, the appointment may be to serve anywhere in or outside of the state.* Figure 11:7 is an example of an order appointing a process server. (Note in Kansas appointments are given freely and may be for a whole calendar year). In states where such appointments are made, the process server has the same authority as the sheriff.

3.   *Certified mail service to the defendant within or without the state by the lawyer or by the office of the sheriff of the county where the court is located.* As with the federal district courts, to reduce costs, state courts have encouraged this service method for some time. This method lacks control if done by the sheriff; preferably, the lawyer should take responsibility and have the legal assistant prepare the documentation and monitor the service of process. The delivery required may or may not be "Restricted Delivery," but usually the court will require that the return receipt or a return envelope be filed with the clerk as evidence of delivery, or refusal of acceptance of delivery as set out in Figure 11:8. If the defendant refuses certified service, then, in some states, service can be made through regular first-class mail. However, failure to claim certified mail is not considered a refusal.

4.   *Service may be made by publication (constructive service) after the filing of an affidavit with the court justifying its use.* Cases in which it can be used include, divorce, maintenance, or annulment of marriage matters; actions against a person who is a nonresident of the state or a foreign corporation having property or debts owing in the state; actions in rem (related to real or personal property in the state); and actions in which the defendant was a resident but departed from the state or secreted himself in the state to avoid service of process. If allowed, a notice of suit similar in form to that in Figure 11:9 is published once a week for three consecutive weeks in a newspaper published in the

county where the complaint is filed and which is authorized to publish legal notices.

FIGURE 11:7

ORDER APPOINTING PROCESS SERVER

IN THE DISTRICT COURT
OF _____, KANSAS

IN THE MATTER OF THE APPOINTMENT OF

                              Miscellaneous Filing
_____
PROCESS SERVER FOR A FIXED PERIOD OF TIME

ORDER APPOINTING _____ AS PROCESS SERVER
FOR A FIXED PERIOD OF TIME

NOW on this ____ day of _____, ____, comes on for consideration petitioner's application, pursuant to K.S.A. 60-303, that _____ be appointed as process server to serve all process anywhere in and out of the State of Kansas and be allowed statutory fees allowed for the sheriff, commencing on January 1, ____ and concluding at 11:59 p.m. on December 31, ____.

IT IS THEREFORE BY THIS COURT ORDERED, ADJUDGED AND DECREED THAT _____ is hereby authorized and appointed as special process server for the petitioner commencing on January 1, ____ and concluding at 11:59 p.m. on December 31, ____, to serve all process in cases generally anywhere in and out of the State of Kansas and to be allowed the fees prescribed by statute for the sheriff.

                              _____
                              JUDGE OF THE DISTRICT COURT

FIGURE 11:8

RETURN OF SERVICE FOR CERTIFIED MAIL

IN THE DISTRICT COURT
OF _____ COUNTY, KANSAS

_____

Plaintiff,

vs.   No.

_____

Defendant.

RETURN OF SERVICE FOR CERTIFIED MAIL

STATE OF KANSAS, COUNTY OF _____, SS.

The undersigned, being duly sworn, state that he or she served the following:
_____ on _____ and that the following Return of
Receipt of Service was served on the defendant by certified mail on
_____, ___, at the time and place as listed on the below attached
card.

SENDER:
- Complete items 1 and/or 2 for additional services.
- Complete items 3, 4a, and 4b.
- Print your name and address on the reverse of this form so that we can return this card to you.
- Attach this form to the front of the mailpiece, or on the back if space does not permit.
- Write *"Return Receipt Requested"* on the mailpiece below the article number.
- The Return Receipt will show to whom the article was delivered and the date delivered.

I also wish to receive the following services (for an extra fee):

1. ☐ Addressee's Address
2. ☐ Restricted Delivery

Consult postmaster for fee.

3. Article Addressed to:

4a. Article Number

4b. Service Type
☐ Registered   ☐ Certified
☐ Express Mail   ☐ Insured
☐ Return Receipt for Merchandise ☐ COD

7. Date of Delivery

5. Received By: *(Print Name)*

8. Addressee's Address *(Only if requested and fee is paid)*

6. Signature: *(Addressee or Agent)*
X

PS Form **3811**, December 1994   Domestic Return Receipt

_____ Check here if service by certified mail was refused.

_____
Name

Subscribed and sworn to before me on this _____ day of _____, ____.

_____

Notary public
My commission expires:

FIGURE 11:9

NOTICE OF SUIT

IN THE DISTRICT COURT
OF _____ COUNTY, KANSAS

_____
Plaintiff,
vs.   No._____

_____
Defendant.

NOTICE OF SUIT

THE STATE OF KANSAS TO (NAME OF DEFENDANT TO WHOM
NOTICE IS GIVEN) AND ALL OTHER PERSONS WHO ARE OR MAY
BE CONCERNED:

You are hereby notified that a petition (or other pleading) has been filed in
(name of court) by (name of pleader) praying for (state briefly the nature of
the pleading and the judgment or other relief sought), and you are hereby
required to plead to the petition (or other pleading) on or before
_____, _____, in the court at _____, Kansas. If you fail to
plead, judgment and decree will be entered in due course upon the petition (or
other pleading).

_____
Name of plaintiff or other party

Personal Service Requirements

For the most part, state statutes and court rules regarding on whom
service of process can be made resemble those discussed for federal
district courts. Some differences apply, however; a state may be more
specific when it comes to service upon a minor or incompetent person.
Minors' parents are their agents, as well as any person having the
minors' care or control or with whom such minors reside. For an
incompetent person, the law designates a guardian or conservator or a

competent adult member of the family with whom the incompetent person resides, or even the director of an institution where he or she resides. In many states the director or commissioner of insurance is designated the agent for service for all insurance companies that do business in the state.

Long-Arm Statutes

To establish jurisdiction over and to effectuate personal service upon persons domiciled outside of their boarders, but who have carried on certain activities within their borders, states have enacted statutes known as long-arm statutes. Under these statutes, the courts of a state have jurisdiction over a defendant as to any cause of action arising from the doing of any of the following or other acts whereby the defendant had sufficient minimum contacts to justify personal jurisdiction:

1. Transaction of any business within the state.

2. Commission of a tortious act within the state (automobile accident).

3. Ownership, use or possession of any real estate situated in the state.

4. Contracting to insure any person, property or risk in the state at the time of the contracting.

5. Entering into an express or implied contract, by mail or otherwise, with a resident of the state to be performed in whole or in part by either party in the state.

6. Acting within the state as director, manager, trustee or other officer of any corporation organized under the laws of or having a place of business in the state, or acting as executor or administrator of any estate within the state.

How service is carried out varies from state to state. Depending upon the activity that gave rise to jurisdiction, some require service to be made on the state's secretary of state or other state official on behalf of the defendant. Others will allow service on the defendant by certified mail as discussed above. Because many defendants claim they are not subject to a state's long-arm statute, the legal assistant must always verify the correct procedures with the lawyer, so that the service of process will not be deemed insufficient by the court when challenged by the defendant. Note, according to Rule 4(c) of the FRCP, federal district courts follow long-arm procedures of the state in which they sit.

Immunities and Exemptions from Service

While service of process must be perfected for the plaintiff's lawsuit to proceed, the legal assistant responsible for such should avoid being overzealous to the extent that the service violates a state's statute granting immunity or exemption. In some instances, persons coming and going from a state to testify at a trial or in some legal proceeding are immune from service. Service may be held invalid if a defendant is fraudulently induced to come to a state for the purpose of serving him or her with process. In some states, service of process may be prohibited on Sundays and holidays.[3]

Basic "Mechanics" of Service of Process

For the legal assistant involved in service of process, several procedures will result in service without any problems:

1. *Service by Certified Mail.* If certified mail is used, delivery procedures and costs requirements should be verified with the local postmaster. Sometimes the post office will attempt delivery more than once, and this can extend the service procedure out over a longer period of time than normally expected. The certification number should be typed on all documents sent to the defendant this way.

2. *Service by Out-of-State Sheriff.* To avoid having the summons and complaint returned unserved for insufficient payment of service fees, incorrect form of payment (personal check when certified or money order required), or insufficient number of copies, the legal assistant must always contact the sheriff's office of the county where out-of-state service will take place before sending the summons and complaint. This ensures that the legal assistant is satisfying current and exact requirements to effect service, and unnecessary delay will be

avoided. Access information can be obtained from the local sheriff or clerk of the court or by using a suitable print or Internet directory.

3.   *Service by the Legal Assistant as a Process Server.* Since federal rules and state statutes and court rules regarding service of process by a process server have become considerably more liberal, legal assistants can expect to engage in this function on behalf of the plaintiff client. It is better for the legal assistant to do this than the lawyer, since if there are any question about the service, the legal assistant will be more suited to being a witness and testifying about the service. As a process server, the legal assistant should act prudently, but the lawyer has the responsibility to refrain from using the legal assistant in situations where the defendant may be considered hostile, aggressive, or even violent. In those cases, a professional process server should be used, or service should be effected through the U.S. Marshall's office.

When the defendants are served personally, the legal assistant does not have to give the summons or complaint or explain what it is. It can even be dropped at their feet. Under no circumstances should the legal assistant attempt to touch the defendant with the papers if he or she refuses to take them.

4.   *Locating the Defendant.* Sometimes a defendant will be difficult to locate, and the lawyer will rely on the legal assistant to accomplish this task. In addition to utilizing the techniques previously discussed for locating witnesses, the legal assistant should develop a "service profile" for the defendant.

If the defendant is an individual, this profile should include helpful information from the client and data pertaining to the defendant's personal and business affairs. Some states recognize this problem and will allow personal service upon a defendant's place of employment, if the plaintiff files an affidavit stating that the defendant is a nonresident or that residence is unknown.

Where the defendant is a business operating from a post office box, 39 CFR Part 265 allows disclosure of the name and street address of the box holder to any person authorized to serve legal process, to the attorney for a party on whose behalf service is to be made, or to a party who is pro se in any actual or prospective litigation. Figure 11:10 illustrates a form letter to be presented to the postmaster in order to obtain such information.

FIGURE 11:10

LETTER REGARDING ACCESS TO
BOX HOLDER INFORMATION

Postmaster

_____Post Office

(Address)

(City, State, Zip)

Re:

Dear Sir:

This is to certify that the name and street address of the holder of P.O. Box _____, (city, state, zip) is needed solely for service of legal process in connection with prospective litigation of the _____(plaintiff) v. _____(defendant). This information will be used in the _____ Court of _____ County, _____ (state). The capacity in which the boxholder is to be served is _____(defendant)(witness) in said action. The nature of the litigation is a suit _____.

Sincerely,

_____

(Capacity: process server, attorney, etc.)

---

5.   *Follow-Up*. One of the most important "mechanical" details for the legal assistant to do is to monitor all service of process activities, particularly when they are being performed by someone else. If service is not perfected within the required time limits, the case could be dismissed. This could prove disastrous if there is a statute of limitations problem and may result in a malpractice claim against the lawyer.

SERVICE OF SUBPOENAS

A subpoena is a document issued by the clerk of a court commanding a person within the jurisdiction of the court to attend and give testimony in proceedings before that court at a designated time and place set out in the subpoena. A subpoena can also be issued to a person directing him or her to produce documentary evidence (a subpoena duces tecum). If the person to whom the subpoena is directed fails to comply with the provisions of the subpoena, the court may find him or her in contempt and assess appropriate sanctions.

1.   ***Subpoenas for Depositions and Production.*** During discovery, subpoenas are issued primarily for the taking of witness depositions and to gain access to documentary evidence under the control of persons who are not parties to the action. A subpoena is not necessary for the taking of the deposition of parties or for the production of documents and things within their possession.

2.   ***Subpoenas for a Hearing or Trial.*** Sometimes during discovery, a witness's attendance may be required at a court hearing. In such cases, a subpoena will be issued by the clerk of the court. Subpoenas will be similarly issued for all witnesses when a case goes to trial.

Federal District Courts

In the federal district courts, Rule 45, FRCP, governs the issuance of subpoenas and their service upon persons named therein. Under Rule 45, FRCP, the clerk issues a subpoena in blank to a party requesting it, who completes it before service, or an attorney as an officer of the court may also issue and sign a subpoena on behalf of the court where he or she is authorized to practice or for a district court where a deposition or production is compelled.

1.   ***Subpoena for Taking Deposition.*** Most clerks issue subpoenas in blank for the taking of depositions, and the party requesting the subpoena must complete it before it is served on the deponent. The clerk will not issue the subpoena, however, until the party serves and files with the court a notice to all other parties stating the time and

place of the taking of the deposition, the name and address of the person to be examined, and (if a subpoena duces tecum is to be served on that person) a designation of the materials to be produced (see Rule 30(b)(1), FRCP). Figure 11:11 is a form of notice.

FIGURE 11:11

NOTICE OF TAKING OF DEPOSITION

IN THE UNITED STATES DISTRICT COURT
FOR THE STATE OF _____

_____
                          Plaintiff,   CIVIL ACTION

v.   NO. _____
_____
Defendant.

NOTICE OF TAKING OF DEPOSITION

TO: (ATTORNEY)
   (ADDRESS)

PLEASE TAKE NOTICE that pursuant to Rule 30 of the Federal Rules of Civil Procedure, that the oral deposition of _____ will be taken on the ____ day of _____, _____, at _____ m. and thereafter from day to day until completed, at the (place of deposition, including address).(If the deponent is to bring documents and things with him or her to the deposition, then such must be specifically identified here).

                                        _____
                                        Attorney for Party
                                        (Address)
                                        (Telephone Number)

---

2.   *Service of Deposition Subpoena.* Upon completion of the subpoena form as required by Rule 45, FRCP, it is then personally served upon the deponent along with the required witness and mileage fees. These are computed according to 28 U.S.C. Section 1821 and must be tendered at the time of service of the subpoena. The clerk of

the district court can advise the correct amounts. Figure 11:12 is the deposition subpoena form used by the district court clerks.

The distance that the deponent will have to travel for the deposition must be verified since Rule 45(b)(2), FRCP, places a 100-mile limit on the distance from where he or she resides, is employed, transacts business, or is served.

To be effective, the subpoena must be personally served on the deponent by any person, including the U.S. Marshal or his or her deputy, who is not a party and is not less than 18 years of age. Unlike a summons and complaint, the service involves the tendering of fees, and the deponent is best informed about the subpoena. After service, the server will file a return of service using the second page of the deposition subpoena in Figure 11:12.

3.   ***Subpoena for a Hearing or Trial***. According to Rule 45(a)(2), FRCP, a subpoena is issued from the court for the district in which the hearing or trial is to be held. Once issued by the clerk or an attorney as an officer of the court, the subpoena may be served at any place within the district, that is within 100 miles of the place of the hearing or trial, or in accordance with the service rules of the state court in the district. Again, attendance and mileage fees must be tendered when the subpoena is served, and the server must file a return of service. Figure 11:12 is the subpoena form used in the district courts. If documents or objects are to be brought, the subpoena should specifically state what will be required.

FIGURE 11:12A

AO 88 (Rev. 1/94) Subpoena in a Civil Case

Issued by the
UNITED STATES DISTRICT COURT

———————————— DISTRICT OF ————————————

V.

SUBPOENA IN A CIVIL CASE

CASE NUMBER:[1]

TO:

☐ YOU ARE COMMANDED to appear in the United States District Court at the place, date, and time specified below to testify in the above case.

PLACE OF TESTIMONY	COURTROOM
	DATE AND TIME

☐ YOU ARE COMMANDED to appear at the place, date, and time specified below to testify at the taking of a deposition in the above case.

PLACE OF DEPOSITION	DATE AND TIME

☐ YOU ARE COMMANDED to produce and permit inspection and copying of the following documents or objects at the place, date, and time specified below (list documents or objects):

PLACE	DATE AND TIME

☐ YOU ARE COMMANDED to permit inspection of the following premises at the date and time specified below.

PREMISES	DATE AND TIME

Any organization not a party to this suit that is subpoenaed for the taking of a deposition shall designate one or more officers, directors, or managing agents, or other persons who consent to testify on its behalf, and may set forth, for each person designated, the matters on which the person will testify. Federal Rules of Civil Procedure, 30(b)(6).

ISSUING OFFICER SIGNATURE AND TITLE (INDICATE IF ATTORNEY FOR PLAINTIFF OR DEFENDANT)	DATE

ISSUING OFFICER'S NAME, ADDRESS AND PHONE NUMBER

———————————————————————————————————
(See Rule 45, Federal Rules of Civil Procedure, Parts C & D on Reverse)

[1] If action is pending in district other than district of issuance, state district under case number.

FIGURE 11:12B

AO 88 (Rev. 1/94) Subpoena in a Civil Case

PROOF OF SERVICE

DATE	PLACE

SERVED

SERVED ON (PRINT NAME)	MANNER OF SERVICE

SERVED BY (PRINT NAME)	TITLE

DECLARATION OF SERVER

I declare under penalty of perjury under the laws of the United States of America that the foregoing information contained in the Proof of Service is true and correct.

Executed on _____
DATE

_____
SIGNATURE OF SERVER

_____
ADDRESS OF SERVER

Rule 45, Federal Rules of Civil Procedure, Parts C & D:

(c) PROTECTION OF PERSONS SUBJECT TO SUBPOENAS.

(1) A party or an attorney responsible for the issuance and service of a subpoena shall take reasonable steps to avoid imposing undue burden or expense on a person subject to that subpoena. The court on behalf of which the subpoena was issued shall enforce this duty and impose upon the party or attorney in breach of this duty an appropriate sanction which may include, but is not limited to, lost earnings and reasonable attorney's fee.

(2) (A) A person commanded to produce and permit inspection and copying of designated books, papers, documents or tangible things, or inspection of premises need not appear in person at the place of production or inspection unless commanded to appear for deposition, hearing or trial.

(B) Subject to paragraph (d) (2) of this rule, a person commanded to produce and permit inspection and copying may, within 14 days after service of subpoena or before the time specified for compliance if such time is less than 14 days after service, serve upon the party or attorney designated in the subpoena written objection to inspection or copying of any or all of the designated materials or of the premises. If objection is made, the party serving the subpoena shall not be entitled to inspect and copy materials or inspect the premises except pursuant to an order of the court by which the subpoena was issued. If objection has been made, the party serving the subpoena may, upon notice to the person commanded to produce, move at any time for an order to compel the production. Such an order to compel production shall protect any person who is not a party or an officer of a party from significant expense resulting from the inspection and copying commanded.

(3) (A) On timely motion, the court by which a subpoena was issued shall quash or modify the subpoena if it

(i) fails to allow reasonable time for compliance;

(ii) requires a person who is not a party or an officer of a party to travel to a place more than 100 miles from the place where that person resides, is employed or regularly transacts business in

person, except that, subject to the provisions of clause (c) (3) (B) (iii) of this rule, such a person may in order to attend trial be commanded to travel from any such place within the state in which the trial is held, or

(iii) requires disclosure of privileged or other protected matter and no exception or waiver applies, or

(iv) subjects a person to undue burden.

(B) If a subpoena

(i) requires disclosure of a trade secret or other confidential research, development, or commercial information, or

(ii) requires disclosure of an unretained expert's opinion or information not describing specific events or occurrences in dispute and resulting from the expert's study made not at the request of any party, or

(iii) requires a person who is not a party or an officer of a party to incur substantial expense to travel more than 100 miles to attend trial, the court may, to protect a person subject to or affected by the subpoena, quash or modify the subpoena, or, if the party in whose behalf the subpoena is issued shows a substantial need for the testimony or material that cannot be otherwise met without undue hardship and assures that the person to whom the subpoena is addressed will be reasonably compensated, the court may order appearance or production only upon specified conditions.

(d) DUTIES IN RESPONDING TO SUBPOENA.

(1) A person responding to a subpoena to produce documents shall produce them as they are kept in the usual course of business or shall organize and label them to correspond with the categories in the demand.

(2) When information subject to a subpoena is withheld on a claim that it is privileged or subject to protection as trial preparation materials, the claim shall be made expressly and shall be supported by a description of the nature of the documents, communications, or things not produced that is sufficient to enable the demanding party to contest the claim.

State Courts

State statutes and court rules are, for the most part, similar to Rule 45, FRCP, but they may place more limits or give more leeway. For example, the travel distance may not be as many miles, or they may require that a request (praecipe) be made prior to issuance of the subpoena. Others are more expansive and already have in place many of the proposed amendments to the federal rules. Where the subpoena is for the taking of a deposition, some allow the court reporter to obtain its issuance and to serve it upon the deponent. When it comes to the production of records of a nonparty business, many statutes and court rules promote this cost-saving discovery devise.

1.   *Local Court Procedures*. Because most of the lawyer's practice will be before the state court where his or her practice is located, the legal assistant must be very familiar with the procedures of that court and its personnel. Normally, the clerk's office of this court will welcome and support the legal assistant who actively seeks its assistance. Local practice manuals and rules are most helpful.

2.   *The Legal Assistant as a Server*. Depending upon the rules of a jurisdiction, the legal assistant may be very involved in serving subpoenas for the taking of depositions, for the production of records of a person not a party, and upon witnesses for their appearance at trial. In this role, the legal assistant must responsibly perform these functions. Although others may have information pertaining to these tasks, the legal assistant should always ascertain, gather, and review current applicable statutes and court rules.

3.   *Friendly Subpoenas*. Often the legal assistant will encounter the situation where a trial witness is "friendly" to the case, and it may seem unnecessary to go to the trouble of wasting time and expense on serving him or her with a subpoena. However, experienced trial lawyers and legal assistants always serve subpoenas on all witnesses to be called at a hearing or trial. This ensures the witness's appearance and dispenses with any potential claim of bias on the witness's part because he or she "voluntarily" appeared without being required to do so.[4]

NOTES

---

[1] J. McCord, *The Litigation Paralegal*, 170 (1988).

[2] Id.

[3] A. Golec, *Techniques of Legal Investigation*, 462 (2nd Ed. 1985).

[4] Id., 70.

Epilogue

After this book was written, a number of events have taken place that substantiate its basic premise: lawyers must investigate their clients' cases thoroughly.

Federal and state court judges have become "judicial activists" and are imposing substantial monetary sanctions on lawyers who file or defend lawsuits without merit or who delay and misuse the formal discovery process. In many cases, they are requiring alternative dispute resolution (ADR) after a lawsuit is filed.

The federal government has made several proposals designed to reduce the number of lawyers and the number of lawsuits filed, including a plan to require the loser of a lawsuit to pay the other side's attorneys' fees as well as their own.

In many urban areas large law firms have disintegrated — some because of the economic problems of their clients, but many others were unable to justify expensive fee structures including those for legal assistants due to inefficiency.

However, legal assistants possessing the interviewing and investigative skills discussed in this book will not only survive but will be significantly utilized in the legal profession as it evolves into the 21st century.

_____

Epilogue 2

_____

Most of the events set out above have evolved further than anticipated. Not only have judges increasingly turned to sanctions, but now many are requiring alternative dispute resolution (ADR) before a lawsuit is filed! And, although the disintegration of law firms continues, we are now witnessing the creation of international megafirms with the largest having over two thousand lawyers and hundreds of legal assistants. These and other trends will continue.

Now, technology and legal assistants are inseparable. With this, the legal assistant has become an indispensable part of the legal system.

BIBLIOGRAPHY

American Bar Association Model Rules of Professional Conduct. Chicago, IL: American Bar Association, 1983.

Berger, Marilyn, Mitchell, John B., and Clark, Ronald H., *Pretrial Advocacy, Planning, Analysis and Strategy*. Boston, MA: Little Brown & Co., 1988.

Berkman, Robert I., *Find It Fast*. New York, NY: Harper & Row, 1987.

Binder, David A. and Bergman, Paul, *Fact Investigation*. St. Paul, MN: West Publishing Co., 1984.

Bruno, Carole A., *Paralegal's Litigation Handbook*. Englewood Cliffs, NJ: Institute for Business Planning, 1980.

Charfoos, Lawrence S. and Christensen, David W., *Personal Injury Practice: Technique and Technology*. Rochester, NY: Lawyers Co-Operative Publishing Co., 1986.

Corrigan, William M., Jr., "Using Judicial Notice in a Personal Injury Case." 47 *Journal of the Missouri Bar* 179. Columbia, MO: Missouri Bar Association, 1991.

Finnigan, Georgia L. and Kennedy, Michael R., *Effective Factual Research for Paralegals*. San Francisco, CA: The Information Store, 1983.

Golec, Anthony M., *Techniques of Legal Investigation*, 2nd Ed. Springfield, IL: Charles C. Thomas, 1985.

Hayakawa, S.I., *Language in Thought and Action*. New York, NY: Harcourt, Brace & Co., 1949.

Horowitz, Lois, *Knowing Where to Look*. Cincinnati, OH: Writer's Digest Books, 1984.

Jacobus, Charles J., *Real Estate Law*. Englewood Cliffs, NJ: Prentice-Hall, 1986.

James, Muriel, Ph.D. and Jongeward, Dorothy, Ph.D., *Born to Win*. Reading, MA: Addison-Wesley, 1971.

Kelner, Joseph and McGovern, Francis E., *Successful Litigation Techniques*, Student Edition. New York, NY: Matthew Bender, 1981.

Lisnek, Paul M. and Kaufman, Michael J., *Depositions, Procedure, Strategy and Technique*, Law School and CLE Edition. St. Paul, MN: West Publishing Co., 1988.

Loftus, Elizabeth F. and Doyle, James M., *Eyewitness Testimony: Civil and Criminal*. New York, NY: Kluwer Law Book Publishers, 1987.

Mason, Mary Ann, *Using Computers in the Law*, 2nd Ed. St. Paul, MN: West Publishing Co., 1988.

McCord, James W.H., *The Litigation Paralegal*. St. Paul, MN: West Publishing Co., 1988.

Morrill, Alan E., *Trial Diplomacy*, 2nd Ed. Chicago, IL: Court Practice Institute, 1972.

National Association of Legal Assistants, Inc., *Manual for Legal Assistants*. St. Paul, MN: West Publishing Co., 1979.

Nierenberg, Gerald I. and Calero, Henry H., *How to Read a Person Like a Book*. New York, NY: E.P. Dutton, 1971.

Pener, Michael A., *Paralegal/Legal Assistant Occupations Catalog of Performance Objectives and Performance Guidelines (Vocational-Technical Education Consortium of States)*. Macomb, IL: Curriculum Publications Clearinghouse (Western Illinois University, Horrabin Hall, Rm 46), 1988.

Philo, Harry M., *Lawyer's Desk Reference, 7th Ed.* Rochester, NY: Lawyers Co-Operative Publishing Co., 1987.

Rhyne, Charles S., *The Law of Local Government Operations*. Kingsport, TN: The Kingsport Press, 1980.

Sarnoff, Dorothy, *Speech Can Change Your Life*. New York, NY: Doubleday, 1970.

Statsky, William, *Legal Thesaurus/Dictionary*. St. Paul, MN: West Publishing Co., 1985.

Strong, Jo, Ph.D. and Hansen, Ida C., Ph.D., *Strong-Hansen Occupational Guide*. Palo Alto, CA: Consulting Psychologist Press, 1987.

Tarantino, John A. and Oliveira, David J., *Personal Injury Forms: Discovery and Settlement*. Santa Anna, CA: James Publishing Group, 1990.

Wydick, Richard, *Plain English for Lawyers*, 2nd Ed. Durham, NC: Carolina Academic Press, 1985.

WHERE TO WRITE
FOR VITAL RECORDS

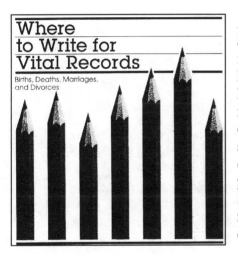

Where to Write for Vital Records
Births, Deaths, Marriages, and Divorces

As part of its mission to provide access to data and information relating to the health of the Nation, the National Center for Health Statistics produces a number of publications containing reference and statistical materials. The purpose of this publication is solely to provide information about individual vital records maintained only on file in State or local vital statistics offices.

An official certificate of every birth, death, marriage, and divorce should be on file in the locality where the event occurred. The federal government does not maintain files or indexes of these records. These records are filed permanently in a state vital statistics office or in a city, county, or other local office.

To obtain a certified copy of any of the certificates, write or go to the vital statistics office in the state or area where the event occurred. Addresses and fees are given for each event in the state or area.

To ensure that you receive an accurate record for your request and that your request is filled expeditiously, please follow these steps for the information in which you are interested:

• Write to the appropriate office to have your request filled.

• Under the appropriate office, information has been included for birth and death records concerning whether the state will accept checks or money orders and to whom they should be made payable.

This same information would apply when marriage and divorce records are available from the state office. However, it is impossible for us to list fees and addresses for all county offices where marriage and divorce records may be obtained.

- For all certified copies requested, make check or money order payable for the correct amount for the number of copies you want to obtain. Cash is not recommended because the office cannot refund cash lost in transit.

- Because all fees are subject to change, a telephone number has been included in the information for each state for use in verifying the current fee.

- Type or print all names and addresses in the letter.

- Give the following facts when writing for birth or death records:
  1. Full name of person whose record is being requested.
  2. Sex.
  3. Parents' names, including maiden name of mother.
  4. Month, day, and year of birth or death.
  5. Place of birth or death (city or town, county, and state, and name of hospital, if known).
  6. Purpose for which copy is needed.
  7. Relationship to person whose record is being requested.

- Give the following facts when writing for marriage records:
  1. Full names of bride and groom.
  2. Month, day, and year of marriage.
  3. Place of marriage (city or town, county, and state).
  4. Purpose for which copy is needed.
  5. Relationship to persons whose record is being requested.

- Give the following facts when writing for divorce records:
  1. Full names of husband and wife.
  2. Date of divorce or annulment.
  3. Place of divorce or annulment.
  4. Type of final decree.
  5. Purpose for which copy is needed.
  6. Relationship to persons whose record is being requested.

Place of event	Cost	Address	Remarks
Alabama			
Birth or Death	$12.00	Center for Health Statistics State Department of Public Health P.O. Box 5625 Montgomery, AL 36103-5625	State office has had records since January 1908. Additional copies at same time are $4.00 each. Fee for special searches is $10.00 per hour. Check or money order should be made payable to Center for Health Statistics. Personal checks are accepted. To verify current fees, call (205) 242-5033.
Marriage	$12.00	Same as Birth or Death	State office has had records since August 1936.
	Varies	See remarks	Probate Judge in county where license was issued.
Divorce	$12.00	Same as Birth or Death	State office has had records since January 1950.
	Varies	See remarks	Clerk or Register of Court of Equity in county where divorce was granted.
Alaska			
Birth or Death	$10.00	Department of Health and Social Services Bureau of Vital Statistics P.O. Box 110675 Juneau, AK 99811-0675	State office has had records since January 1913. Money order should be made payable to Bureau of Vital Statistics. Personal checks are not accepted. To verify current fees, call (907) 465-3391.
Marriage	$10.00	Same as Birth or Death	State office has had records since January 1913.
Divorce	$10.00	Same as Birth or Death	State office has had records since 1950.
	Varies	See remark	Clerk of Superior Court in judicial district where divorce was granted. Juneau and Ketchikan (First District), Nome (Second District), Anchorage (Third District), Fairbanks (Fourth District).

Place of event	Cost	Address	Remarks
American Samoa			
Birth or Death	$2.00	Registrar of Vital Statistics Vital Statistics Section Government of American Samoa Pago Pago, AS 96799	Registrar has had records since 1900. Money order should be made payable to ASG Treasurer. Personal checks are not accepted. To verify current fees, call (684) 633-1222, ext. 214. Personal identification required before record will be sent.
Marriage	$2.00	Same as Birth or Death	
Divorce	$1.00	High Court of American Samoa Tutuila, AS 96799	
Arizona			
Birth (long form) Birth (short form) Death	$8.00 $5.00 $5.00	Vital Records Section Arizona Department of Health Services P.O. Box 3887 Phoenix, AZ 85030	Check or money order should be made payable to Office of Vital Records. Personal checks are accepted. To verify current fees, call (602) 255-3260. Applicants must submit a copy of picture identification or have their request notarized.
Marriage	Varies	See remarks	Clerk of Superior Court in county where license was issued.
Divorce	Varies	See remarks	Clerk of Superior Court in county where divorce was granted.
Arkansas			
Birth Death	$5.00 $4.00	Division of Vital Records Arkansas Department of Health 4815 West Markham Street Little Rock, AR 72201	Additional copies of death record requested at the same time are $1.00 each. Check or money order should be made payable to Arkansas Department of Health. Personal checks are accepted. To verify current fees, call (501) 661-2336.
Marriage	$5.00	Same as Birth or Death	Coupons since 1917.
	Varies	See remarks	Full certified copy may be obtained from County Clerk in county where license was issued.

Place of event	Cost	Address	Remarks
Divorce	$5.00	Same as Birth or Death	Coupons since 1923.
	Varies	See remarks	Full certified copy may be obtained from Circuit or Chancery Clerk in county where divorce was granted.
California			
Birth Death	$12.00 $8.00	Vital Statistics Section Department of Health Services P.O. Box 730241 Sacramento, CA 94244-0241	Check or money order should be made payable to State Registrar, Department of Health Services or Vital Statistics. Personal checks are accepted. To verify current fees, call (916) 445-2684.
Heirloom Birth	$31.00	Not available until further notice	Decorative birth certificate (11" x 14") suitable for framing
Marriage	$13.00	Same as Birth or Death	State office has had records since July 1905. For earlier records, write to County Recorder in county where event occurred.
Divorce	$13.00	Same as Birth or Death	Fee is for search and identification of county where certified copy can be obtained. Certified copies are not available from State Health Department.
	Varies	See remarks	Clerk of Superior Court in county where divorce was granted.
Canal Zone			
Birth or Death	$2.00	Panama Canal Commission Vital Statistics Clerk APOAA 34011	Records available from May 1904 to September 1979.
Marriage	$1.00	Same as Birth or Death	Records available from May 1904 to September 1979.
Divorce	$0.50	Same as Birth or Death	Records available from May 1904 to September 1979.

Place of event	Cost	Address	Remarks
Colorado			
Birth or Death	$12.00	Vital Records Section Colorado Department of Health 4300 Cherry Creek Drive South Denver, CO 80222-1530	Additional copies of the same record ordered at the same time are $6.00. Check or money order should be made payable to Colorado Department of Health. Personal checks are accepted. To verify current fees, call (303) 756-4464.
Marriage	See remarks	Same as Birth or Death	Certified copies are not available from State Health Department. Statewide index of records for 1900-39 and 1968 to present. Fee for verification is $12.00.
	Varies	See remarks	Copies available from County Clerk in county where license was issued.
Divorce	See remarks	Same as Birth or Death	Certified copies are not available from State Health Department. Statewide index of records for 1900-39 and 1968 to present. Fee for verification is $12.00.
	Varies	See remarks	Copies available from Clerk of District Court in county where divorce was granted.
Connecticut			
Birth or Death	$5.00	Vital Records Department of Public Health 150 Washington Street Hartford, CT 06106	State office has had records since July 1897.[1] Check or money order should be made payable to Department of Public Health. Personal checks are accepted. FAX requests are not accepted. Must have original signature on request. To verify current fees, call (203) 566-2334.

[1] . For earlier records, write to Registrar of Vital Statistics in town or city where event occurred.

Place of event	Cost	Address	Remarks
Marriage	$5.00	Same as Birth or Death	Records since July 1897 at State Registry.
		See remarks	For older records, contact the Registrar of Vital Statistics in town where marriage occurred.
Divorce		See remarks	Applicant must contact Clerk of Superior Court where divorce was granted. State office does not have divorce decrees and cannot issue certified copies.
Delaware			
Birth or Death	$5.00	Office of Vital Statistics Division of Public Health P.O. Box 637 Dover, DE 19903	State office has death records since 1955 and birth records since 1923. Additional copies of the same record requested at the same time are $4.00 each.
			Check or money order should be made payable to Office of Vital Statistics. Personal checks are accepted. To verify current fees, call (302) 739-4721.
Marriage	$5.00	Same as Birth or Death	Records since 1955. Additional copies of the same record requested at the same time are $4.00 each.
Divorce	See remarks	Same as Birth or Death	Records since 1935. Inquiries are forwarded to appropriate office. Fee for search and verification of essential facts of divorce is $5.00 for each 5-year period searched. Certified copies are not available from state office.
	$2.00	See remarks	Prothonotary in county where divorce was granted up to 1975. For divorces granted after 1975, the parties concerned should contact Family Court in county where divorce was granted.

Place of event	Cost	Address	Remarks
District of Columbia			
Birth or Death	$12.00 $18.00 for long form birth certificate	Vital Records Division 800 9th Street, S.W. 1st Floor Washington, DC 20024-2480	Office has had death records since 1855 and birth records since 1874 but no death records were filed during the Civil War. Cashiers check or money order should be made payable to DC Treasurer. To verify current fees, call (202) 727-9281.
Marriage	$5.00	Marriage Bureau 515 5th Street, NW Washington, DC 20001	
Divorce	$2.00	Clerk, Superior Court for the District of Columbia Family Division 500 Indiana Ave, NW Washington, DC 20001	Records since September 16, 1956.
	Varies	Clerk, U.S. District Court for the District of Columbia Washington, DC 20001	Records before September 16, 1956.
Florida			
Birth Death	$9.00 $5.00[2]	Department of Health and Rehabilitative Services Office of Vital Statistics P.O. Box 210 1217 Pearl Street Jacksonville, FL 32231	The majority of records date from January 1917. Additional copies are $4.00 each when requested at the same time. Check or money order should be made payable to Office of Vital Statistics. Personal checks are accepted. To verify current fees, call (904) 359-6900.

[2] If the exact date is unknown, the fee is $9.00 (births) or $5.00 (deaths) for the first year searched and $2.00 for each additional year up to a maximum of $50.00. Fee includes one certification of record if found or certified statement stating record not on file.

Place of event	Cost	Address	Remarks
Marriage	$5.00[3]	Same as Birth or Death	Records since June 6, 1927. Additional copies are $4.00 each when requested at the same time.
Divorce	$5.00[4]	Same as Birth or Death	Records since June 6, 1927. Additional copies are $4.00 each when requested at the same time.
Georgia			
Birth or Death	$10.00	Georgia Department of Human Resources Vital Records Unit Room 217-H 47 Trinity Avenue, SW Atlanta, GA 30334	State office has had records since January 1919.[5] Additional copies of same record ordered at same time are $5.00 each except birth cards, which are $10.00 each. Money order should be made payable to Vital Records, GA. DHR. Personal checks are not accepted. To verify current fees, call (404) 656-4900.
Marriage	$10.00	Same as Birth or Death	Centralized State records since June 9, 1952. Certified copies are issued at State office. Inquiries about marriages occurring before June 9, 1952, will be forwarded to appropriate Probate Judge in county where license was issued.
	Varies	See remarks	Probate Judge in county where license issued, cost varies.

[3] If the exact date is unknown, the fee is $5.00 for the first year searched and $2.00 for each additional year up to a maximum of $50.00. Fee includes one copy of record if found or certified statement stating record not on file.

[4] If the exact date is unknown, the fee is $5.00 for the first year searched and $2.00 for each additional year up to a maximum of $50.00. Fee includes one copy of record if found or certified statement stating record not on file.

[5] For earlier records in Atlanta or Savannah, write to County Health Department in county where event occurred.

Place of event	Cost	Address	Remarks
Divorce	$2.00 for certification plus $0.50 per page	See remarks	Centralized State records since June 9, 1952. Certified copies are not issued at State office. Inquiries will be forwarded to appropriate Clerk of Superior Court in county where divorce was granted.
		See remarks	Clerk of Superior Court in county where divorce was granted.
Guam			
Birth or Death	$5.00	Office of Vital Statistics Department of Public Health and Social Services Government of Guam P.O. Box 2816 Agana, GU, M.I. 96910	Office has had records since October 16, 1901.

Money order should be made payable to Treasurer of Guam. Personal checks are not accepted. To verify current fees, call (671) 734-4589. |
Marriage	$5.00	Same as Birth or Death	
Divorce	Varies	Clerk, Superior Court of Guam Agana, GU, M.I. 96910	
Hawaii			
Birth or Death	$2.00	Office of Health Status Monitoring State Department of Health P.O. Box 3378 Honolulu, HI 96801	State office has had records since 1853.

Check or money order should be made payable to State Department of Health. Personal checks are accepted for the correct amount only. To verify current fees, call (808) 586-4533. |
Marriage	$2.00	Same as Birth or Death	
Divorce	$2.00	Same as Birth or Death	Records since July 1951.
	Varies	See remarks	Circuit Court in county where divorce was granted.

Place of event	Cost	Address	Remarks
Idaho			
Birth Wallet card Death	$8.00 $8.00 $8.00	Vital Statistics Unit Center for Vital Statistics and Health Policy 450 West State Street, 1st floor P.O. Box 83720 Boise, ID 83720-0036	State office has had records since July 1911. For records from 1907 to 1911, write to County Recorder in county where event occurred.
Heirloom Birth	$30.00		Check or money order should be made payable to Idaho Vital Statistics. Personal checks are accepted. To verify current fees, call (208) 334-5988.
Marriage	$8.00	Same as Birth or Death	Records since May 1947. Earlier records are with County Recorder in county where license was issued.
	Varies	See remarks	County Recorder in county where license was issued.
Divorce	$8.00	Same as Birth or Death	Records since May 1947. Earlier records are with County Recorder in county where divorce was granted.
	Varies	See remarks	County records in county where divorce was granted.

Place of event	Cost	Address	Remarks
Illinois			
Birth or Death	$15.00 certified copy $10.00 certification	Division of Vital Records Illinois Department of Public Health 605 West Jefferson Street Springfield, IL 62702-5097	State office has had records since January 1916. The fee for a search of the state files is $10.00. If the record is found, one certification is issued at no additional charge. Additional certifications of the same record ordered at the same time are $2.00 each. The fee for a full certified copy is $15.00. Additional certified copies of the same record ordered at the same time are $2.00 each.[6] Money orders, certified checks, or personal checks should be made payable to Illinois Department of Public Health. To verify current fees, call (217) 782-6553.
Marriage	$5.00	Same as Birth or Death	Marriage Index since January 1962. Selected items may be verified (fee $5.00). Certified copies are NOT available from state office. For certified copies, write to the County Clerk in county where license was issued.
Divorce	$5.00	Same as Birth or Death	Divorce Index since January 1962. Selected items may be verified (fee $5.00). Certified copies are NOT available from State office. For certified copies, write to the Clerk of Circuit Court in county where divorce was granted.

[6] For earlier records and for copies of State records since January 1916, write to County Clerk in county where event occurred (county fees vary).

Place of event	Cost	Address	Remarks
Indiana			
Birth Death	$6.00 $4.00	Vital Records Section State Department of Health 1330 West Michigan Street P.O. Box 7125 Indianapolis, IN 46206-7125	State office has had birth records since October 1907 and death records since 1900. Additional copies of the same record ordered at the same time are $1.00 each. For earlier records, write to Health Officer in city or county where event occurred.
			Check or money order should be made payable to Indiana State Department of Health. Personal checks are accepted. To verify current fees, call (317) 633-0274.
Marriage	See remarks	Same as Birth or Death	Marriage index since 1958. Certified copies are not available from State Health Department.
	Varies	See remarks	Clerk of Circuit Court or Clerk of Superior Court in county where license was issued.
Divorce	Varies	See remarks	County Clerk in county where divorce was granted.
Iowa			
Birth or Death	$10.00	Iowa Department of Public Health Vital Records Section Lucas Office Building 321 East 12th Street Des Moines, IA 50319-0075	State office has had records since July 1880.
			Check or money order should be made payable to Iowa Department of Public Health. To verify current fees, call (515) 281-4944.
Marriage	$10.00	Same as Birth or Death	State office has had records since July 1880.
Divorce	See remarks	Same as Birth or Death	Brief statistical record only since 1906. Inquiries will be forwarded to appropriate office. Certified copies are not available from State Health Department.
	$6.00	See remarks	Clerk of District Court in county where divorce was granted.

Place of event	Cost	Address	Remarks
Kansas			
Birth Death	$10.00 $7.00	Office of Vital Statistics Kansas State Department of Health and Environment Landon State Office Building 900 SW Jaskson Street Rm. 151 Topeka, Kansas 66612-2221	State office has had records since July 1911. For earlier records, write to County Clerk in county where event occurred. Additional copies of same record ordered at same time are $5.00 each. Check or money order should be made payable to State Registrar of Vital Statistics. Personal checks are accepted. To verify current fees, call (913) 296-1400.
Marriage	$10.00	Same as Birth or Death	State office has had records since May 1913.
	Varies	See remarks	District Judge in county where license was issued.
Divorce	$10.00	Same as Birth or Death	State office has had records since July 1951.
	Varies	See remarks	Clerk of District Court in county where divorce was granted.
Kentucky			
Birth Death	$7.00 $6.00	Office of Vital Statistics Department for Health Services 275 East Main Street Frankfort, KY 40621	State office has had records since January 1911. Check or money order should be made payable to Kentucky State Treasurer. Personal checks are accepted. To verify current fees, call (502) 564-4212.
Marriage	$6.00	Same as Birth or Death	Records since June 1958.
	Varies	See remarks	Clerk of County Court in county where license was issued.
Divorce	$6.00	Same as Birth or Death	Records since June 1958.
	Varies	See remarks	Clerk of Circuit Court in county where decree was issued.

Place of event	Cost	Address	Remarks
Louisiana			
Birth (long form) Birth (short-form) Death	$10.00 $7.00 $5.00	Vital Records Registry Office of Public Health 325 Loyola Avenue New Orleans, LA 70112	State office has had records since July 1914.[7] Check or money order should be made payable to Vital Records. Personal checks are accepted. To verify current fees, call (504) 568-5152.
Marriage Orleans Parish	$5.00	Same as Birth or Death See remarks	Certified copies are issued by Clerk of Court in parish where license was issued.
Other Parishes	Varies	See remarks	
Divorce	Varies	See remarks	Clerk of Court in parish where divorce was granted.
Maine			
Birth or Death	$10.00	Office of Vital Statistics Main Department of Human Services State House Station 11 Augusta, ME 04333-0011	Records for 1892-1922 are available at the Maine State Archives. For earlier records, write to the municipality where the event occurred. Additional copies of same record ordered at same time are $4.00 each. Check or money order should be made payable to Treasurer, State of Maine. Personal checks are accepted. To verify current fees, call (207) 289-3184.
Marriage	$10.00	Same as Birth or Death	Same as Birth or Death.
Divorce	$10.00 Varies	Same as Birth or Death See remarks	Same as Birth or Death. Clerk of District Court in judicial division where divorce was granted.

[7] Birth records for City of New Orleans are available from 1892. Death records are available since 1942. Older birth, death, and marriage records are available through the Louisiana State Archives, P.O. Box 94125, Baton Rouge, LA 70804.

Place of event	Cost	Address	Remarks
Maryland			
Birth or Death	$4.00	Division of Vital Records Department of Health and Mental Hygiene Metro Executive Building 4201 Patterson Avenue P.O. Box 68760 Baltimore, MD 21215-0020	State office has had records since August 1898. Records for City of Baltimore are available from January 1875.[8] Check or money order should be made payable to Division of Vital Records. Personal checks are accepted. To verify current fees, call (301) 225-5988.
Marriage	$4.00	Same as Birth or Death	Records since June 1951.
	Varies	See remarks	Clerk of Circuit Court in county where license was issued or Clerk of Court of Common Pleas of Baltimore City (for licenses issued in City of Baltimore).
Divorce Verification only	No fee	Same as Birth or Death	Records since January 1961. Certified copies are not available from State office. Some items may be verified.
	Varies	See remarks	Clerk of Circuit Court in county where divorce was granted.
Massachusetts			
Birth or Death	$6.00 (In person) $11.00 (Mail request) $3.00 (State Archives)	Registry of Vital Records and Statistics 470 Atlantic Avenue, 2nd Floor Boston, MA 02210-2224	State office has records since 1901.[9] Check or money order should be made payable to the Commonwealth of Massachusetts. Personal checks are accepted. To verify current fees, call (617) 727-7388.

[8] Will not do research for genealogical studies. Must apply to State of Maryland Archives, 350 Rowe Blvd., Annapolis, MD 21401 (301) 974-3914.

[9] . For earlier records, write to The Massachusetts Archives at Columbia Point, 220 Morrissey Boulevard, Boston, MA 02125 (617) 727-2816.

Place of event	Cost	Address	Remarks
Marriage	Same as Birth or Death	Same as Birth or Death	Records since 1901.
Divorce	See remarks	Same as Birth or Death	Index only since 1952. Inquirer will be directed where to send request. Certified copies are not available from State office.
Michigan			
Birth or Death	$13.00	Michigan Department of Community Health Office of the State Registrar 3423 N. Logan St. P.O. Box 30195 Lansing, MI 48909	State office has had records since 1867. [10] Check or money order should be made payable to State of Michigan. Personal checks are accepted. To verify current fees, call (517) 335-8655.
Marriage	$13.00	Same as Birth or Death	Records since April 1867.
	Varies	See remarks	County Clerk in county where license was issued.
Divorce	$13.00	Same as Birth or Death	Records since 1897. Will search for document by phone.
	Varies	See remarks	County Clerk in county where divorce was granted.

[10] Copies of most records since 1867 may also be obtained from County Clerk in county where event occurred. Fees vary from county to county. Detroit records may be obtained from the City of Detroit Health Department for births occurring since 1893 and for deaths since 1897.

Place of event	Cost	Address	Remarks
Minnesota			
Birth	$11.00	Minnesota Department of Health Section of Vital Statistics 717 Delaware Street, SE P.O. Box 9441 Minneapolis, MN 55440	State office has had records since January 1908.
Death	$8.00		Additional copies of the birth record when ordered at the same time are $5.00 each. Additional copies of the death record when ordered at the same time are $2.00 each.
			Check or money order should be made payable to Treasurer, State of Minnesota. Personal checks are accepted. To verify current fees, call (612) 623-5121.
Marriage	See remarks	Same as Birth or Death	Statewide index since January 1958. Inquiries will be forwarded to appropriate office. Certified copies are not available from State Department of Health.
	$8.00	See remarks	Local Registrar in county where license was issued. Additional copies of the marriage record when ordered at the same time are $2.00 each.
Divorce	See remarks	Same as Birth or Death	Index since January 1970. Certified copies are not available from State office.
	$8.00	See remarks	Local Registrar in county where divorce was granted.
Mississippi			
Birth	$12.00	Vital Records State Department of Health 2423 North State Street Jackson, MS 39216	State office has had records since 1912. Full copies of birth certificates obtained within 1 year after the event are $7.00. Additional copies of same record ordered at same time are $3.00 each for birth; $2.00 each for death and marriage.
Birth (short-form)	$7.00		
Death	$10.00		Personal checks are accepted only for in-state requests. To verify current fees, call (601) 960-7981. A recorded message may be reached on (601) 960-7450

Place of event	Cost	Address	Remarks
Marriage	$10.00	Same as Birth or Death	Statistical records only from January 1926 to July 1, 1938, and since January 1942.
	$3.00	See remarks	Circuit Clerk in county where license was issued.
Divorce	See remarks	Same as Birth or Death	Records since January 1926. Certified copies are not available from State office. Index search only available at $6.00 for each 5-year increment. Book and page number for county record provided.
	Varies	See remarks	Chancery Clerk in county where divorce was granted.
Missouri			
Birth or Death	$10.00	Missouri Department of Health Bureau of Vital Records 1730 East Elm P.O. Box 570 Jefferson City, MO 65102-0570	State office has had records since January 1910.[11]
			Personal checks are accepted. To verify current fees on birth and death records, call (314) 751-6400.
Marriage	No fee	Same as Birth or Death	Indexes since July 1948. Correspondent will be referred to appropriate Recorder of Deeds in county where license was issued.
	Varies	See remarks	Recorder of Deed in county where license was issued.
Divorce	No fee	Same as Birth or Death	Indexes since July 1948. Certified copies are not available from State Health Department. Inquiries are forwarded to appropriate office.
	Varies	See remarks	Clerk of Circuit Court in county where divorce was granted.

[11] If event occurred in St. Louis (City), St. Louis County, or Kansas City before 1910, write to the City or County Health Department. Copies of these records are $10.00 each in St. Louis City and St. Louis County. In Kansas City, the fee is $6.00 for the first copy and $3.00 for each additional copy ordered at same time.

Place of event	Cost	Address	Remarks
Montana			
Birth or Death	$10.00	Bureau of Vital Records and Health Statistics Montana Department of Public Health and Human Services Helena, MT 59620	State office has had records since late 1907. Check or money order should be made payable to Montana Department of Public Health and Human Services. Personal checks are accepted. To verify current fees, call (406) 444-2614.
Marriage	See remarks	Same as Birth or Death	Records since July 1943. Some items may be verified. Inquiries will be forwarded to appropriate office. Apply to county where license was issued if known. Certified copies are not available from State Office.
	Varies	See remarks	Clerk of District Court in county where license was issued.
Divorce	See remarks	Same as Birth or Death	Records since July 1943. Some items may be verified. Inquiries will be forwarded to appropriate office. Apply to court where divorce was granted if known. Certified copies are not available from State office.
	Varies	See remarks	Clerk of District Court in county where divorce was granted.
Nebraska			
Birth Death	$8.00 $7.00	Bureau of Vital Statistics State Department of Health 301 Centennial Mall South P.O. Box 95007 Lincoln, NE 68509-5007	State office has had records since late 1904. If birth occurred before then, write the state office for information. Check or money order should be made payable to Bureau of Vital Statistics. Personal checks are accepted. To verify current fees, call (402) 471-2871.
Marriage	$7.00	Same as Birth or Death	Records since January 1909.
	Varies	See remarks	County Court in county where license was issued.

Place of event	Cost	Address	Remarks
Divorce	$7.00	Same as Birth or Death	Records since January 1909.
	Varies	See remarks	Clerk of District Court in county where divorce was granted.
Nevada			
Birth	$11.00	Division of Health – Vital Statistics	State office has records since July 1911. For earlier records, write to County Recorder in county where event occurred.
Death	$8.00	Capitol Complex 505 East King Street #102 Carson City, NV 89710	Check or money order should be made payable to Section of Vital Statistics. Personal checks are accepted. To verify current fees, call (702) 687-4480.
Marriage	See remarks	Same as Birth or Death	Indexes since January 1968. Certified copies are not available from State Health Department. Inquiries will be forwarded to appropriate office.
	Varies	See remarks	County Recorder in county where license was issued.
Divorce	See remarks	Same as Birth or Death	Indexes since January 1968. Certified copies are not available from State Health Department. Inquiries will be forwarded to appropriate office.
	Varies	See remarks	County Clerk in county where divorce was granted.
New Hampshire			
Birth or Death	$10.00	Bureau of Vital Records Health and Welfare Building 6 Hazen Drive Concord, NH 03301	State office has had records since 1640. Copies of records may be obtained from State office or from City or Town Clerk in place where event occurred. Additional copies ordered at the same time are $6.00 each. Check or money order should be made payable to Treasurer, State of New Hampshire. Personal checks are accepted. To verify current fees, call (603) 271-4654.

Place of event	Cost	Address	Remarks
Marriage	$10.00	Same as Birth or Death	Records since 1640.
	$10.00	See remarks	Town Clerk in town where license was issued.
Divorce	$10.00	Same as Birth or Death	Records since 1808.
	Varies	See remarks	Clerk of Superior Court where divorce was granted.
New Jersey			
Birth or Death	$4.00	State Department of Health Bureau of Vital Statistics South Warren and Market Streets, CN 370 Trenton, NJ 08625	State office has had records since June 1878. Additional copies of same record ordered at same time are $2.00 each. If the exact date is unknown, the fee is an additional $1.00 per year searched.
		Archives and History Bureau State Library Division State Department of Education Trenton, NJ 08625	For records from May 1848 to May 1878.
			Check or money order should be made payable to New Jersey State Department of Health. Personal checks are accepted. To verify current fees, call (609) 292-4087.
Marriage	$4.00	Same as Birth or Death	If the exact date is unknown, the fee is an additional $1.00 per year searched.
	$2.00	Archives and History Bureau State Library Division State Department of Education Trenton, NJ 08625	For records from May 1848 to May 1878.
Divorce	$10.00	Public Information Center CN 967 Trenton, NJ 08625	The fee is for a certified Blue Seal copy. Make check payable to Clerk of the Superior Court.

Place of event	Cost	Address	Remarks
New Mexico			
Birth Death	$10.00 $5.00	Vital Statistics New Mexico Health Services Division P.O. Box 26110 Santa Fe, NM 87502	State office has had records since 1920 and delayed records since 1880. Check or money order should be made payable to Vital Statistics. Personal checks are accepted. To verify current fees, call (505) 827-2338.
Marriage	Varies	See remarks	County Clerk in county where license was issued.
Divorce	Varies	See remarks	Clerk of Superior Court where divorce was granted.
New York (Except New York City)			
Birth or Death	$15.00	Vital Records Section State Department of Health Empire State Plaza Albany, NY 12237-0023	State office has had records since 1880. For records before 1914 in Albany, Buffalo, and Yonkers, or before 1880 in any other city, write to Registrar of Vital Statistics in city where event occurred. For the rest of the State, except New York City, write to State Office. Check or money order should be made payable to New York State Department of Health. Personal checks are accepted. To verify current fees, call (518) 474-3075.
Marriage	$5.00	Same as Birth or Death	Records from 1880 to present.
	$10.00	See remarks	For marriage licenses issued before 1908 in the cities of Albany, Buffalo, or Yonkers, apply to Albany: City Clerk, City Hall, Albany, NY 12207; Buffalo: City Clerk, City Hall, Buffalo, NY 14202; Yonkers: Yonkers City Clerk, Room 207 City Hall, Yonkers, NY 10701.
Divorce	$15.00	Same as Birth or Death	Records since January 1963.
	Varies	See remarks	For records before 1963, write to the County Clerk in county where divorce was granted.

Place of event	Cost	Address	Remarks
New York City			
Birth or Death	$15.00	Division of Vital Records New York City Department of Health 125 Worth Street Room 133 New York, NY 10013	Office has birth records since 1910 and death records since 1949 for those occurring in Manhattan, Brooklyn, Bronx, Queens, Staten Island. [12] Certified check or money order should be made payable to New York City Department of Health. To verify current fees, call (212) 619-4530 or (212) 693-4637.
Marriage Bronx Borough	$10.00	City Clerk's Office 1780 Grand Concourse Bronx, NY 10457	Additional copies of same record ordered at same time are $5.00 each. [13]
Brooklyn Borough	$10.00	City Clerk's Office Municipal Building Brooklyn, NY 11201	
Manhattan Borough	$10.00	City Clerk's Office Municipal Building New York, NY 10007	

[12] For birth records prior to 1910 and death records prior to 1949, write to Archives Division, Department of Records and Information Services, 31 Chambers Street, New York, NY 10007.

[13] Records from 1847 to 1865: Archives Division, Department of Records and Information Services, 31 Chambers Street, New York, NY 10007, except Brooklyn records for this period, which are filed with County Clerk's Office, Kings County, Supreme Court Building, Brooklyn, NY 11201. Records from 1866 to 1907: City Clerk's Office in borough where marriage was performed. Records from 1908 to May 12, 1943. New York City residents write to City Clerk's Office in the borough of bride's residence; nonresidents write to City Clerk's Office in borough where license was obtained.

Place of event	Cost	Address	Remarks
Queens Borough	$10.00	City Clerk's Office 120-55 Queens Boulevard Kew Gardens, NY 11424	Records since May 13, 1943: City Clerk's Office in borough where license was issued.
Staten Island Borough (no longer called Richmond)	$10.00	City Clerk's Office Staten Island Borough Hall Staten Island, NY 10301	
Divorce			See New York State
North Carolina			
Birth or Death	$10.00	Department of Environment, Health and Natural Resources Division of Epidemiology Vital Records Section 225 North McDowell P.O. Box 29537 Raleigh, NC 27626-0537	State office has had birth records since October 1913 and death records since January 1, 1946.[14] Additional copies of the same record ordered at the same time are $5.00 each. Check or money order should be made payable to Vital Records Section. Personal checks are accepted. To verify current fees, call (919) 733-3526.
Marriage	$10.00	Same as Birth or Death	Records since January 1962.
	$3.00	See remarks	Registrar of Deeds in county where marriage was performed.
Divorce	$10.00	Same as Birth or Death	Records since January 1958.
	Varies	See remarks	Clerk of Superior Court where divorce was granted.

[14] Death records from 1913 through 1945 are available from Archives and Records Section, 109 East Jones Street, Raleigh, NC 27611.

Place of event	Cost	Address	Remarks
Northern Mariana Islands			
Birth or Death	$3.00	Superior Court Vital Records Section P.O. Box 307 Saipan, MP 96950	Records from 1945 to 1950 are incomplete. Money order or bank cashiers check should be made payable to Superior Court. Personal checks are not accepted. To verify current fees, call (670) 234-6401, ext. 15.
Marriage	$3.00	Same as Birth or Death	
Divorce	$0.50 per page for Divorce Decree plus $2.50 for certification	Same as Birth or Death	Office has had records for divorce since 1960.
North Dakota			
Birth Death	$7.00 $5.00	Division of Vital Records State Capitol 600 East Boulevard Avenue Bismarck, ND 58505-0200	State office has had some records since July 1893. Years from 1894 to 1920 are incomplete. Additional copies of birth records are $4.00 each; death records are $2.00 each. Money order should be made payable to Division of Vital Records. To verify current fees, call (701) 224-2360.
Marriage	$5.00	Same as Birth or Death	Records since July 1925. Requests for earlier records will be forwarded to appropriate office. Additional copies are $2.00 each.
	Varies	See remarks	County Judge in county where license was issued.

Place of event	Cost	Address	Remarks
Divorce	See remarks	Same as Birth or Death	Index of records since July 1949. Some items may be verified. Certified copies are not available from State Health Department. Inquiries are forwarded to appropriate office.
	Varies	See remarks	Clerk of District Court in county where divorce was granted.
Ohio			
Birth or Death	$7.00	Bureau of Vital Statistics Ohio Department of Health Columbus, OH 43215-0098	State office has had birth records since December 20, 1908. For earlier birth and death records, write to the Probate Court in the county where the event occurred.
			Check or money order should be made payable to State Treasury. Personal checks are accepted. To verify current fees, call (614) 466-2531.
Marriage	See remarks	Same as Birth or Death	Records since September 1949. All items may be verified. Certified copies are not available from State Health Department. Inquiries are referred to appropriate office.
	Varies	See remarks	Probate Judge in county where license was issued.
Divorce	See remarks	Same as Birth or Death	Records since September 1949. All items may be verified. Certified copies are not available from State Health Department. Inquiries are referred to appropriate office.
	Varies	See remarks	Clerk of Court of Common Pleas in county where divorce was granted.

Place of event	Cost	Address	Remarks
Oklahoma			
Birth	$5.00	Vital Records Section	State office has had records since October 1908.
Death	$5.00	State Department of Health 1000 Northeast 10th Street P.O. Box 53551 Oklahoma City, OK 73152	Check or money order should be made payable to Oklahoma State Department of Health. Personal checks are accepted. To verify current fees, call (405) 271-4040.
Marriage	Varies	See remarks	Clerk of Court in county where license was issued.
Divorce	Varies	See remarks	Clerk of Court in county where divorce was granted.
Oregon			
Birth or Death	$13.00	Oregon Health Division Vital Statistics Section P.O. Box 14050 Portland, OR 97293-0050	State office has had records since January 1903.[15] Money order should be made payable to Oregon Health Division. To verify current fees, call (503) 731-4095.
Heirloom Birth	$28.00	Same as Birth or Death	
Marriage	$15.00	Same as Birth or Death	Records since January 1906.
	Varies	See remarks	County Clerk in county where license was issued. County Clerks also have some records before 1906.
Divorce	$15.00	Same as Birth or Death	Records since 1925.
	Varies	See remarks	County Circuit Court Clerk in county where divorce was granted. County Clerks also have some records before 1925.

[15] Some earlier records for the City of Portland since approximately 1880 are available from the Oregon State Archives, 1005 Broadway, NE, Salem, OR 97310.

Place of event	Cost	Address	Remarks
Pennsylvania			
Birth	$4.00	Division of Vital Records	State office has had records since January 1906.[16]
Wallet card	$5.00	State Department of Health	
Death	$3.00	Central Building	Check or money order should be made payable to Division of Vital Records. Personal checks are accepted. To verify current fees, call (412) 656-3100.
		101 So. Mercer Street	
		P.O. Box 1528	
		New Castle, PA 16103	
Marriage	Varies	See remarks	Make application to the Marriage License Clerks, County Court House, in county where license was issued.
Divorce	Varies	See remarks	Make application to the Prothonotary, Court House, in county seat of county where divorce was granted.
Puerto Rico			
Birth or Death	$2.00	Department of Health	Central office has had records since July 22, 1931. Copies of earlier records may be obtained by writing to local Registrar (Registrador Demografico) in municipality where event occurred or by writing to central office for information.
		Demographic Registry	
		P.O. Box 11854	
		Fernandez Juncos Station	
		San Juan, PR 00910	Money order should be made payable to Secretary of the Treasury. Personal checks are not accepted. To verify current fees, call (809) 728-7980.
Marriage	$2.00	Same as Birth or Death	
Divorce	$2.00	Same as Birth or Death	Superior Court where divorce was granted.
		See remarks	

---

[16] For earlier records, write to Register of Wills, Orphans Court, in county seat of county where event occurred. Persons born in Pittsburgh from 1870 to 1905 or in Allegheny City, now part of Pittsburgh, from 1882 to 1905 should write to Office of Biostatistics, Pittsburgh Health Department, City-County Building, Pittsburgh, PA 15219. For events occurring in City of Philadelphia from 1860 to 1915, write to Vital Statistics, Philadelphia Department of Public Health, 401 North Broad Street, Room 942, Philadelphia, PA 19108.

Place of event	Cost	Address	Remarks
Rhode Island			
Birth or Death	$10.00	Division of Vital Records Rhode Island Department of Health 3 Capitol Hill Room 101 Providence, RI 02908-5097	State office keeps birth and marriage records for 100 years and death records for 50 years. Additional copies of the same record ordered at the same time are $5.00 each.[17] Money order should be made payable to General Treasurer, State of Rhode Island. To verify current fees, call (401) 277-2811.
Marriage	$15.00	Same as Birth or Death	Records since January 1853. Additional copies of the same record ordered at the same time are $5.00 each.
Divorce	$3.00	Clerk of Family Court 1 Dorrance Plaza Providence, RI 02903	
South Carolina			
Birth or Death	$8.00	Office of Vital Records and Public Health Statistics South Carolina Department of Health and Environmental Control 2600 Bull Street Columbia, SC 29201	State office has had records since January 1915. Additional copies of the same birth records ordered at the same time of certification are $3.00. Check or money order should be made payable to Department of Health and Environmental Control. Personal checks are accepted. To verify current fees, call (803) 734-4830.
Marriage	$8.00	Same as Birth or Death	Records since July 1950.
	Varies	See remarks	Records since July 1911. Probate Judge in county where license was issued.

[17] For earlier records, write to the city/town clerk where the event occurred or to the Rhode Island State Archives, 337 Westminster Street, Providence, RI 02903.

Place of event	Cost	Address	Remarks
Divorce	$8.00	Same as Birth or Death	Records since July 1962.
	Varies	See remarks	Records since April 1949. Clerk of county where petition was filed.
South Dakota			
Birth or Death	$5.00	State Department of Health Health Policy and External Affairs Vital Records 445 East Capitol Pierre, SD 57501-3185	State office has had records since July 1905 and access to other records for some events that occurred before then. Personal checks are accepted. To verify current fees, call (605) 773-3355. This will be a recorded message.
Marriage	$5.00	Same as Birth or Death	Records since July 1905.
		See remarks	County Treasury in county where license was issued.
Divorce	$5.00	Same as Birth or Death	Records since July 1905.
	Varies	See remarks	Clerk of Court in county where divorce was granted.
Tennessee			
Birth (long form) Birth (short-form) Death	$10.00 $5.00 $5.00	Tennessee Vital Records Dept. of Health Cordell Hull Building Nashville, TN 37247-0350	Additional copies of the same birth, marriage, or divorce record, requested at the same time, are $2.00 each.[18] Check or money order should be made payable to Tennessee Vital Records. Personal checks are accepted. To verify current fees, call (615) 741-1763.
Marriage	$10.00	Same as Birth or Death	Records since July 1945.
	Varies	See remarks	County Clerk in county where license was issued.

[18] State office has had birth records for entire State since January 1914, for Nashville since June 1881, for Knoxville since July 1881, and for Chattanooga since January 1882.

Place of event	Cost	Address	Remarks
Divorce	$10.00	Same as Birth or Death	Records since July 1945.
	Varies	See remarks	Clerk of Court in county where divorce was granted.
Texas			
Birth	$11.00	Bureau of Vital Statistics	State office has had records since 1903. Additional copies of death record ordered at same time are $3.00 each.
Death	$9.00	Texas Department of Health P.O. Box 12040 Austin, TX 78711-2040	Check or money order should be made payable to Texas Department of Health. Personal checks are accepted. To verify current fees, call (512) 458-7111.
Marriage	See Remarks		Records since January 1966. Certified copies are not available from State office. Fee for search and verification of essential facts of marriage is $9.00 each.
	Varies	See remarks	County Clerk in county where license was issued.
Divorce	See Remarks		Records since January 1968. Certified copies are not available from State office. Fee for search and verification of essential facts of divorce is $9.00 each.
	Varies	See remarks	Clerk of District Court in county where divorce was granted.
Utah			
Birth	$12.00	Bureau of Vital Records	State office has had records since 1905. Additional copies requested at the same time are $5.00 each.[19]
Death	$9.00	Utah Department of Health 288 North 1460 West P.O. Box 142855 Salt Lake City, UT 84114-2855	Check or money order should be made payable to Utah Department of Health. Personal checks are accepted. To verify current fees, call (801) 538-6105.

---

[19] If event occurred from 1890 to 1904 in Salt Lake City or Ogden, write to City Board of Health. For records elsewhere in the State from 1898 to 1904, write to County Clerk in county where event occurred.

Place of event	Cost	Address	Remarks
Marriage	$9.00	Same as Birth or Death	State office has had records since 1978. Only short form certified copies are available.
	Varies		County Clerk in county where license was issued.
Divorce	$9.00	Same as Birth or Death	State office has had records since 1978. Only short form certified copies are available.
	Varies		County Clerk in county where divorce was granted.
Vermont			
Birth or Death	$5.00	Vermont Dept. of Health Vital Records Section Box 70 60 Main St. Burlington, VT 05402	State office has had records since 1981. Check or money order should be made payable to Vermont Department of Health. Personal checks are accepted. To verify current fees, call (802) 863-7275.
Birth, Death or Marriage	$5.00	Division of Public Records US Route 2-Middlesex 133 State Street Montpelier, VT 05633	Records prior to 1981. To verify current fees, call (802) 828-3286.
	$5.00	See remarks	Town or City Clerk of town where birth or death occurred.
Marriage	$5.00	Same as Birth or Death	State office has had records since 1981.
	$5.00	See remarks	Town Clerk in town where license was issued.
Divorce	$5.00	Same as Birth or Death	State office has had records since 1981.
	$5.00	See remarks	Town Clerk in town where divorce was granted.

Place of event	Cost	Address	Remarks
Virgin Islands			
Birth or Death St. Croix	$10.00	Registrar of Vital Statistics Charles Harwood Memorial Hospital Christiansted St. Croix, VI 00820	Registrar has had birth and death records on file since 1840.
St. Thomas and St. John	$10.00	Registrar of Vital Statistics Knud Hansen Complex Hospital Ground Charlotte Amalie St. Thomas, VI 00802	Registrar has had birth records on file since July 1906 and death records since January 1906. Money order for birth and death records should be made payable to Bureau of Vital Statistics. Personal checks are not accepted. To verify current fees, call (809) 774-9000 ext. 4621 or 4623.
Marriage	See remarks	Bureau of Vital Records and Statistical Services Virgin Islands Dept. of Health Charlotte Amalie St. Thomas, VI 00801	

Place of event	Cost	Address	Remarks
St. Croix	$2.00	Chief Deputy Clerk Family Division Territorial Court of the Virgin Islands P.O. Box 929 Christiansted St. Croix, VI 00820	Certified copies are not available. Inquiries will be forwarded to the appropriate office.
St. Thomas and St. John	$2.00	Clerk of the Territorial Court of the Virgin Islands Family Division P.O. Box 70 Charlotte Amalie St. Thomas, VI 00801	
Divorce	See remarks	Same as Marriage	Certified copies are not available. Inquiries will be forwarded to appropriate office.
St. Croix	$5.00	Same as Marriage	Money order for marriage and divorce records should be made payable to Territorial Court of the Virgin Islands. Personal checks are not accepted.
St. Thomas and St. John	$5.00	Same as Marriage	
Virginia			
Birth or Death	$5.00	Division of Vital Records State Health Department P.O. Box 1000 Richmond, VA 23208-1000	State office has had records from January 1853 to December 1896 and since June 14, 1912. [20] Check or money order should be made payable to State Health Department. Personal checks are accepted. To verify current fees, call (804) 786-6228.

[20] Only the cities of Hampton, Newport News, Norfolk, and Richmond have records between 1896 and June 14, 1912.

Place of event	Cost	Address	Remarks
Marriage	$5.00	Same as Birth or Death	Records since January 1853.
Divorce	Varies	See remarks	Clerk of Court in county or city where license was issued.
Washington			
Birth or Death	$5.00	Same as Birth or Death	Records since January 1918.
	Varies	See remarks	Clerk of Court in county or city where divorce was granted.
	$11.00	Department of Health Center for Health Statistics P.O. Box 9709 Olympia, WA 98507-9709	State office has had records since July 1907. For King, Pierce, and Spokane counties copies may also be obtained from county health departments. County Auditor of county of birth has registered births prior to July 1907.

Check or money order should be made payable to Department of Health. To verify current fees, call (360) 753-5936. |
Marriage	$11.00	Same as Birth or Death	State office has had records since January 1968.
Divorce	$2.00	See remarks	County Auditor in county where license was issued.
	$11.00	Same as Birth or Death	State office has had records since January 1968.
	Varies	See remarks	County Clerk in county where divorce was granted.
West Virginia			
Birth or Death	$5.00	Vital Registration Office Division of Health State Capitol Complex Bldg. 3 Charleston, WV 25305	State office has had records since January 1917. For earlier records, write to Clerk of County Court in county where event occurred.

Check or money order should be made payable to Vital Registration. Personal checks are accepted. To verify current fees, call (304) 558-2931. |

Place of event	Cost	Address	Remarks
Marriage	$5.00	Same as Birth or Death	Records since 1921. Certified copies available from 1964.
Divorce	Varies	See remarks	County Clerk in county where license was issued.
	See remarks	Same as Birth or Death	Index since 1968. Some items may be verified (fee $5.00). Certified copies are not available from State office.
	Varies	See remarks	Clerk of Circuit Court, Chancery Side, in county where divorce was granted.
Wisconsin			
Birth	$10.00	Vital Records	Additional copies of the same record ordered at the same
Death	$7.00	1 West Wilson Street	time are $2.00 each.[21]
		P.O. Box 309	
		Madison, WI 53701	Check or money order should be made payable to Center for Health Statistics. Personal checks are accepted. To verify current fees, call (608) 266-1371.
Marriage	$7.00	Same as Birth or Death	Additional copies of the same record ordered at the same time are $2.00 each.[22]
Divorce	$7.00	Same as Birth or Death	Records since October 1907. Additional copies of the same record ordered at the same time are $2.00 each.

[21] State Office has scattered records earlier than 1857. Records before October 1, 1907, are very incomplete.

[22] Records since April 1836. Records before October 1, 1907, are incomplete.

Wyoming			
Birth	$8.00	Vital Records Services	State office has had records since July 1909.
Death	$6.00	Hathaway Building	Money order should be made payable to Vital Records
		Cheyenne, WY 82002	Services. To verify current fees, call (307) 777-7591.
Marriage	$8.00	Same as Birth or Death	Records since May 1941.
	Varies	See remarks	County Clerk in county where license was issued.
Divorce	$8.00	Same as Birth or Death	Records since May 1941.
	Varies	See remarks	Clerk of District Court where divorce took place.

INTERNET RESOURCES

(All Internet addresses preceded by http://)

Business

www.thomasregister.com/index.html	Thomas Register of American Manufacturers
www.law.cornell.edu/ucc.table.html	Uniform Commercial Code

Court Systems (Federal)

www.law.cornell.edu/supct	Decisions of U.S. Supreme Court
www.fjc.gov	Federal Judicial Center
www.uscourts.gov	US Federal Courts Site
www.law.cornell.edu/rules/frcp	Federal Rules of Civil Procedure
www.law.cornell.edu/rules/fre	Federal Rules of Evidence

Court Systems (State & Local)

www.ncsc.dni.us	National Center for State Courts

Experts

www.intr.net/tab	Technical Assistance Bureau
www.lawinfo.com	Legal Industry Directory
www.tasanet.com	Technical Advisory Services for Attorneys

Government (Federal)

www.house.gov	U.S. House of Representatives
www.law.vill.edu/fed-agency	Villanova Center for Information, Law and Policy
www.irs.ustreas.gov	Internal Revenue Service
www.fedworld.gov	FedWorld Information Network
law.house.gov/usc.htm	United States Code
law.house.gov/cfr.htm	Code of Federal Regulations
law.house.gov/7.htm	Federal Register

www.nhtsa.dot.gov   National Highway Traffic Safety
                                     Administration

www.cpsc.gov   Consumer Product Safety
                                     Commission

thomas.loc.gov   Thomas Site for Legislation

www.ssa.gov   Social Security Administration

Government (State)

www.nasire.org   National Association of State
                                     Resource Executives

Investigative Services

www.litnet.com   Litigation Investigations Service

www.usps.gov/GILS/mainlist.html   Postal Information Locator Service

Law Schools/Libraries

law.wuacc.edu   Washburn University School of
                                     Law

www.law.indiana   Indiana University School of Law

www.law.cornell   Cornell Law School

Legal Directories

www.wld.com   West Publishing Company

www.martindale.com   Martindale-Hubbell

Legal Ethics

www.law.cornell.edu/lawyers   Rules of Professional Conduct

www.lawref.com/cpra/cpra.html   California Rules of Professional
                                     Conduct

Legal Forms

192.41.429/forma.htm   'Lectric Law Library Law Practice
                                     Forms

www.gama.com/forms.htm   Miscellaneous Legal Forms

Legal Organizations

www.abanet.org   American Bar Association (ABA)

www.atlanet.com   American Trial Lawyers
                                     Association

www.nala.org   National Association of Legal
                                     Assistants

www.paralegals.org	National Federation of Paralegal Associations
www.aafpe.org	American Association for Paralegal Education

Legal Research Databases

www.westlaw.com	West Publishing Company
www.lexis.com	Lexis-Nexis
www.pita.com	Law Office Information Systems

Legal Research/Information

www.findlaw.com	Internet Legal Research Sites
www.lectlaw.com	'Lectric Law Library
www.catalaw.com	Index of Law & Government Sites
www.law.house.gov	U.S. House of Representatives Law Library
www.lawinfo.com	Links to Legal Research Sites
www.abanet.org/lawlink	ABA's Legal Research Sites
shell.rmi.net/~jflax/jmf_invs.htm	Jeff Flax's Investigative Resources

Legal Terms/Glossaries/Dictionaries

www.bailey-law.com/terms.html	Glossary of Legal Terminology
www.lectlaw.com/d-g.htm	'Lectric Law Library Legal Terms
www.bucknell.edu/~rbeard/diction.html	On-line Dictionaries

Libraries

lcweb.loc.gov/homepage/lchp.html	Library of Congress
thorplus.lib.purdue.edu	Extensive Search Databases
ipl.sils.umich.edu	Internet Public Library

Locating Search Sites/Services

www.real-time-data.com	National Credit Information Network
www.yahoo.com/search/people	Yahoo's People Search
www.abii.com	American Directory Assistance
www.angelfire.com/pages0/ultimates	Ultimate White Pages
www.worldpages.com	World Pages
www.ameri.com	American Information Network
www.cdb.com	CDB Infotek

www.databaseamerica.com	Database America
www.infoam.com	Information America
www.switchboard.com	Switchboard

Medical

www.ama-assn.org	American Medical Association
www.cdc.gov	Center for Disease Control
www.nih.gov	National Institute for Health
www.healthgate.com	Medical Resources

Miscellaneous

www.courttv.com	Court TV's Site
www.usc.edu.dept/law-lib	USC Index of Legal/Law-Related Journals

National Newspapers

www.wsj.com	Wall Street Journal
www.nytimes.com	New York Times
www.usatoday.com	USA Today
www.nlj.com	National Law Journal

Search Engines

www.albany.net	All-In-One Search
www.altavista.digital/com	Alta Vista Web Crawler/Software
www.excite.com	Excite Service of Arcitext Software
www2.infoseek.com	InfoSeek Net Search
www.lycos.com	Lycos Web Index
www.mckinley.com	McKinley Internet Directory
www.yahoo.com	Yahoo List of Directories

Vital Records

www.vitalcheck.com	Vital Records Resource

INDEX

A

ABA. *See* American Bar Association
ABA Model Code of Professional
    Responsibility, 11
abuse of the legal process, 20
accident reconstruction, 157, 210
accident reports
    obtaining, 151
Administrative Dispute Resolution Act, 5
administrative evidence, 33
administrative law, 66
ADRA. *See* Administrative Dispute
    Resolution Act
advertising by lawyers, 17
agency relationships, 84
    duty of agent to principal, 85
ALR Digest, 64
Am. Jur. 2d, 64
Am. Jur. Pleading and Practice Forms, 37
American Bar Association, 11, 21, 23, 140
American Jurisprudence 2d, 62
American Law Reports, 64
American Library Directory, 261
American Trial Lawyers Association, 188
analysis
    evidentiary, 209
    technical, 210
analytical methods, 72
    deductive thinking, 73
    inductive thinking, 72
analytical process, 73
    background and knowledge, 74
    legal methods, 75
        recording, 75
        selection of method, 76
        storyboarding, 76
        time sequencing, 75
    limitations, 74
annotated materials, 64
annual reports, 90
appropriate legal research, 60
articles of incorporation, 91
assessment and tax records, 228
Attorney General of the United States, 280
authenticated copies, 239
automobile accident investigation plan
    checklist, 50
Automobile Accident Law and Practice, 37

automobile accident topical outline, 51
Automobile Law and Practice, 37, 62

B

bad faith liability, 129
bailments, 100
Best Evidence Rule, 195
Biography Index, 257
birth records
    necessary facts, 306
Book of the States, 251
BRS, 189, 267
Bureau of Alcohol, Tobacco and Firearms,
    249
business entities, 84
Business Periodical Index, 256
business records, 230
bylaws, 91

C

case law, 67
case or direct evidence, 196
case reports, 117
Census Bureau, 225, 249
Center for Disease Control, 261
Central Intelligence Agency, 219
certified copies, 239
CFR. *See Code of Federal Regulations*
chain of custody, 195
character of the evidence, 28
Chemical Exposure, 266
citators, 68
civil court records, 229
Civil Cover Sheet Form, 270
Civil Service Commission, 223
Claims/U.S. Patent Abstracts, 266
client evaluations, 146
client information sheets, 140, 147
client profiles, 81
closely-held corporations, 90
Code of Ethics and Professional
    Responsibility, 11
Code of Federal Regulations, 66, 291
Cohen v. Everett City Council, 535 P.2d
    801, 254
Cole, 162
Collier's on Bankruptcy, 61

F

fact control, 48
fact synthesis, 48
Facts on File, 262
Federal Aviation Administration, 248, 249
Federal Bureau of Investigation, 219, 223, 249
Federal Communications Commission, 223, 249
Federal Emergency Management Agency, 249
Federal Energy Regulatory Commission, 249
federal government
immunities, 92
Federal Highway Administration, 249, 267
Federal Housing Authority, 98
Federal Railroad Administration, 249
Federal Register, 66
Federal Rules of Civil Procedure, 35, 36, 37, 38, 41, 67, 80, 183, 187, 270, 273, 275, 276, 277, 278, 279, 289, 292, 293, 294, 296
Federal Trade Commission, 244, 250
Federal-State-Local Government Directory, 251
fees, 126
fees agreements, 139
financial records, 231
Find It Fast, 263
First Facts, 262
FOIA. *See* Freedom of Information Act
follow-up letters, 147
Food and Drug Administration, 108, 223, 250
formal discovery
escalation in cost, 2
Formal Opinion 316, 21
Forms of Discovery, 37
FRCP. *See* Federal Rules of Civil Procedure
Freedom of Information Act, 164, 213, 219, 236, 243, 244, 248, 250, 252
exemptions to law, 246
request letter, 244
Freedom of Information Clearinghouse, 247

G

Gale's Biographical Index, 258
general warranty deeds, 97
Gold v. McDermott, 347 A.2d 643, 254
Government Printing Office, 221, 247, 252
government sources

federal government, 240
departments, agencies, and commissions, 249
Internet, 241, 249
publications, 247
source identification, 241
telephone directories, 249
local government, 253
accessing information, 254
state government, 250
departments and agencies, 252
Internet resources, 251
open records acts, 251
publications, 252
source identification, 250
state manuals, 251
government sources of information, 240
governmental entities, 92
Gray's Human Anatomy, 263
Guide to Reference Books, 262

H

Hammond Almanac, 262
health and vital records, 228
health records, 231
hearsay rule, 30
exceptions
business records, 31
declarations against self-interest, 30
public records, 31
spontaneous statements, 31
unavailability of declarant as witness, 30
How to Find Information about Companies, 255

I

identification of parties, 79, 80
agency relationships, 84
business entities, 84
client profiles, 81
clients, 81
clubs, fraternities, and leagues, 93
corporations, 89
employment relationships, 85
federal government, 92
governmental entities, 92
individuals
legal relationships, 83
limited liability companies, 91
opposing parties, 82
other entities, 93

T